GREEK
PHRASEBOOK

Markella A. Callimassia

Greek phrasebook
2nd edition – September 2000

Published by
Lonely Planet Publications Pty Ltd A.C.N. 005 607 983
192 Burwood Rd, Hawthorn, Victoria 3122, Australia

Lonely Planet Offices
Australia PO Box 617, Hawthorn, Victoria 3122
USA 150 Linden St, Oakland CA 94607
UK 10a Spring Place, London NW5 3BH
France 1 rue du Dahomey, 75011 Paris

Cover illustration
Kidnap on Lesbos by Patrick Marris

ISBN 0 86442 683 6

text © Lonely Planet Publications 2000
cover illustration © Lonely Planet 2000

Printed by The Bookmaker International Ltd
Printed in China

About the Author

Markella Calimassia grew up in Athens spending most of her summers travelling around the Aegean Islands and the Greek mainland. After completing a BSc in genetics at the University of St Andrews in Scotland, followed by a PhD at the Royal Botanic Gardens in Kew, West London. After her studies she worked in Greece, Denmark, and England translating and editing, teaching modern Greek and English, meddling with genetics and acquiring a few more languages as well as a Danish husband along the way. In between work she managed to squeeze in a few trips to the USA, India, and various parts of Europe. In her spare time she reads up on classical art and ancient history while cooking Greek food.

Being unable to decide between a career in languages or genetics, she is embarking on an around-the-world odyssey.

From the Author

Markella would like to thank her brother Georgios Callimassias for his help with political and sports issues, John Burke for his invaluable corrections and suggestions, and her husband for making sure she was fed properly while writing this phrasebook.

From the Publisher

This book is based on the first edition of Lonely Planet's *Greek Phrasebook* written by Paul Hellander.

The unstoppable force behind the production of this edition was: Jo Adams who laid out with great enthusiasm. Olivier Breton who edited as usual. Patrick Marris whose illustrations and cover art graced this book. Karin Vidstrup Monk who proofed and proofed. Natasha Velleley who did the lovely map. John Burke, reader extraordinaire who left no stone unturned. Peter D'Onghia the overseer who also did his fair share of proofing. Sally Steward who gave birth to one Iggy Joe.

CONTENTS

6   Contents

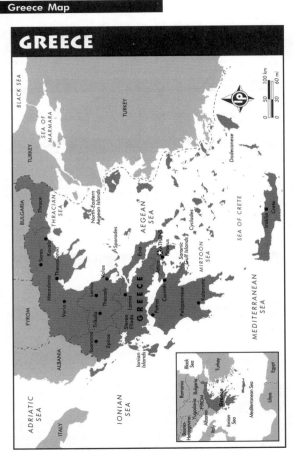

INTRODUCTION

The role of Greek in the development of Western European civilization barely needs an introduction. Some of the most influential texts in Western European history have been written in Greek: the works of Homer, the first ever history by Herodotus, the philosophical works of Plato and Aristotle, the historical accounts of Xenophon, Plutarch and Thucidides, the plays of Sofocles, Euripides and Aristofanes, the New Testament.

Greek has been spoken since about the 18th century BC, maybe even earlier. The first, rather fragmented, records of the greek language come from clay tablets dating from the 14th to 12th century BC written in *linear B*, a syllabic alphabet (each symbol representing a syllable, not a sound). Between the 10th and 8th century BC the Greeks adopted the Phoenician alphabet, and by the 5th century BC this alphabet had developed into the 24-letter alphabet that Greeks use today.

From about the 10th century BC, three and later four dialects of Greek were distinguishable. *Aeolian* was spoken in the north-east Aegean (the island of Lesvos) and northwest Asia Minor, and in Arcadia, the area around Thebes and Cyprus. *Doric* was the dialect of northwestern Greece, the western mainland, most of the Peloponnese including Sparta, the southern Aegean islands and the later colonies of Sicily and the Black Sea coast. *Ionian* was spoken in Attica, Evvia, the islands of Andros, Samos and Chios, and most of the coast of Asia Minor. The extremely influential *Attic* dialect, used in Athens and Attica, developed out of a predominantly Ionian dialect, with some elements of doric. All these dialects were mutually understood, and their differences consisted mainly of the variation in word endings and use of vowels, variations that to some extent have persisted to the present day.

With the rise in power of the Athenian state in the 5th century BC, *Attic* became the predominant dialect used in literary works and all forms of intellectual expression. Another factor played a vital role in the later evolution of the greek language; Alexander's teacher and mentor, Aristotle, used the *Attic* dialect in his writings.

This form of Greek spread with Alexander the Great's Empire, that stretched from Macedon to the shores of the Indus river, was a simplified form of *Attic*. By the end of the first millennium BC, the conquered people of western Asia, Egypt and southern Italy used Greek to conduct all their commercial, administrative and military affairs.

This was the foundation of *Koine*, 'the common language' – a very simplified form of *Attic*, devoid of much of its syntactical and grammatical complexity, that had assimilated elements of dialects spoken by the conquered peoples.

In the 6th century AD, Greek as an almost unadulterated form of *Attic*, became the official language of the Eastern Roman, or Byzantine Empire, of which Constantinople was the capital. This version of Greek established itself as the language of the Orthodox church, and the administrative language of the Empire.

After the fall of Constantinople in 1453, which saw Greece become part of the Ottoman Empire, the use of formal *Attic* became almost obsolete, as levels of literacy dropped dramatically. *Koine* however, was still spoken by the Greek population. A wealth of poems known as *dhimotika traghoudia* (popular songs) were written and sung in *Koine*. At various stages, *Koine* was enriched by Slavic, Albanian and Turkish words, residue from the regular waves of conquest and migration.

After the liberation of Greece in 1832, the dilemma of which language to adopt as its official language split scholars into two camps. It was clear that *Attic* in its pure, classical form was no longer viable, but many supported a language, close to *Attic*, that was 'cleansed' of all foreign elements. From this movement sprang

Katharevousa (*katharos* means clean). *Koine* or *laiki* (meaning popular) had equally strong support as the language most people used and understood, and one that could be implemented into the education system to raise literacy levels. By the early 20th century, the *Koine*, now known as *Dhimotiki* (demotic or popular) became the accepted form of Greek. *Dhimotiki* suffered a temporary blow during the years of the military dictatorship (1967-1974) when the purist *Katharevousa* was 'declared' as the official language, and many works written in demotic Greek were banned. However, *Dhimotiki* was re-established as the official language in 1974. The language underwent another wave of simplification in 1981 when all the accents, aspiration marks and archaic noun endings were abolished (at least in theory). More recently, and despite efforts from scholars, it has been impossible to stop the invasion of English-American and French words from being accepted into the language.

This strong linguistic dichotomy between purist *Katharevousa* and *Dhimotiki* has plagued education and the development of the language to the present day. Doctors, lawyers, professors and even some journalists use *Katharevousa* for all legal and official documents, and *Dhimotiki* for everything else. Some newspapers are even published entirely in *Katharevousa*. A 'smartened-up', austere *Dhimotiki* almost verging on *Katharevousa* is still the mark of a well-educated person. Another paradox: ancient Greek, taught in schools today is written using the full aspiration and accent system – developed for the benefit of modern Greek – that it never had in classical times, but modern Greek no longer uses them.

INTRODUCTION

To a learner of Greek, it must be most frustrating to have to cope with two or three different forms of the same word. But whether you are a speaker of English, French, German, or even a Slavonic language, you'll soon recognize similarities to Greek words in your own language (such as father, *Vater*, *père*, *pater* which all resemble the Greek πατήρ patir). After all, Greek is an Indo-European language with grammar and syntax that are very similar to most European languages. Having mastered some Greek, you will have the satisfaction of having learnt a small part of a 4000 year old piece of history.

Dhimotiki has been used throughout this book.

ABBREVIATIONS USED IN THIS BOOK

acc	accusative case	m	masculine
adj	adjective	n	neuter
adv	adverb	nom	nominative case
f	feminine	pl	plural
gen	genetive case	pol	polite/formal
inf	informal	sg	singular
lit	literal		

Where nouns have two genders, for example some professions, the masculine form has been given first. Adjectives have three genders and they have been listed in the order masculine/feminine/neuter.

PRONUNCIATION

THE GREEK ALPHABET

The Greek alphabet may look daunting and unfriendly at first sight. However, at closer inspection you will recognize several of the letters from the English alphabet. Only about half will be completely new to you.

There are 24 letters in the Greek alphabet, listed below together with a pronunciation guide and the transliteration that has been used throughout this phrasebook. You may notice that the Greek alphabet does not run from 'A to Z' (in fact Z is the sixth letter) but from 'A to Ω' (alpha to omegha).

Name	Upper case	Lower case
alpha	A	α
vita	B	β
ghama	Γ	γ
dhelta	Δ	δ
epsilon	E	ε
zita	Z	ζ
ita	H	η
thita	Θ	θ
yiota	I	ι
kapa	K	κ
lamdha	Λ	λ
mi	M	μ
ni	N	ν
ksi	Ξ	ξ
omikron	O	o
pi	Π	π
ro	P	ρ
sighma	Σ	σ/ς (at the end of a word)
taf	T	τ
ipsilon	Y	υ

fi	Φ	φ
chi	X	χ
psi	Ψ	ψ
omegha	Ω	ω

VOWELS

There are seven vowels α, ε, η, ι, ο, υ, ω, but only four vowel sounds in Greek. Vowels are only ever pronounced one way.

A α	as the 'a' in 'lap' (but pronounced with the mouth slightly more open)
E ε	as the 'e' in 'bet'
I/H/Y ι/η/υ	as the 'i' in 'lid'
O/Ω ο/ω	as the 'o' in 'lot'

Eliding

When a word that ends in a vowel is followed by another word that starts with the same or a similar vowel sound, one vowel can usually be omitted. The two words are pronounced as if they were one, this is called eliding. For example:

Σε ευχαριστώ.	se efcharisto	Thank you.
becomes		
Σ' ευχαριστώ.	sefcharisto	

Μου αρέσει.	mu aresi	I like it.
becomes		
Μ' αρέσει.	maresi	

Θα έρθω.	tha ertho	I will come.
becomes		
Θα' ρθω.	thartho	

TI OR TIN

You'll sometimes hear the final letter ν being omitted from the accusative articles τον ton, την tin, εναν enan, the negation particles δεν dhen, μην min, and the female direct object pronoun την tin (see page 22).

FALSE FRIENDS

False Friends
B H P Y X
β η ρ υ χ

These five letters are the tricky ones – they look as if you should know them (at least in their upper case form), but they sound quite different in Greek from what they do in English. See pages 14-16 to see what they sound like.

DIPHTHONGS

Although these are technically termed diagraphs, and represent only one sound phonetically, they are still often referred to as diphthongs.

αι	as the 'e' in 'bet'
ει/οι/υι	as the 'i' in 'lid'
ου	as the 'u' in put
αυ	as 'av' in 'average' or the 'af' in 'after'
ευ	as the 'ev' in 'ever' or the 'ef' in 'left'

If two vowels occur together and are not listed above, they should be pronounced separately, as in ζώο zo-o animal.

CONSONANTS

There are only two Greek consonants that are unfamiliar to the English ear, Γ/γ and Χ/χ.

Γ/γ before an 'i' or 'e' sound, is pronounced as the 'y' in 'yes' or 'yellow', as in γιατρός yiatros 'doctor' or, γέρος yeros 'old'. Before an 'a', 'u' or 'o' sound and before other consonants, γ becomes a guttural sound, something between a hard 'g' and the 'ch' in 'loch', as if you have something stuck in your throat and you are trying to clear it. Some examples are: γάτα ghata 'cat', γόνατο ghonato 'knee', γράφω ghrafo 'to write'.

PRONUNCIATION

X/χ before an 'i' or 'e' sound is a bit like a hissing sound, as in χέρι cheri 'hand'. Before an 'a', 'o', or 'u' sound and before other consonants, again it becomes rather guttural, like a Scot would pronounce 'loch'. For example χώρα chora 'country', χρώμα chroma 'colour'. All sounds are transliterated as stated below unless otherwise specified.

B β	as the 'v' in 'vase'
Γ γ	as the 'y' in 'yellow' (before 'e', and 'i' sounds). Transliterated as y.
	guttural sound somewhere between the 'g' in 'goat' and the 'ch' in 'loch' (before all other sounds). Transliterated as gh.
Δ δ	as the 'th' in 'the'. Transliterated as dh.
Z ζ	as the 'z' in 'zoo'
Θ θ	as the 'th' in 'theatre'
K κ	as the 'k' in 'kit'
Λ λ	as the 'l' in 'let'
M μ	as the 'm' in 'mat'
N ν	as the 'n' in 'not'

DID YOU KNOW ...   In classical times, the sound of non-Greeks talking in their native tongues sounded like 'var, var, var ...' to Greek ears – hence they called anyone who didn't speak Greek βάρβαρος varvaros, 'a barbarian'.

OLD FRIENDS

Old Friends
Α Ε Ζ Ι Κ Μ Ν Ο Τ
α ε ζ ι κ μ ν ο τ

You will recognize these letters from the English alphabet, at least in their upper case form. Their sound in Greek more or less corresponds to their sound in English.

Ξ ξ	as the 'ks' in 'yaks'
Π π	as the 'p' in 'pin'
Ρ ρ	as the 'r' in 'red', but more trilled
Σ σ (ς at the end of a word)	as the 's' in 'sad', can sound like the 'z' in 'zoo' in front of 'v', 'gh' and 'm' sounds.
Τ τ	as the 't' in 'top'
Φ φ	as the 'f' in 'fit'
Χ χ	as the 'h' in 'heath' but with more emphasis (before 'e' and 'i' sounds); or as the 'ch' in 'loch' (before all other sounds). Always transliterated as ch.
Ψ ψ	as the 'ps' in 'lapse'

There are several consonant combinations that may sound unfamiliar to English speakers. These take a bit of practice:

μπ	as the 'b' in 'bed' at the beginning of a word; or as the 'mb' in 'amber' in the middle of a word

PRONUNCIATION

ντ	as the 'd' in 'dog' at the beginning of a word; or as the 'nd' in 'indigo' in the middle of a word.
γκ/γγ	as the 'g' in 'gap' at the beginning of a word; or as in the 'ng' in 'English' in the middle of a word. The combination γγ never occurs at the beginning of word.
γχ	there is no real equivalent in English: try saying 'ng' followed immediately by the 'ch' in 'loch' from quite deep in the throat. Transliterated as nch.
τσ	as the 'ts' in 'hats'
τζ	as the 'dds' in 'adds'. Transliterated as dz.

Unlike vowels, double consonants are not pronounced twice, for example άλλος meaning 'other' is pronounced alos.

ACCENTS & STRESS

You may notice that Greek words are quite long and can often have five syllables or more. The stress on Greek words can fall on any of the last three syllables, but never beyond that. Fortunately, in written Greek the stressed syllable is always indicated by an accent ('). Words with only one syllable are generally not accented.

The accent is written only on the vowels and in the case of diphthongs on the second letter as in ού, οί, αί, αύ, εύ. Where the accent is placed on the first of two vowels, it means that those two vowels do not form a diphthong and the two letters should

---

NEW FRIENDS

New Friends
Γ Δ Θ Λ Ξ Π Σ Φ Ψ Ω
γ δ θ λ ξ π σ φ ψ ω

These letters will be new to you, as they are particular to the Greek alphabet.

be read separately, for example Μάιος ma-ios 'May'. Where this is not clear a dialysis (¨) is used, to indicate that the two vowels should be pronounced separately, as in λαϊκός la-ikos 'popular'.

Text written entirely in upper case does not take any accents. However, upper case letters in normal text do, as in Άρης Aris, or Έλλη Eli.

> The stressed vowel is shown in bold in the transliteration throughout this book.

The stress on a word is quite important, as stressing the wrong syllable could change the meaning of the word quite drastically, as in μισός, misos 'half' but μίσος misos 'hatred'.

Some street signs or books that are over 20 years old may still have the old system of stressing words which was abolished in 1981. This included two aspiration symbols (') and ('), which can be ignored when reading, and two stress symbols (´) and (~), which can be both treated as (´).

INTONATION

Mainland Greek, especially Athenian can sound rather flat to the ear – there is a change in intonation only when asking a question, when the voice is raised at the end of the sentence. However, many of the local dialects have a much more colourful intonation. That of the Ionian islands sounds very much like the singing intonation of Italian (undoubtedly, an Italian influence from the 15th century). Also, in many of the Aegean islands, notably Samos and Chios, and on Crete, the local dialects sound a lot more 'sung' – with extra vowels added to the end of words.

Cypriot Greek is much more nasal, with clipped vowels in the middle of a word. Often, words end in an extra 'n' or 'en', and intonation is much less flat than that of mainland Greek.

PRONUNCIATION

GRAMMAR

Greek grammar, despite popular misconceptions, is no more difficult than many grammars of languages in the Indo-European family group. The main drawback of Greek for newcomers is its generally unfamiliar vocabulary. Greek does not have any closely related languages, so its vocbulary tends to be isolating for most people. However Greek's rich contribution to the scientific language of English means that a few words may be familiar to you.

GRAMMATICAL TERMS

A number of terms are used in this chapter. Masculine, feminine and neuter refer to the classification of words (nouns) usually by their endings, rather than by sense of physical gender or sex, although nouns which are clearly feminine (such as woman) are feminine, and likewise obviously masculine nouns (such as man) are masculine. Neuter nouns refer to nouns without gender, such as inanimate objects. Neuter nouns can also be words like 'child' which is considered not to have reached sexual maturity. By and large the 'sex definition' ends here. Adjectives also have masculine, feminine and neuter endings dependent on the classification of the noun they refer to (see page 29).

(see page 29)

Common noun endings:
You may be able to recognise the gender of some words by looking for these common endings. Nouns in all three genders can finish in -ος.

Masculine: -ης, -ας
Feminine: -η, -α also most names of countries and Greek cities
Neuter: -ι, -α, -ο and all nouns ending in -ακι

The term 'subject' refers to the noun which operates the verb. With a sentence such as 'The man sees.', 'the man' is the subject, as he is 'seeing'. The 'object' is a noun that is affected by the verb. In this case, whatever it is that the man sees. The term 'possessive' is applied to a noun that relates directly to another noun.

WORD ORDER

Because of the elaborate forms of cases and genders, it is clear whether a noun is the object or the subject of a sentence, and who the verb refers to. Apart from a few cases where word order is very specific (possessive pronouns, direct and indirect relative pronouns), all possible combinations of 'subject-verb-object' are correct. Emphasised words generally are at the beginning of the sentence.

ARTICLES

Articles differ according to gender and for singular and plural. They also differ according to case (see page 23).

Definite Articles

These are equivalent to the English 'the'.

Masculine	Feminine	Neuter
o	i	to
Singular		
the road	the city	the village
o dhromos	i poli	to chorio
Plural		
i	i	ta
the roads	the cities	the villages
i dhromi	i polis	ta choria

Indefinite Articles

These are equivalent to the English 'a' or 'an'. There is no plural for the indefinite article.

Masculine	**Feminine**	**Neuter**
enas	mia	ena
a road	a city	a village
enas dhromos	mia poli	ena chorio

NOUNS

Case indicates the function of a noun or pronoun in a sentence, such as subject, object, indirect object etc. Greek nouns (and adjectives) have three main cases, the nominative, the genitive and the accusative. There is also a case called the vocative, used only when addressing people.

The Nominative Case

The nominative is the case you use when a noun is the subject of a sentence, for example:

husband	o andhras
My husband is English.	o andhras mu ine anglos
	(lit: the husband my is English)
friend	i fili
My friend (f) is here.	i fili mu ine edho
	(lit: the friend my is here)

In dictionaries, nouns always appear in the nominative case.

The Accusative Case

The accusative is the direct object of the sentence.

street	o dhromos
I see the street	vlepo ton dhromo
	(lit: I-see the street)

You'll notice that both the article and the noun ending change slightly to denote that the noun is the object of the sentence.

A WORD ABOUT CASE

In English, we're able to recognise the 'role' of a noun in a sentence (whether it's a subject, direct object or indirect object) by its position in the sentence and/or by the use of prepositions. However, like Latin, German and many other languages, Greek employs what are known as 'cases' to make these distinctions. Different 'case endings' (suffixes) act like labels on the nouns to indicate their role and their relationship to other words in a sentence. The case endings of the other words in the sentence, such as the articles, adjectives, adverbs or pronouns, must agree in number and gender with the case ending of the noun to which they refer.

Greek has three cases, and their application relates to grammatical usage in English. Here's a brief explanation of each case.

1. The **nominative** case refers to the the subject of a verb in a sentence, and is also the form you'll find in a dictionary. It indicates what or who is performing an action:

The thief who robbed the banker's house gave presents to his friends. (the thief 'robbed' and the thief 'gave').

2. The **accusative** is the direct object of a sentence. It indicates what or whom the verb refers to. Here it indicates what was given:

The thief who robbed the banker's house gave **presents** to his friends.

3. The **genitive** case refers to possession, a bit like the English 'of' or the possessive 's' ('s). It indicates **whose** or **of what/of whom**:

The thief who robbed **the banker's** house gave presents to his friends.

The Genitive Case

The genitive case denotes possession, as in 'John's car' or 'the teacher's class'. Again in Greek, both article and noun ending change slightly to denote the genitive.

John	o yianis
John's car	to aftokinito tu yiani
	(lit: the car of John)
the city	i poli
the city centre	to kendro tis polis
	(lit: the centre the city)

The Vocative Case

This case is used only when you are addressing someone (see page 48). This has the same ending as the nominative case except for masculine names which drop the final s ς.

Declension of Nouns

If you've done Latin or Ancient Greek at school, you will have had plenty of practice at this. A declension is essentially a fixed pattern of changes that applies to a group of nouns of the same gender and of the same ending.

Declension tables can initially look very daunting, but they are actually quite logical. You can try them out with any of the nouns in the dictionary. Once you know the gender, place the noun in the appropriate declension group according to its ending. The ending of the noun is the only part of the word that changes; the rest of the word, known as the stem, stays the same.

SINGULAR

	Masculine	Feminine	Neuter
Article	the	the	the
Nom	o	i	to
Gen	tu	tis	tu
Acc	ton	tin	to
	the road	the drachma	the child
Nom	dhrom-os	dhrachm-i	pedh-i
Gen	dhrom-u	dhrachm-is	pedh-iu
Acc	dhrom-o	dhrachm-i	pedh-i

PLURAL

	Masculine	Feminine	Neuter
Article	the	the	the
Nom	i	i	ta
Gen	ton	ton	ton
Acc	tus	tis	ta
	the roads	the drachmas	the children
Nom	dhrom-i	dhrachm-es	pedh-ia
Gen	dhrom-on	dhrachm-on	pedh-ion
Acc	dhrom-us	dhrachm-es	pedh-ia

GRAMMAR

THEY MAY SAY ...

kali tichi!	Καλή τύχη!	Good luck!
kali andamosi!	Καλή αντάμωση!	Until soon!
kalo taksidhi	Καλό ταξίδι.	Safe journey.
kales dhiakopes	Καλές διακοπές.	Have a nice holiday.

PRONOUNS
Subject Pronouns

The equivalents of 'I', 'you', 'he', 'she' etc are rarely used in Greek. This is because it is obvious from the verb ending, who the verb is referring to (see Verbs page 30). They are only used for emphasis or when there is no verb in the sentence.

I	egho	εγώ
you	esi	εσύ
he/she/it	aftos/afti/afto	αυτός/αυτή/αυτό
we	emis	εμείς
you (pl/pol)	esis	εσείς
they (m/f/n)	afti/aftes/afta	αυτοί/αυτές/αυτά

Direct Object Pronouns

These replace an object or a person in the sentence, equivalent to the English me, you, him, etc. They are placed before the verb.

me	me	με
you	se	σε
him/masculine nouns	ton	τον
her/feminine nouns	tin	την
it/neuter nouns	to	το
us	mas	μας
you (pl/pol)	sas	σας
them (m/f/n)	tus/tis/ta	τους/τις/τα

I see Maria.	vlepo tin maria
	(lit: I-see her Maria)
I see her.	tin vlepo
	(lit: her I-see)
I eat the grapes.	troo ta stafilia
	(lit: I-eat the grapes)
I eat them.	ta troo
	(lit: them I-eat)

Indirect Object Pronouns

You use these when there is a preposition (to, at) in front of the person or object that the pronoun is replacing. The indirect object pronouns are also placed before the verb.

to me	mu	μου
to you	su	σου
to him/masculine nouns	tu	του
to her/feminine nouns	tis	της
to it/neuter nouns	tu	του
to us	mas	μας
to you (pl/pol)	sas	σας
to them (m/f/n)	tus	τους

When you are using both a direct and an indirect object pronoun, the order is: indirect pronoun + direct pronoun + verb.

Helen is giving the glass to her sister.	i eleni dhini to potiri stin adhelfi tis (lit: the Helen gives the glass her sister to-her)
She is giving it to her.	tis to dhini (lit: to-her the gives)
I speak to John.	milao ston yianni (lit: I-speak to John)
I speak to him.	tu milao (lit: to-him I-speak)

OMIT ν SOMETIMES

You will hear the final letter ν n being omitted sometimes in the accusative articles τον ton, την tin, έναν enan, the negation particles δεν dhen, μην min, and the female direct object pronoun την tin.

GRAMMAR

POSSESSION

The possessive pronouns go after the noun, and they agree with the 'possessor'.

| my handbag | i tsanda mu | η τσάντα μου |
| your watch | to roloi su | το ρολόι σου |

Note that the article is retained, a bit like saying 'the handbag of me'.

my	mu	μου
your	su	σου
his/her/its	tu/tis/tu	του/της/του
our	mas	μας
your (pl/pol)	sas	σας
their	tus	τους

ADJECTIVES

Adjectives in Greek have to agree in gender and case with the noun that they qualify. They are usually placed before the noun. Placing them after the noun gives them more emphasis. Note that you have to use the article twice in the second construction.

to aspro forema   'the white dress'
but:
to forema to aspro   'the white dress'
(lit: the white the dress)

The majority of adjectives end in -os in the masculine, -i or -a in the feminine and -o in the neuter. They decline in exactly the same way as would the nouns with those endings (see page 25).

	SINGULAR		
	Masculine	Feminine	Neuter
	tall	tall	tall
Nom	psilos	psili	psilo
Gen	psilu	psilis	psilu
Acc	psilo	psili	psilo

	PLURAL		
	Masculine	**Feminine**	**Neuter**
	tall	tall	tall
Nom	psili	psiles	psila
Gen	psilon	psilon	psilon
Acc	psilus	psiles	psila

COMPARATIVE & SUPERLATIVE

You form the comparative by adding the ending -oteros, -oteri, -otero to the masculine, feminine and neuter form of the adjective respectively. Use the preposition apo for 'than'.

| The train is more expensive than the bus. | to treno ine akrivotero apo to leoforio (lit: the train is expensive-more than the bus) |

To form the superlative, add the appropriate article in front of the comparative form of the adjective.

| It's the cheapest ticket. | ine to fthinotero isitirio (lit: is the cheapest ticket) |

VERBS
Active & Passive Voice

Passive verbs are verbs that indicate a subject's action on itself. Active verbs are those that affect an action on someone or something else for example subject on to object.

> **DICTIONARY FORM**
>
> In their dictionary form all Greek verbs end in either -ω -o or -μαι mai.

Verbs are always listed in the dictionary in the first person, present tense. For example 'to write' is listed in a Greek dictionary as ghrafo, 'I write'. There is no equivalent to the English infinitive 'to …'.

The ending o belongs to verbs of the active voice, which usually expresses an action (dhiavazo I read); the ending -ame belongs to verbs of the passive voice, which denote a state (kimame I

GRAMMAR

sleep), a condition (fovame I'm afraid) or an action that is happening to the subject of the verb (kovome I cut myself). Some verbs have both an active and a passive form.

to cut	kovo
to cut myself	kovome
to lose	chano
to be lost	chanome

Some verbs with the active ending are:

to have	echo
to eat	troo
to go	piyeno
to see	vlepo
to open	anigho
to put	vazo

Some verbs with the passive ending are:

to be	ime
to sleep	kimame
to dress (oneself)	dinome
to sit	kathome
to be in a hurry	viazome

Each type of verb follows a different pattern of conjugation, so it's important to know whether a verb is active or passive.

LOOK OUT FOR DOTS

When you have two vowels together that normally form a diphthong, αι, ει, οι, and you see a dialisis sign (¨) over the second, it means that the two vowels have to be pronounced separately. It can make a difference: παΐδια pa-idhia means 'ribs', but παιδιά pedhia means 'children'!

GENDER

Some commonly used adjectives have irregular gender, and/or comparative and superlative forms. Gender is shown in the following order – masculine, feminine, neuter.

good	better
kalos/kali/kalo	kaliteros/kaliteri/kalitero
bad	worse
kakos/kakia/kako	chiroteros/chiroteri/chirotero
many	more
polis/poli/poli	perisoteros/perisoteri/perisotero
long	longer
makris/makria/makri	makriteros/makriteri/makritero

Several adjectives used to describe dimensions behave like this last example, including: makris 'long', vathis 'deep', platis 'wide' and fardhis 'broad'.

Present Tense

This tense can be translated as both 'I write' and 'I am writing'.

Some verbs have a stem (the part of the verb that doesn't change in conjugation) that ends in a vowel, for example:

to speak	milao
to ask	rotao
to laugh	yelao

ACTIVE VOICE
to write*

I	ghraf-o
you	ghraf-is
he/she/it	ghraf-i
we	ghraf-ume
you (pl/pol)	ghraf-ete
they	ghraf-un

*ghraf-usi in some spoken dialects

PASSIVE VOICE
to think

I	skeft-ome
you	skeft-ese
he/she/it	skeft-ete
we	skeft-omaste
you (pl/pol)	skeft-osaste/skeft-este
they	skeft-onde

The Simple Past

This is equivalent to the English 'I wrote', 'I spoke'.

To form the active simple past, you add the following endings to the end of the verb and move the accent to the third last syllable. The accent can move no further than three syllables from the end. Endings for the active voice are: -a, -es, -e, -ame, ate, an. For the passive voice the endings are: ika, ikes, ike, ikame, ikate, an.

This seems simple enough; however when the sounds s or th find themselves next to another consonant, they change, merge or disappear all together. For example y or gh+s and k+s usually become x, f+s, v+s and p+s usually become ps. This is simply because these and many other combinations of consonants are totally cacophonous to the Greek ear.

This is a difficult tense to form and has tormented generations of students of Greek. It is impossible to give all combinations of endings in a limited space. The most common verbs are listed in the Key Verbs box (page 41).

ACTIVE VOICE
to write

I	e-ghraps-a
you	e-ghraps-es
he/she/it	e-ghraps-e
we	ghraps-ame
you (pl/pol)	ghraps-ate
they	e-ghraps-an

GRAMMAR

PASSIVE VOICE
to think

I	skeft-ika
you	skeft-ikes
he/she/it	skeft-ike
we	skeft-ikame
you (pl/pol)	skeft-ikate
they	skeft-an

Note that each verb has now acquired a different stem. The modified stem has arisen from the merging of the sound s (active voice) or -th- (passive voice) with the final letter of the original stem. For example, ghraf- is the original stem of the verb ghrafo 'to write'. When the ending -sa is added, the sound f becomes ps, and the stem is now ghraps-. It is this modified stem that is used to form the past participle, the simple future and the subjunctive.

The Future

The Simple Future is the future tense you will come across most often, and corresponds to the English 'I will write', 'I will eat'. It is formed by using the modified stem from the simple past (see page 33), together with the endings below and the word tha in front of the verb.

ACTIVE VOICE
to write

I	tha ghraps-o
you	tha ghraps-is
he/she/it	tha ghraps-i
we	tha ghraps-ete
you (pl/pol)	tha ghraps-ume
they	tha ghraps-un

PASSIVE VOICE
to think

I	tha skeft-o
you	tha skeft-is
he/she/it	tha skeft-i
we	tha skeft-ume
you (pl/pol)	tha skeft-ite
they	tha skeft-un

MODALS
To Want

To express an intention, a desire, a feeling or a possibility of doing something, but not the action of doing it, you use the same structure as the simple future (see page 34), but with na in front of the verb instead of tha: na ghrapso. Where in English you would say 'I am afraid to swim' or 'I want to leave', with the verbs 'to swim' and 'to leave' in Greek you would use this structure.

I want to go to the museum.	thelo na pao sto musio
	(lit: I-want na go to museum)
I want to speak to you.	thelo na su miliso
Can you help me?	boris na me voithisis?
I like to travel.	mu aresi na taksidevo

Some expressions always use this structure:

It's possible to ...	ine dhinato na ...
It's necessary to ...	ine aparetito na ...
I have to ...	prepi na ...
Perhaps ...	isos na ...

GRAMMAR

Must/Have To

The verb 'I must' prepi is slightly unusual in Greek, in that it is not conjugated. It loosely translates as 'It is imperative that ...' and always takes the same structure as 'to want' (na ...). The verb chriazete denoting necessity, behaves in the same way.

I must get up early tomorrow.	prepi na ksipniso noris avrio (lit: prepi na I-wake early tomorrow)

The Imperative

The Imperative is the 'commanding' form of the verb as in 'Go!' or 'Come here!'. The imperative, especially the polite form, is much more widely used in Greek than English, as it's not considered an impolite way of asking for something.

	Informal	Polite
Come!	ela!	elate!
Give (me)!	dhose (mu)!	dhoste (mu)!
Bring (me) ...!	fere (mu)!	ferte (mu)!
Drink (it)!	pies (to)!	pyite (to)!
Tell (me)!	pes (mu)!	pite (mu)!

TO HAVE

The verb 'to have' presents a few irregularities:

The future tense uses tha ... followed by the verb in the present tense, for example tha echo. To express possibility use the same structure except put na in front of the word (see page 35). Apart from the present and the simple past, there are no other tenses for this verb.

TO HAVE		
	Present	**Simple Past**
I	echo	icha
you	echis	iches
he/she/it	echi	iche
we	echume	ichame
you (pl)	echete	ichate
they	echun	ichan

GRAMMAR

TO BE

The verb 'to be' is formed in the same way as 'to have' can also only be formed in the present, simple past and future.

	TO BE	
	Present	**Simple Past**
I	ime	imun
you	ise	isun
he/she/it	ine	itan
we	imaste	imaste/imastan
you (pl)	isaste/iste	isaste/isastan
they	ine	itan

NEGATIVES

You form a negative sentence by adding dhen in front of the verb.

I know.	ksero
	(lit: know-I)
I don't know.	dhen ksero
	(lit: not know-I)

In Greek, a double negative is used:

I (don't) know nothing.	dhen ksero tipota
	(lit: not know-I nothing)
I (don't) see nobody.	dhen vlepo kanena
	(lit: not see-I nobody)

To express possibilities or the imperative use min instead of dhen.

Don't touch.	min angizete
	(lit: not touch-you)
Maybe he/she won't come.	isos na min erthi
	(lit: maybe na not come)

QUESTIONS

There is no particular way of forming questions – simply raise your voice at the end of the sentence in the way that you would do when asking a question in English.

The bus stop is here.	i stasi ine edho
	(lit: the stop is here)
Is the bus stop here?	i stasi ine edho? (raise your voice at edho)

Note that the Greek question mark is (;). An English semi colon is a full-stop mark written as a superscript, for example καλά.

Question Words

The three options given are masculine/feminine/neuter respectively.

QUESTION WORDS	
Who/Which pios/pia/pio (sg) pi-i/pies/pia (pl)	Who's there? pios ine eki? (lit: who is there) Which street is this? pia odhos ine afti? (lit: which street is this)
What ti	What's this? ti ine afto? (lit: what is this)
Where pu	Where's the harbour? pu ine to limani? (lit: where is the harbour)
When pote	When does the boat leave? pote fevghi to plio? (lit: when leaves the boat)
Why yiati	Why are you laughing? yiati yelas? (lit: why laugh-you)

GRAMMAR

QUESTION WORDS

How
  pos
	How is your family?
	  pos ine i ikoyenia su?
	  (lit: how is the family your)

How (many/much)
  posos/posi/poso (sg)
  posi/poses/posa (pl)
	How many children
	  do you have?
	  posa pedia echete?
	  (lit: how children have-you)
	How (much)?
	  poso?
	How much is it?
	  poso kani?
	  (lit: how costs)

PREPOSITIONS

All the prepositions in the box below are followed by the noun in the accusative case, except metaksi 'between', which takes the genitive.

I'm from England.

> ime apo tin anglia
> (lit: I-am from the England)

The bank is between the
hotel and the coffee shop.

> i trapeza ine metaksi tu
> ksenodhochiu ke tu kafeniu
> (lit: the bank is between the
> hotel and the coffee shop)

to/at	se	σε
from	apo	από
with	me	με
for	ya	για
between	metaksi	μεταξύ
towards	pros	προς
under	kato apo	κάτω από
on	pano se	πάνω σε

When the preposition σε se is in front of an accusative article, it merges with it.

Prepositions	m, sg	f, sg	n, sg
singular to/at+the	ton ston	tin stin	to sto
plural to/at+the	tus stus	tis stis	ta sta

at the station   ston stathmo
in the cities   stis polis

CONJUNCTIONS

and	ke	και
because	yiati/epidhi	γιατί/επειδή
but	ala/omos	αλλά/όμως
therefore	lipon/ara	λοιπόν/άρα
or	i	ή
then	tote	τότε
although	an ke	αν και

CHEATING WITH TENSES

You'll most probably have trouble remembering your tenses, especially at the beginning. Don't panic, there are simple ways around this problem. If you can't get the future tense right just add tha in front of the verb, and that alone will signify that you are talking about the future. For the past tense just use the words chtes 'yesterday' or persi 'last year' as appropriate. Although this approach won't sound grammatically correct, you'll be clearly undertsood.

GRAMMAR

USEFUL VERBS

Useful verbs Verbs are given in first person singular

	Present	Simple Past	Simple Future
to answer	apandao/ apando	apandisa	tha apandiso
to ask	rotao/roto	rotisa	tha rotiso
to do something	kano	ekana	tha kano
to drive	odhigho	odhiyisa	tha odhiyiso
to enter	beno	bika	tha bo
to hear/listen	akuo	akusa	tha akuso
to know	ksero	iksera	tha ksero
to learn	matheno	ematha	tha matho
to leave	fevgho	efigha	tha figho
to live/stay	meno	emina	tha mino
to look for	psachno	epsaksa	tha psakso
to lose	chano	echasa	tha chaso
to sleep	kimame	kimithika	tha kimitho

KEY VERBS

Some of the more commonly used verbs also happen to be very irregular, especially in the way they form the Simple Past.

	Present	Imperfect	Simple Past	Simple Future
to eat troo				
I	troo	etrogha	efagha	tha fao
you	tros	etroghes	efaghes	tha fas
he/she/it	troi	etroghe	efaghe	tha fai
we	trome	troghame	faghame	tha fame
you (pl)	trote	troghate	faghate	tha fate
they	trone	etroghan	efaghan	tha fane

GRAMMAR

KEY VERBS

	Present	Imperfect	Simple Past	Simple Future
to drink pino				
I	pino	epina	ipia	tha pyo
you	pinis	epines	ipies	tha py-is
he/she/it	pini	epine	ipie	tha py-i
we	pinume	piname	ipiame	tha pyume
you (pl)	pinete	pinate	ipiate	tha py-ite
they	pinun	epinan	ipian	tha pyun
to go piyeno				
I	piyeno/ pao	piyena	pigha	tha pao
you	piyenis/ pas	piyenes	pighes	tha pas
he/she/it	piyeni/ pai	piyene	pighe	tha pai
we	piye-nume/ pame	piyename	pighame	tha pame
you (pl)	piyenete/ pate	piyenate	pighate	tha pate
they	piyenun/ pane	piyenan	pighan	tha pane
to say leo				
I	leo	elegha	ipa	tha po
you	les	eleyes	ipes	tha pis
he/she/it	lei	eleye	ipe	tha pi
we	leme	leghame	ipame	tha pume
you (pl)	lete	leghate	ipate	tha pite
they	lene	eleghan	ipan	tha pun

KEY VERBS

	Present	Imperfect	Simple Past	Simple Future
to see vlepo				
I	vlepo	evlepa	idha	tha dho
you	vlepis	evlepes	idhes	tha dhis
he/she/it	vlepi	evlepe	idhe	tha dhi
we	vlepume	vlepame	idhame	tha dhume
you (pl)	vlepete	vlepate	idhate	tha dhume
they	vlepun	evlepan	idhan	tha dhun
to take perno				
I	perno	eperna	pira	tha paro
you	pernis	epernes	pires	tha paris
he/she/it	perni	eperne	pire	tha pari
we	pernume	pername	pirame	tha parume
you (pl)	pernete	pernate	pirate	tha parete
they	pernun	epernan	piran	tha parun
to come erchome				
I	erchome	erchomun	irtha	tha ertho (thartho)
you	erchese	erchosun	irthes	tha erthis (tharthis)
he/she/it	erchete	erchotan	irthe	tha erthi (tharthi)
we	erchomaste	erchomaste/ erchomastan	irthame	tha erthume (tharthume)
you (pl)	erchosaste/ ercheste	erchosaste/ erchosastan	irthate	tha erthete (tharthete)
they	erchonde	erchodan	irthan	tha erthun (tharthun)

KEY VERBS

	Present	Imperfect	Simple Past	Simple Future
to give dhino				
I	dhino	edhina	edhosa	tha dhoso
you	dhinis	edhines	edhoses	tha dhosis
he/she/it	dhini	edhine	edhose	tha dhosi
we	dhinume	dhiname	dhosame	tha dhosume
you (pl)	dhinete	dhinate	dhosate	tha dhosete
they	dhinun	edhinan	edhosan	tha dhosun
to want thelo				
I	thelo	ithela	none	none
you	thelis	itheles		
he/she/it	theli	ithele		
we	thelume	thelame		
you (pl)	thelete	thelate		
they	thelun	ithelan		

GRAMMAR

ΣΥΝΑΝΤΩΝΤΑΣ ΚΟΣΜΟ
MEETING PEOPLE

YOU SHOULD KNOW

ΘΑ ΠΡΕΠΕΙ ΝΑ ΞΕΡΕΙΣ

Yes.	ne	Ναι.
No.	ochi	Όχι.
Hello.	yia sou (inf)/sas (pol)	Γειά σου/σας.
Goodbye.	cherete andio	Χαίρετε/Αντίο.
Please.	parakalo	Παρακαλώ.
Thank you.	efcharisto	Ευχαριστώ.
You're welcome.	parakalo	Παρακαλώ.
Excuse me.	sighnomi	Συγγνώμη.
OK.	endaksi	Εντάξει.

NO MEANS YES

Remember: ναι ne might sound like 'no', but it actually means YES.

GREETINGS

ΧΑΙΡΕΤΙΣΜΟΙ

Greeks greet each other by shaking hands, both upon meeting and parting. When you get to know people a bit better, you will probably be greeted with a kiss on both cheeks. It's quite acceptable to kiss people of either sex, irrespective of their age.

Good morning.	kalimera	Καλημέρα.
Good afternoon/ evening.	kalispera	Καλησπέρα.
Good night.	kalinichta	Καληνύχτα.
How are you?	ti kanis (inf)/ kanete? (pol)	Τι κάνεις/ κάνετε;

(Very) well, thanks.	(poli) kala, efcharisto	(Πολύ) καλά, ευχαριστώ.
So so.	etsi ki etsi	Έτσι κι έτσι.
And you?	kesi (inf)/kesis? (pol)	Και εσύ/Και εσείς;

'Good morning', 'good afternoon' and 'good evening' in the English sense don't have direct equivalents in Greek. You greet people with καλημέρα kalimera, from the start of the day until the start of siesta time, at about 3pm. If someone is going off for their afternoon rest, you can wish them καλό μεσημέρι kalo mesimeri (lit: good midday). When Greeks refer to το απόγευμα apoyevma 'afternoon', they really mean the hours after siesta time – 5.30pm onwards – when they greet each other with καλησπέρα kalispera. You use καληνύχτα kalinichta, when you leave in the evening. If unsure, use the general greeting χαίρετε cherete.

BODY LANGUAGE
Η ΓΛΩΣΣΑ ΤΟΥ ΣΩΜΑΤΟΣ

Greeks can sometimes be laconic with their replies. The single most confusing gesture is the tilting of the head backwards once, which means 'no' (όχι ochi). This gesture is sometimes reduced to a mere raise of the eyebrows, and is often accompanied by a tongue-clicking sound. On the other hand, 'yes' (ναι ne) is signified by a sideways tilt of the head, while shrugging one's shoulders or raising one's hands in the air (or both together) means 'I don't know' (δεν ξέρω dhen ksero).

An outward-facing palm with all five fingers splayed out (as if you're signifying the number five) is a very rude gesture, and it normally means that you've done something very offensive. Unsurprisingly, it's often used by angry taxi drivers to fellow drivers. Normally, only one hand is raised, but if the offender has been particularly obtuse, both hands are used. As a visitor, it is best not to use this gesture yourself, but if you see it directed to you, you know you're not popular!

FORMS OF ADDRESS

ΠΩΣ ΑΠΕΥΘΥΝΟΜΑΙ ΣΕ ΚΑΠΟΙΟΝ

There is an informal and a polite way of addressing people in Greece. To address people in the polite way use the plural of 'you' sas σας (see page 27).

Use the informal with your friends, people of your age group, children, and whenever someone asks you:

Μίλα μου στον ενικό.   mila mu ston eniko
Speak to me in the singular.

Use the polite form with older people, people you don't know well, in a professional capacity or in a formal environment.

If you're addressed in the informal way by someone in the above categories, it doesn't mean that you can do likewise – wait until asked.

Mr	kirios	Κύριος (κ.)
Mrs	kiria	Κυρία (κ.)
Miss	dhespinis	Δεσποινίς
Excuse me! (to catch someone's attention)	parakalo!	Παρακαλώ!

You may hear Greeks addressing people of a high professional status by their professional title:

Doctor!	yiatre!	γιατρέ!
Professor! (m)	kirie kathiyita!	κύριε Καθηγητά!
Director! (m)	kirie dhiefthinda!	κύριε Διευθυντά!

The vast majority of Greek male names end in -s, like Nikos, Kostas, Christos, Ioannis and so on. However, when you address the person, you have to drop the final 's'- you therefore call out Niko, Kosta, Christo, Ioanni. With a few names you have to change the final vowel to -ε e : Αλέξανδρε aleksandhre, Φίλιππε filipe, Κωνσταντίνε konstandine. Κύριος kirios 'Mr' becomes κύριε kirie, when you are talking to a man. Female names don't change in this way.

FIRST ENCOUNTERS

ΠΡΩΤΕΣ ΓΝΩΡΙΜΙΕΣ

What's your name?
    pos se (inf)/sas (pol) lene?   Πώς σε/ σας λένε;

My name is ...
    me lene ...   Με λένε ...

I'd like to introduce you to ...
    na se sistiso ston/stin ... (inf)   Να σε συστήσω στον/στην ...
    na sas sistiso ston/stin ... (pol)   Να σας συστήσω στον/στην ...

His/her name is ...
    to onoma tu/tis ine ...   Το όνομα του/της είναι ...

Pleased to meet you.
    chero poli   Χαίρω πολύ.

Do you live here?
    menis (inf)/menete (pol)   Μένεις/Μένετε εδώ;
    edho?

Where do you live;
are you staying?
    pu menis (inf)/menete (pol)?   Πού μένεις/μένετε;

I'm/We're staying at ...
    meno/menume sto ...   Μένω/Μένουμε στο ...

Do you like it here?
    saresi (inf)/(sas aresi) (pol)   Σ'αρέσει/(Σας αρέσει) εδώ;
    edho?

I like it here very much.
    m'aresi poli edho   Μ' αρέσει πολύ εδώ.

Are you here on holiday?
    ise (inf)/iste (pol) edho ya   Είσαι/Είστε εδώ για
    dhiakopes?   διακοπές;

I am here on/to ...	ime edho ...	Είμαι εδώ ...
holiday	ya dhiakopes	για διακοπές
business	ya dhulia	για δουλειά
study	ya spudhes	για σπουδές

MEETING PEOPLE

How long are you here for?
   ya poso kero ise (inf)/   Για πόσο καιρό είσαι/
   iste (pol) edho?   είστε εδώ;
I'm/we're here for ...
(days/weeks).
   tha ime/imaste edho ya ...   Θα είμαι/είμαστε εδώ για ...
   (meres/evdhomadhes)   (μέρες/εβδομάδες).
Enjoy your stay.
   kali dhiamoni   Καλή διαμονή.
Goodbye, nice to meet you.
   andio, charika ya tin   Αντίο, χάρηκα για την
   ghnorimia   γνωριμία.

I'm with (my/a) ...	ime edho me ...	Σίμαι εδώ με ...
friend	ton filo mu/ tin fili mu	τον φίλο μου/ την φίλη μου
partner	to zevghari mu	το ζευγάρι μου
business associate	ton/tin sinetero mu	τον/την συνέταιρο μου
family	tin ikoyenia mu	την οικογένεια μου
group	ena grup	ένα γκρουπ

It's OK.	endaksi	Εντάξει.
It's fine.	kala	Καλά.
Just a minute.	miso lepto	Μισό λεπτό.
It doesn't matter.	dhen pirazi	Δεν πειράζει.
Is it possible?	yinete?	Γίνεται;
It's (not) possible.	(dhen) yinete	(Δεν) γίνεται.
Of course/Sure.	veveos	Βεβαίως.
Good luck!	kali tichi!	Καλή τύχη!
I don't know.	dhen ksero	Δεν ξέρω.
Do you mind?	se (inf)/ sas (pol) pirazi?	Σε/Σας πειράζει;
Don't worry about it.	min stenochoriese!	Μην στενοχωριέσαι!

Excuse me! (to attract attention)	parakalo!	Παρακαλώ!
Excuse me. (apology)	sighnomi	Συγγνώμη.
Be careful!	proseche (inf)/ prosekste!(pol)	Πρόσεχε/Προσέξτε!
Come here!	ela dho!	Έλα δω!
I don't believe it!	ela christe ke panayia!	Έλα Χριστέ και Παναγία!

NATIONALITIES   ΕΘΝΙΚΟΤΗΤΕΣ

Unfortunately we can't include all countries here. Most names of countries sound similar in Greek to English. A notable exception is Greece itself, which is called Ελλάς elas.

What nationality are you?
  ti ethnikotita ise (inf)/ iste (pol)?   Τι εθνικότητα είσαι/είστε;

Have you been to my country?
  echis (inf)/echete (pol) pai stin chora mu?   Έχεις/Έχετε πάει στην χώρα μου;

Where are you from?
  apo pu ise (inf)/apo (pol) pu iste?   Από πού είσαι/Από πού είστε;

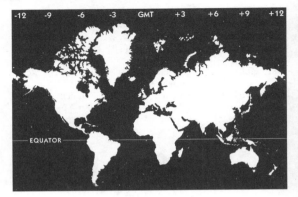

I'm from ...	ime apo ...	Είμαι από ...
Australia	tin afstralia	την Αυστραλία
Canada	ton kanadha	τον Καναδά
Cyprus	tin kipro	την Κύπρο
England	tin anglia	την Αγγλία
Ireland	tin irlandhia	την Ιρλανδία
Japan	tin iaponia	την Ιαπωνία
New Zealand	ti nea zilandhia	τη Νέα Ζηλανδία
Scotland	tin skotia	την Σκωτία
South Africa	ti notio afriki	τη Νότιο Αφρική
Spain	tin ispania	την Ισπανία
the USA	tis ipa/tin ameriki	τις ΗΠΑ/την Αμερική

THE FEMININE COUNTRIES

The majority of countries are feminine in Greek. Some exceptions are ο Καναδάς ο kanadhas Canada (m), οι ΗΠΑ i ipa the USA (f, pl), το Μεξικό to meksiko Mexico (n).

CULTURAL DIFFERENCES

ΔΙΑΦΟΡΕΣ ΚΟΥΛΤΟΥΡΑΣ

Is this a local custom?
afto ine topiko ethimo?

Αυτό είναι τοπικό έθιμο;

How do you do this in your country?
pos to kanete afto sti chora sas?

Πώς το κάνετε αυτό στη χώρα σας;

I don't want to offend you.
dhen thelo na se (inf)/ sas (pol) prozvalo

Δεν θέλω να σε/σας προσβάλω.

I'm sorry, it's not the custom in my country.
sighnomi, ala dhen to sinithizume afto stin chora mu

Συγγνώμη, αλλά δεν το συνηθίζουμε αυτό στην χώρα μου.

My culture/religion doesn't allow me to ...	ta ethima mu/i thriskia mu dhen mu epitrepun na ...	Τα έθιμα μου/η θρησκεία μου δεν μου επιτρέπουν να ...
practise this	kano afto	κάνω αυτό
eat this	fao afto	φάω αυτό
drink this	pio afto	πιω αυτό

AGE

ΗΛΙΚΙΑ

How old are you?
poson chronon ise (inf)/ iste (pol)?

Πόσων χρονών είσαι/είστε;

I am ... years old.
ime ... chronon

Είμαι ... χρονών.

(see page 229 for your age)

MEETING PEOPLE

OCCUPATIONS

Where do you work?
    pu dhulevis (inf)/
    dhulevete (pol)?
What work do you do?
    ti dhulia kanis (inf)/
    kanete (pol)?

ΕΠΑΓΓΕΛΜΑΤΑ

Πού δουλεύεις/δουλεύετε;

Τι δουλειά κάνεις/κάνετε;

I'm a/an ...	ime ...	Είμαι ...
artist	kalitechnis	καλλιτέχνης
business person	epichirimatias	επιχειρηματίας
doctor	yiatros	γιατρός
farmer	aghrotis	αγρότης
journalist	dhimosioghrafos	δημοσιογράφος
lawyer	dhikighoros	δικηγόρος
mechanic	michanikos	μηχανικός
nurse	nosokomos/	νοσοκόμος/
	nosokoma	νοσοκόμα
sailor	naftis	ναύτης
student	fititis/fititria	φοιτητής/
		φοιτήτρια
teacher	dhaskalos/	δάσκαλος/
	dhaskala	δασκάλα
waiter	servitoros/	σερβιτόρος/
	servitora	σερβιτόρα

I'm unemployed.
    ime anerghos/aneryi
I'm retired.
    ime sindaksiuchos
Do you enjoy your work?
    saresi (inf)/(sas aresi) (pol)
    i dhulia su (inf)/sas (pol)?

Είμαι άνεργος/άνεργη.

Είμαι συνταξιούχος.

Σ' αρέσει/(Σας αρέσει) η
δουλειά σου/σας;

MEETING PEOPLE

STUDYING   ΣΠΟΥΔΕΣ

What are you studying?
  ti spudhazis? (inf)   Τι σπουδάζεις;

I'm studying ...	spudhazo ...	Σπουδάζω ...
archaeology	archeoloyia	αρχαιολογία
art	kales technes	καλές τέχνες
arts/humanities	filoloyia	φιλολογία
biology	violoyia	βιολογία
Classical Greek	archea elinika	Αρχαία Ελληνικά
engineering	michanoloyia	μηχανολογία
languages	ksenes ghloses	ξένες γλώσσες
law	nomiki	νομική
medicine	iatriki	ιατρική
Modern Greek	nea elinika	Νέα Ελληνικά
teaching	pedhaghoyia	παιδαγωγία

FEELINGS   ΑΙΣΘΗΜΑΤΑ

cold	kriono	Κρυώνω
hot	zestenome	Κεσταίνομαι
hungry	pinao	Κεινάω
thirsty	dhipsao	Διψάω
afraid	fovame	Φοβάμαι
sorry (regret)	lipame	Λυπάμαι
sorry (apology)	sighnomi	Συγγνώμη
I'm ...	lip ...	Καλά
happy	charumenos/ charumeni	Χαρούμενος/ χαρούμενη
sad	lipimenos/ lipimeni	Λυπημένος/ λυπημένη
well	kala	Καλά
angry	thimomenos/ thimomeni	Θυμωμένος/ θυμωμένη
tired	kurazmenos/ kurazmeni	Κουρασμένος/ Κουρασμένη

BREAKING THE LANGUAGE BARRIER

ΣΠΑΖΩ ΤΟ ΦΡΑΓΜΑ ΤΗΣ ΓΛΩΣΣΑΣ

Do you speak English?
milas (inf)/milate (pol) anglika?

Μιλάς/Μιλάτε Αγγλικά;

Yes, I do (speak English).
ne, (milao anglika)

Ναι, (μιλάω Αγγλικά).

No, I don't (speak English).
ochi, (dhen milao anglika)

Όχι, (δεν μιλάω Αγγλικά).

I don't speak (much) Greek.
dhen milao (pola) elinika

Δεν μιλάω (πολλά) Ελληνικά.

Does anyone speak English?
milai kanis anglika?

Μιλάει κανείς Αγγλικά;

Do you understand?
katalavenis (inf)/
katalavenete (pol)?

Καταλαβαίνεις/
Καταλαβαίνετε;

I (don't) understand.
(dhen) kataleno

(Δεν) καταλαβαίνω.

Could you speak more slowly?
boris (inf)/borite (pol) na
milas/milate pio argha?

Μπορείς/ Μπορείτε να μιλάς/
μιλάτε πιο αργά;

Could you repeat that?
boris (inf)/borite (pol) na
to epanalavis/epanalavete?

Μπορείς/Μπορείτε να το
επαναλάβεις/επαναλάβετε;

Please write it down.
ghrapse (inf)/ghrapste (pol)
to, parakalo

Γράψε/Γράψτε το, παρακαλώ.

How do you say... in Greek?
pos lene ... sta elinika?

Πώς λένε ... στα Ελληνικά;

What does ... mean?
ti simeni ...?

Τι σημαίνει ...;

STAYING IN TOUCH

ΚΡΑΤΑΩ ΕΠΑΦΗ

I'm leaving tomorrow.
  fevgho avrio

Φεύγω αύριο.

I'd like to write to you.
  thathela na su (inf)/sas (pol)
  ghrapso

Θα'θελα να σου/ σας γράψω.

What's your address?
  pia ine i dhiefthinsi u (inf)/
  sas (pol)?

Ποιά είναι η διεύθυνση
σου/σας;

Do you have email?
  echis email?

Έχεις e-mail;

Come to visit me.
  ela (inf)/elate (pol) na
  mepiskefthis (inf)/
  mepiskefthite (pol)

Έλα/Έλατε να μ'επισκεφθείς/
επισκεφθείτε.

You're always welcome.
  ise (inf)/iste (pol) panda
  efprosdhektos (m)/
  efprosdhekti (f)

Είσαι/Είστε πάντα
ευπρόσδεκτος/
ευπρόσδεκτη.

DID YOU KNOW ... Ελλάς elas or Ελλάδα eladha is the Greek name for Greece, from which the word 'hellenic' is derived. The official name in Greek is η Ελληνική Δημοκρατία i eliniki dhimokratia 'the Hellenic Republic'. The language is ελληνικά elinika, the people Έλληνας elinas (m) or Ελληνίδα elinidha (f) which means 'a Greek'. 'Greek' the adjective is ελληνικός/ελληνική/ελληνικό elinikos/eliniki/eliniko.

MEETING PEOPLE

WRITING LETTERS   ΓΡΑΦΩ ΓΡΑΜΜΑΤΑ

Formal letters are quite difficult to write, as they are written in a very stylized, elaborate way using some katharevusa (purist) forms. An official letter can be written in English, as most business people will be able to understand it. However, if you'd like to keep in touch with a friend you made in Greece, here are some phrases to help you.

Dear (Kostas) ...	Αγαπημένε μου (Κώστα) ...
Dear Mr (Michalakis)	Αγαπημένε μου κ. (Μιχαλάκη)
Dear Mrs (Michalaki)	Αγαπημένη μου κ. (Μιχαλάκη)

Polite forms for the phrases below are in brackets.

How are you?	Τι κάνεις (κάνετε);
Are you well?	Είσαι (είστε) καλά;
Is your family well?	Η οικογένεια σου (σας) είναι καλά;
I had a good trip.	Είχα καλό ταξίδι.
I'm sorry I took so long to write.	Συγγνώμη που άργησα να σου (σας) γράψω.

HOW'S YOUR GREEKNESS?

The word 'Greece' comes from Γραικός ghrekos, a word originating in classical times, and used to refer to a tribe in western Greece – it was taken up later by the Italians mistakenly to refer to all Greeks. Sometimes, the Greeks refer to themselves as Ρωμιός romios, meaning 'Roman', an inhabitant of the Byzantine (eastern Roman) empire. Ρωμιοσύνη romiosini stands for 'Greekness'.

I'm sending you the photos from the holiday.	Σου (Σας) στέλνω τις φωτογραφίες από τις διακοπές.
Thank you for your hospitality.	Σ' (Σας) ευχαριστώ για την φιλοξενία.
Say hello to ... from me.	Δώσε (Δώστε) χαιρετισμούς στον/στην ... από μένα.
I miss you a lot.	Μου λείπεις (λείπετε) πολύ.
I miss Greece.	Μου λείπει η Ελλάδα.
I hope to come again next year.	Ελπίζω να ξανάρθω του χρόνου.
When will you come here?	Πότε θα'ρθεις (θα'ρθετε) εδώ;
I'm waiting for you.	Σε (σας) περιμένω.

THEY MAY SAY ...

Greeks love the term 'Have a nice ...!', so there's a greeting for every occasion:

kali evthomadha	Have a good week. (on Mondays)
kalo mina	Have a good month. (on the 1st of every month)
kalo kalokeri	Have a good summer.
kalo chimona	Have a good winter.
kali dhiaskedhasi	Have a nice time.
kali ora	literally 'good hour' (when you are expecting someone to return)

MEETING PEOPLE

Write to me soon.	Γράψε (γράψτε) μου σύντομα.
Lots of kisses	Με πολλά φιλιά.
Lots of love	Με πολλή αγάπη.
Greetings	Χαιρετισμούς.
P.S.	Υ.Γ.

ΚΥΚΛΟΦΟΡΩΝΤΑΣ
GETTING AROUND

FINDING YOUR WAY ΚΑΤΑΤΟΠΙΖΟΜΑΙ

Be prepared when asking directions in Greece! People are a bit more laid back when it comes to direction giving. That 'five minutes' may be 25 minutes; 'near' the post office may mean on the opposite side of town from the post office.

Where's the ...?	pu ine ... ?	Πού είναι ...;
bus stop	i stasi leoforiu	η στάση λεωφορείου
trolley stop	i stasi trolei	η στάση τρόλλεϋ
train station	o sidhirodhromikos stathmos	ο σιδηροδρομικός σταθμός
port	to limani	το λιμάνι
taxi rank	o stathmos taxi	ο σταθμός ταξί
ticket office	to ekdhotirio isitirion	το εκδοτήριο εισιτηρίων
airport	to aerodhromio	το αεροδρόμιο

DON'T MISS IT!

What time does the ... leave?	ti ora fevyi to... ?	Τι ώρα φεύγει το ...;
plane	aeroplano	αεροπλάνο
ferry-boat	feribot	φερυμπώτ
boat	plio/to vapori	πλοίο/το βαπόρι
bus	leoforio	λεωφορείο
coach	pulman	πούλμαν
train	treno	τραίνο

Can you show me on the map?
  borite na mu dhiksete sto charti?
  Μπορείτε να μου δείξετε στο χάρτη;

Where am I (on the map)?
  pu vriskome (sto charti)?
  Πού βρίσκομαι (στο χάρτη);

How do I get to ...?
  pos pane sto ...?
  Πώς πάνε στο ...;

Is it far from here?
  ine makria apo dho?
  Είναι μακριά από δω;

Can I walk there?
  boro na perpatiso os eki?
  Μπορώ να περπατήσω ως εκεί;

What street is this?
  ti odhos ine afti?
  Τι οδός είναι αυτή;

DIRECTIONS   ΟΔΗΓΙΕΣ

Straight ahead.	olo efthia	Όλο ευθεία.
Turn left/right at the next ...	stripste aristera/ dheksia	Στρίψτε αριστερά/ δεξιά ...
corner	stin epomeni ghonia	στην επόμενη γωνία
block	sto epomeno tetraghono	στο επόμενο τετράγωνο
traffic lights	sta fota	στα φώτα
in front of	brosta apo	μπροστά από
behind	piso apo	πίσω από
next to	dhipla	δίπλα
opposite	apenandi apo	απέναντι από
far	makria	μακριά
near	konda	κοντά
north	voria	βόρεια
south	notia	νότια
west	dhitika	δυτικά
east	anatolika	ανατολικά

ADDRESSES ΔΙΕΥΘΥΝΣΕΙΣ

Greek addresses are written as follows:

4ος όροφος
Οδ. Αχιλλέως 44
Π. Φάληρο
GR-175 33 Αθήνα

This is deciphered as follows.

4ος όροφος	4th floor (floor number isn't always given as part of the address)
Οδ.	abbreviation for Οδός odhos 'Street'
Αχιλλέως 44	street name and number
Π. Φάληρο:	name of suburb, not always included in smaller towns. Π is an abbreviation of Παλαιό paleo meaning 'old'
Αθήνα	name of city
175 33	postal code

BUYING TICKETS ΑΓΟΡΑΖΩ ΕΙΣΙΤΗΡΙΑ

Where can I buy a ticket?
pu boro na aghoraso isitirio? — Πού μπορώ να αγοράσω εισιτήριο;

How much is a/(the cheapest) ticket to Thessaloniki?
poso kani to (fthinotero) isitirio ya tin thesaloniki? — Πόσο κάνει το (φθηνότερο) εισιτήριο για την Θεσσαλονίκη;

Do I need to book a seat?
chriazete na kliso thesi? — Χρειάζεται να κλείσω θέση;

Is it full?
ine yemato? — Είναι γεμάτο;

GETTING AROUND

I'd like (a) ...	tha ithela (ena) ...	Θα ήθελα (ένα) ...
one-way ticket	aplo isitirio	απλό εισιτήριο
return ticket	ena isitirio metepistrofis	ένα εισιτήριο μετ' επιστροφής
two tickets	dhio isitiria	δύο εισιτήρια
first/second class ticket	ena isitirio protis/ dhefteris thesis	ένα εισιτήριο πρώτης/δεύτερης θέσης
student ticket	ena fititiko isitirio	ένα φοιτητικό εισιτήριο
children's ticket	ena pedhiko isitirio	ένα παιδικό εισιτήριο

THEY MAY SAY ...

aplo i me epistrofi?	Single or return?
fititiko?	Student? (student ticket)
kapnizondes i mi kapnizondes?	Smoking or non-smoking?
echete klisi thesi?	Have you booked a seat?
ine yemato	It's full.

AT CUSTOMS

I have something to declare.
  echo kati na dhiloso.
Do I have to declare this?
  prepi na to dhiloso afto?
I didn't know I had to declare this.
  dhen iksera oti eprepe na to dhiloso

ΣΤΟ ΤΕΛΩΝΕΙΟ

Έχω κάτι να δηλώσω.

Πρέπει να το δηλώσω αυτό;

Δεν ήξερα ότι έπρεπε να το δηλώσω.

AIR

When is the next flight
to (Iraklion)?
    pote ine i epomeni ptisi
    ya (to Iraklio)?
How long is the flight?
    posi ora ine i ptisi?
I've lost my luggage.
    echasa tis aposkeves mu
My luggage hasn't arrived.
    i aposkeves mu dhen
    echun ftasi
Where is the lost &
found desk?
    pu ine to ghrafio
    apolesthendon?

ΑΕΡΟΠΟΡΙΚΩΣ

Πότε είναι η επόμενη πτήση
για (το Ηράκλειο);

Πόση ώρα είναι η πτήση;

Έχασα τις αποσκευές μου.

Οι αποσκευές μου δεν
έχουν φτάσει.

Πού είναι το γραφείο
απωλεσθέντων;

STON IT BABY

In general, where you would use 'in', 'at' or 'to'
before the article 'the', articles in Greek change
from ο o (m), η i (f), το to (n) το στον ston, στην stin,
στο sto, in the singular and στους stous, στις stis, στα
sta, in the plural. For example:

Where is **the** station?   pu ine **o** stathmos?
                                Πού είναι ο σταθμός;
How do I get **to the**   pos pane **ston** stathmo?
station?   Πώς πάνε στον σταθμό;
I'm **at the** port.   ime **sto** limani
                                  Είμαι στο λιμάνι.

Note that the noun 'station' also changes (see
page 25).

GETTING AROUND

BUS & TROLLEY BUS

ΛΕΩΦΟΡΕΙΟ & ΤΡΟΛΛΕΫ

Athens has a well-developed bus service that covers most suburbs of Athens, though it can be confusing finding the right bus from the city centre to the suburbs. In several Greek cities, Athens included, you have to buy your bus tickets beforehand. They can be bought from little booths marked ΕΙΣΙΤΗΡΙΑ at main stops or from the omnipresent yellow kiosks, known as περίπτερο periptero. Punch them in the machine as you board.

Where is the bus/trolley stop?
    pu ine i stasi tu
    leoforiu/trolei?

Πού είναι η στάση του
λεωφορείου/τρόλλεϋ;

Is this the bus stop for number (14)?
    afti ine i stasi ya to
    (dhekatesera)?

Αυτή είναι η στάση για το
(δεκατέσσερα);

Does this bus go to (Sintagma)?
    pai afto to leoforio (sto
    sindaghma)?

Πάει αυτό το λεωφορείο (στο
Σύνταγμα);

Which bus goes to (Piraeus)?
    pio leoforio pai
    (ston pirea)?

Ποιο λεωφορείο πάει
(στον Πειραιά);

Where can I buy a ticket for the bus?
    apo pu boro na aghoraso
    isitiriu ya to leoforio?

Από πού μπορώ να αγοράσω
εισιτήριο για το λεωφορείο;

One ticket, please.
    ena isitirio, parakalo

Ένα εισιτήριο, παρακαλώ.

A bunch of (10) tickets.
    mia dhesmidha (dheka)
    isitirion

Μια δεσμίδα (δέκα)
εισιτηρίων.

SIGNS

ΣΤΑΣΗ ΛΕΩΦΟΡΕΙΟΥ	**BUS STOP**
ΣΤΑΣΗ ΤΡΟΛΛΕΥ	**TROLLEY STOP**
ΕΙΣΙΤΗΡΙΑ	**TICKETS**

When is the ... bus?   pote erchete to   Πότε έρχεται το ...
                        ... leoforio?   λεωφορείο;
    next   epomeno   επόμενο
    first   proto   πρώτο
    last   telefteo   τελευταίο

Do you stop at (Likavitos)?
    kanete stasi (ston   Κάνετε στάση (στον
    likavito)?   Λυκαβηττό);
Can you tell me when we
get to (the museum)?
    borite na mu pite otan   Μπορείτε να μου πείτε όταν
    ftasume (sto musio)?   φτάσουμε (στο μουσείο);
Stop, please!
    stamatiste, parakalo!   Σταματήστε, παρακαλώ!

TRAIN   ΤΡΑΙΝΟ

Greece's train system has always come second to its road transport
system – at least in the minds of most Greek travellers – and has
generally been regarded as somewhat inferior and slower. Admit-
tedly it is cheaper, however the express intercity services linking
north and south have made travel much more comfortable and
are highly recommendable.

N FOR SOUTH

On greek maps and road signs N stands for Νότος notos
'south', while B marks the North (Βορράς voras).

GETTING AROUND

When is the next train for
Thessaloniki?
    pote ine to epomeno
    treno ya (tin thesaloniki)?

Πότε είναι το επόμενο τραίνο
για (την Θεσσαλονίκη);

Which platform does the train
to (Patra) leave from?
    apo pia apovathra fevyi to
    treno ya (tin patra)?

Από ποια αποβάθρα φεύγει
το τραίνο για (την Πάτρα);

Is this the train to (Munich)?
    afto ine to treno ya (to
    monacho)?

Αυτό είναι το τραίνο για (το
Μόναχο);

The train is delayed.
    to treno echi kathisterisi

Το τραίνο έχει καθυστέρηση.

Do you accept Interail?
    dhecheste karta interail?

Δέχεστε κάρτα Interail;

METRO

The long-awaited Athens metro (το μετρό to metro)
started operating on New Year's Eve 1999. The
original line links the port of Piraeus (ΠΕΙΡΑΙΑΣ) to
the northern suburb of Kifisia (ΚΗΦΙΣΙΑ) via
Monastiraki (ΜΟΝΑΣΤΗΡΑΚΙ) at the foot of the
Acropolis and Omonia square (ΟΜΟΝΟΙΑ). Stations
show antiqtuities on site, as they were found during
the digging of the tunnels.

BOAT   ΠΛΟΙΟ

In the course of your travels to Greece, you will almost certainly
need to catch a ferry (φερυμπώτ feribot) to one of the islands, and
often it is the only way of getting there. You are likely to start
your journey from the main port of Piraeus Πειραιάς or
Πειραιεύς, pronounced pireas or pireefs.

As long as you avoid weekends and public holidays (screaming kids, smoked-filled, packed lounges), a trip on an island ferry can be a pleasant experience.

Boats are often named after islands, for example Νήσος Σάμος nisos samos (the island of Samos). They're usually named after their destination, but it's worth checking before boarding!

Where does the boat to
(Chania) leave from?

   apo pu fevyi to plio ya (ta   Από πού φεύγει το πλοίο για
   chania)?   (τα Χανιά);

When is the next boat for
(Naxos)?

   pote ine to epomeno   Πότε είναι το επόμενο πλοίο
   plio ya (ti naxo)?   για (την Νάξο);

Does this ferry go to (Rodos)?

   afto to feribot pai   Αυτό το φερυμπώτ πάει
   (sti rodho)?   (στην Ρόδο);

Can I have the cheapest ticket
to (Santorini)?

   boro na echo to fthinotero   Μπορώ να έχω το φθηνότερο
   isitirio ya (tin sandorini)?   εισιτήριο για (την Σαντορίνη);

Do I get a discount with
an Interail card?

   kanete ekptosi me karta   Κάνετε έκπτωση με κάρτα
   interail?   Interail;

On Board   Στο πλοίο

Where is the ...?	pu ine ... ?	Πού είναι ...;
deck	to katastroma	το κατάστρωμα
cabin number ...	i kabina ...	η καμπίνα ...
car deck	to garaz	το γκαράζ
reception	i resepsion	η ρεσεψιόν
restaurant	to estiatorio	το εστιατόριο
purser's office	to loyistirio	το λογιστήριο

boat	to plio/vapori/karavi	το πλοίο/βαπόρι/καράβι
ferryboat	to feribot	το φερυμπώτ
sailing boat	to istioplo-iko	το ιστιοπλοϊκό
yacht	to kotero/to yiot	το κότερο, το γιωτ
caique (large fishing boat)	to ka-iki	το καΐκι
small fishing boat	i psarovarka/varka	η ψαρόβαρκα/βάρκα

I'd like an inside/outside cabin.
 tha ithela mia esoteriki/
 eksoteriki kabina
Θα ήθελα μια εσωτερική/
εξωτερική καμπίνα.

A cabin for one/two people, please.
 mia kabina ya ena/dhio
 atoma, parakalo
Μια καμπίνα για ένα/δύο
άτομα, παρακαλώ.

Which island is this?
 pio nisi ine afto?
Ποιο νησί είναι αυτό;

How many hours is it (to Milos)?
 poses ores ine os
 (tin milo)?
Πόσες ώρες είναι ως
(την Μήλο);

FOR THE CHEAPSKATES

If you want the cheapest ticket for the ferry ask for ένα
εισιτήριο τουριστικής θέσης ena isitirio turistikis thesis 'one
tourist class ticket', or μια θέση κατάστρωμα mia thesi
katastroma 'one deck class ticket'. This gives you access
to the entire boat, except areas marked ΣΑΛΟΝΙ ΠΡΩΤΗΣ
ΘΕΣΕΩΣ 'first class lounge', or Α΄ΘΕΣΗ 'first class'.

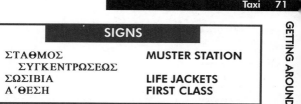

ΣΤΑΘΜΟΣ ΣΥΓΚΕΝΤΡΩΣΕΩΣ	**MUSTER STATION**
ΣΩΣΙΒΙΑ	**LIFE JACKETS**
Α΄ΘΕΣΗ	**FIRST CLASS**

TAXI   ΤΑΞΙ

You've heard of all the scams – dodgy meters, taking the 'scenic route', anything to get some more money out of the unsuspecting traveller. Unfortunately, Greece is no exception, although by no means are all taxi drivers like that. So here's a few tips in taxi etiquette.

When you get to the airport, have a look at the taxi price lists posted in the baggage reclaim hall, and don't let any taxi driver charge you more. If in doubt, ask the driver prices before you get in the car. Taxi drivers, especially in Athens, like taking a full load, so don't be disturbed when you have to share the taxi with another three people. It also means that you can hail a taxi even if there are a couple of passengers in it already, as long as you are all going towards the same direction – but don't expect to share the fare, as each passenger pays the full value displayed on the meter. Taxi drivers charge more for carrying luggage, being called out, working at 'unsociable hours', and they take a double tariff on holidays.

Where is the taxi rank?
    pu ine i stasi taxi?   Πού είναι η στάση ταξί;
Are you free?
    iste eleftheros?   Είστε ελεύθερος;
Can you take me to ...?
    borite na me pate sto ...?   Μπορείτε να με πάτε στο ...;
How much is it to ...?
    poso ine os to ...?   Πόσο είναι ως το ...;

GETTING AROUND

How much do you charge
for the luggage?
    poso chreonete ya tis
    aposkeves?   Πόσο χρεώνετε για τις
                                   αποσκευές;

Do you have change for
(1000) drachmas?
    echete resta apo (chilies)
    drachmes?   Έχετε ρέστα από (χίλιες)
                                   δραχμές;

You've overcharged me!
    me chreosate parapano!   Με χρεώσατε παραπάνω!

Please, wait.
    perimenete, parakalo   Περιμένετε, παρακαλώ.

Could you slow down, please?
    borite na pate pio argha,
    parakalo?   Μπορείτε να πάτε πιο αργά,
                                   παρακαλώ.

CAR   ΑΥΤΟΚΙΝΗΤΟ

Where can I rent a car/
motorbike?
    pu boro na nikiaso
    aftokinito/motosikleta?   Πού μπορώ να νοικιάσω
                                     αυτοκίνητο/μοτοσυκλέτα;

How much is it daily/weekly/
per kilometre?
    poso kani tin imera/tin
    evdhomadha/to chiliometro?   Πόσο κάνει την ημέρα/την
                                     εβδομάδα/το χιλιόμετρο;

Does this include insurance?
    simberilamvanete i
    asfalia?   Συμπεριλαμβάνεται η
                                     ασφάλεια;

I prefer a small/large car
(with air-conditioning).
    protimo ena mikro/meghalo   Προτιμώ ένα μικρό/μεγάλο
    aftokinito (me klimatismo)   αυτοκίνητο (με κλιματισμό).

Can I return it in another city?
    boro na to epistrepso se   Μπορώ να το επιστρέψω σε
    mia ali poli?   μια άλλη πόλη;

Where is the next petrol
station?
    pu ine to epomeno   Πού είναι το επόμενο
    venzinadhiko?   βενζινάδικο;

Fill it up, please.
    yemiste to parakalo   Γεμίστε το, παρακαλώ.

Ten thousand drachmas, please.
    dheka chiliadhes, parakalo   Δέκα χιλιάδες, παρακαλώ.

It takes ...	perni ...	Παίρνει ...
super (leaded)	super	σούπερ
unleaded	amolivdhi	αμόλυβδη
diesel	dizel	ντίσελ

ODDS OR EVENS IN THE RING

The expressions μονά-ζυγά mona-zigha 'odds-evens'
and δακτύλιος dhaktilios 'ring', are not some strange
form of Greek gambling. They refer to Athens' traffic
restrictions in order to curb the notorious νέφος nefos
'smog'. On odd days of the month, only cars with
number plates ending in odd numbers are allowed
to enter the restricted ring area dhaktilios, and vice
versa on even days. On days when the pollution is
particularly bad, only buses and taxis are allowed in,
and of course bikes and trolley buses. Look out for
road signs showing a yellow hexagonal shape on a
white background – they mark the boundary of the
restricted area.

GETTING AROUND

Can you check the ... please.	borite na elenchsete ... parakalo	Μπορείτε να ελέγξετε ... παρακαλώ.
oil	ta ladhia	τα λάδια
tyres	ta lasticha	τα λάστιχα

Is this the road to (Meteora)?
    aftos o dhromos pai (sta meteora)?   Αυτός ο δρόμος πάει (στα Μετέωρα);

Can I park here?
    boro na parkaro edho?   Μπορώ να παρκάρω εδώ;

Car Problems   Προβλήματα με το αυτοκίνητο

My car has broken down.
    epatha vlavi   Έπαθα βλάβη.

I need a mechanic.
    chriazome michaniko   Χρειάζομαι μηχανικό.

What make is it?
    ti marka ine?   Τι μάρκα είναι;

Where is the nearest garage?
    pu ine to kondinotero garaz?   Πού είναι το κοντινότερο γκαράζ;

I have a puncture.
    epatha lasticho   Έπαθα λάστιχο.

I've run out of oil.
    emina apo ladhi   Έμεινα από λάδι.

My brakes don't work.
    dhen dhulevun ta frena mu   Δεν δουλεύουν τα φρένα μου.

It's overheating.
    zestathike   Ζεστάθηκε.

I've locked my keys in the car.
    klidhosa ta klidhia mu mesa sto aftokinito   Κλείδωσα τα κλειδιά μου μέσα στο αυτοκίνητο.

I need to be towed.
    chriazome rimulkisi   Χρειάζομαι ρυμούλκηση.

I need a jump start.
    chriazome ekinisi anangis   Χρειάζομαι εκκίνηση ανάγκης.

BICYCLE   ΠΟΔΗΛΑΤΟ

If you've got the stamina, cycling is a wonderful way of getting around and seeing the country. However, remember that the terrain in Greece in very mountainous, with flat areas few and far in between. It's worth making sure that your brakes work properly, and bearing in mind that 100 km on mountainous terrain at 30°C might take longer than you anticipated!

ENGLISH OR GREEK?

Travel brochures and guide books often use the anglicized form of a Greek place name, which can sound quite different from its name in Greek. This is a list of some that may cause confusion:

English name	Greek name	
Athens	Αθήνα	athina (sometimes Αθήναι athine)
Corfu	Κέρκυρα	kerkira
Mitilini	Λέσβος	lesvos (Mitilini Μυτιλήνη is the main town)
Salonica	Θεσσαλονίκη	thessaloniki
Santorini	Θήρα/Σαντορίνη˙	thira/sandorini
Rhodes	Ρόδος	rodhos
Zante	Ζάκυνθος	zakinthos

And in Cyprus ...

Nicosia	Λευκωσία	lefkosia
Limassol	Λεμεσός	lemesos
Famagusta	Αμμόχωστος	amochostos (in Northern Cyprus)

Road signs display the Greek version only, in both Greek and Latin characters.

At the moment and for the near future, Greek cities are poorly equipped for cyclists – there are no cycling paths, cars are often parked on both sides of the pavement, or worse, on the pavement, and as a cyclist you may not get noticed.

Where can I hire a bicycle?
  apo pu boro na nikiaso podhilato?

Από πού μπορώ να νοικιάσω ποδήλατο;

How much is it per hour/day?
  poso kani tin ora/imera?

Πόσο κάνει την ώρα/ημέρα;

Is this road OK for bikes?
  aftos o dhromos kani ya podhilata?

Αυτός ο δρόμος κάνει για ποδήλατα;

I have a flat tyre.
  epatha lasticho

Έπαθα λάστιχο.

bicycle pump	i troba	η τρόμπα
brakes	ta frena	τα φρένα
chain	i alisidha	η αλυσίδα
gears	i tachitites	οι ταχύτητες
handlebars	ta cherulia timoniu	τα χερούλια τιμονιού

ΔΙΑΜΟΝΗ
ACCOMMODATION

FINDING ACCOMMODATION
ΒΡΙΣΚΩ ΔΙΑΜΟΝΗ

Finding accommodation in Greece should not be a problem for most of the year, except perhaps during the first fortnight of August when all of the Athenian population spills out into the countryside. The cheapest form of accommodation is probably camping, which is feasible in the lowlands throughout the year, although not many campsites stay open all year round (see page 187).

Athens has several reasonably priced, official and unofficial, youth hostels. Outside big cities, your best option for budget accommodation is δωμάτια dhomatia rooms; these are usually attached to a house, where the family lives, and it really is the best way of meeting some of the local people.

I'm looking for ...	psachno yia ...	Ψάχνω για ...
a hotel	ena ksenodhochio	ένα ξενοδοχείο
a room	ena dhomatio	ένα δωμάτιο
a youth hostel	ena ksenona neotitas	ένα ξενώνα νεότητας
the campsite	tin kataskinosi	την κατασκήνωση

Where can I find a cheap/ good hotel?

pu boro na vro ena ftino/ kalo ksenodhochio?

Πού μπορώ να βρω ένα φτηνό/ καλό ξενοδοχείο;

ACCOMMODATION

BOOKING AHEAD

ΚΛΕΙΝΩ ΔΩΜΑΤΙΟ ΕΚ ΤΩΝ ΠΡΟΤΕΡΩΝ

I'd like to book a room, please.
   thelo na kliso ena
   dhomatio, parakalo.

Θέλω να κλείσω ένα
δωμάτιο, παρακαλώ.

Are there any rooms free?
   iparchun elefthera
   dhomatia?

Υπάρχουν ελεύθερα
δωμάτια;

I'd like a room for ...	tha ithela ena dhomatio ya ...	Θα ήθελα ένα δωμάτιο για ...
one person	ena atomo	ένα άτομο
two people	dhio atoma	δύο άτομα
two nights	dhio nichtes	δύο νύχτες
one week	mia evdhomadha	μια εβδομάδα

How much is it ...?	poso kani ... ?	Πόσο κάνει ...;
per night	tin vradhia	την βραδιά
for a week	ya mia evdhomadha	για μια εβδομάδα

CHECKING IN

Η ΑΦΙΞΗ

If you want a single room ask for ένα μονόκλινο παρακαλώ ena monoklino parakalo. For a double room ask for ένα δίκλινο παρακαλώ ena dhiklino parakalo, which usually implies twin beds. Few places have double beds, but you can try asking for ένα διπλό κρεβάτι ena dhiplo krevati.

Very often you'll be asked to surrender your passport when you check into a hotel, or even private rooms. This is for the purposes of registration and security, though in the former case you are entitled to ask for your passport back after registration is completed, especially since you will probably need it for identification when changing travellers cheques or even purchasing tickets.

Do you have any rooms
available?
   echete elefthera dhomatia?   Έχετε ελεύθερα δωμάτια;

Sorry, we're full.
    dhistichos ine ghemato   Δυστυχώς είναι γεμάτο.
I'd like a single/double room.
    tha ithela ena monoklino/   Θα ήθελα ένα μονόκλινο/
    dhiklino   δίκλινο.

I want a room with a ...	thelo ena dhomatio me ...	Θέλω ένα δωμάτιο με ...
private bathroom	idhiotiko banio	ιδιωτικό μπάνιο
shared bathroom	kino banio	κοινό μπάνιο
double bed	dhiplo krevati	διπλό κρεβάτι
shower	dus	ντους
balcony	balkoni	μπαλκόνι
window	parathiro	παράθυρο
view	thea	θέα

ACCOMMODATION

ACCOMMODATION

Can I see it?	boro na to dho?	Μπορώ να το δω;
Is there anything ...?	iparchi tipota ... ?	Υπάρχει τίποτα ...;
bigger	meghalitero	μεγαλύτερο
smaller	mikrotero	μικρότερο
quieter	pio isicho	πιο ήσυχο
else	alo	άλλο

Is there hot water all day?
    iparchi zesto nero oli tin
    imera?
Υπάρχει ζεστό νερό όλη την
ημέρα;

Is breakfast included?
    simberilamvanete to proino?
Συμπεριλαμβάνεται το πρωινό;

Where is the bathroom?
    pu ine to banio?
Πού είναι το μπάνιο;

Do you accept credit cards/
(travellers cheques)?
    dhecheste pistotiki karta/
    (taksidhiotikes epitayes)?
Δέχεστε πιστωτική κάρτα/
(ταξιδιωτικές επιταγές);

Do you need a deposit?
    chriazeste prokatavoli?
Χρειάζεστε προκαταβολή;

It's fine. I'll take it.
    ine endaksi
Είναι εντάξει.

THEY MAY SAY ...

ena dhiavatirio, parakalo.	Your passport, please.
poso tha minete?	How long are you staying?
... tin vradhia	... per night.
dhistichos to ksenodhochio ine yemato.	Sorry, the hotel is full.

Hotel rooms are at a fixed price, but for δωμάτια dhomatia rooms, especially off season, you can probably haggle. The general rule is: the longer you are staying, the more you can lower the daily price. You can ask:

Can we have it for (10,000) drachmas?

    mas to afinete ya (dheka   Μας το αφήνετε για
    chiliadhes) dhrachmes?   (δέκα χιλιάδες) δραχμές;

We'll stay for a week.

    tha minume mia   Θα μείνουμε μια
    evdhomadha   εβδομάδα.

REQUESTS & COMPLAINTS

ΑΙΤΗΣΕΙΣ & ΠΑΡΑΠΟΝΑ

Can I have another ...?	mu dhinete akomi ... ?	Μού δίνετε ακόμη ...;
blanket	mia kuverta	μια κουβέρτα
pillow	ena maksilari	ένα μαξιλάρι
pillowcase	mia maksilarothiki	μια μαξιλαροθήκη
sheet	ena sendoni	ένα σεντόνι
towel	mia petseta	μια πετσέτα

ETIQUETTE POINTER

Starting a question with μήπως mipos makes it sound more polite, equivalent to the English 'Do you by any chance ...? '

Μήπως έχετε ένα δωμάτιο με θέα;
mipos echete ena dhomatio me thea?
'Do you by any chance have a room with a view?'

Can you put a cot in the room?
    borite na valete ena pedhiko
    krevati sto dhomatio?   Μπορείτε να βάλετε ένα
                                    παιδικό κρεβάτι στο δωμάτιο;

Can you put the heating/
air conditioning on?
    borite nanapsete tin
    thermansi/ton klimatismo?   Μπορείτε ν' ανάψετε την
                                    θέρμανση/τον κλιματισμό;

Where can I leave valuables?
    pu boro nafiso politima
    andikimena?   Πού μπορώ ν' αφήσω
                                    πολύτιμα αντικείμενα;

Can I use the kitchen?
    boro na chrisimopi-iso tin
    kuzina?   Μπορώ να χρησιμοποιήσω την
                                    κουζίνα;

Where can I wash clothes?
    pu boro na plino rucha?   Πού μπορώ να πλύνω ρούχα;

Can you clean my room?
    borite na katharisete to
    dhomatio mu?   Μπορείτε να καθαρίσετε το
                                    δωμάτιο μου;

Please change my sheets.
    alakste ta sendonia mu,
    parakalo   Αλλάξτε τα σεντόνια μου,
                                    παρακαλώ.

Can you put some mosquito
repellent in my room?
    mu vazete sto dhomatio
    apothitiko ya ta kunupia?   Μου βάζετε στο δωμάτιο
                                    απωθητικό για τα κουνούπια;

Do I have any mail/telephone
messages?
    mipos echo aliloghrafia/
    kapio minima?   Μήπως έχω αλληλογραφία/
                                    κάποιο μηνύμα;

Can I leave a message for ...?
    boro nafiso ena minima
    ya ...?   Μπορώ ν' αφήσω ένα μήνυμα
                                    για ...;

My room isn't clean.
    to dhomatio mu dhen ine
    katharo   Το δωμάτιο μου δεν είναι
                                    καθαρό.

The toilet won't flush.
    dhen dhulevi to kazanaki   Δεν δουλεύει το καζανάκι.
The window won't open.
    dhen aniyi to parathiro   Δεν ανοίγει το παράθυρο.
I locked myself out.
    klidhothika apekso   Κλειδώθηκα απ' έξω.
My room is too cold/hot.
    to dhomatio mu ine poli   Το δωμάτιο μου είναι πολύ
    krio/zesto   κρύο/ζεστό.

WHO'S WHO

As you wander around Greek cities and towns, you may notice that many streets and buildings are named after prominent figures of Greek history.

Ελευθέριος Βενιζέλος **Eleftherios Venizelos (1864-1936)** – from Crete, seven times Prime Minister between 1910-1933. It was during his government that large areas of Macedonia, Thraki and Crete became part of Greece.

Ιωάννης Μεταξάς **Ioannis Metaksas (1871-1941)** – from Kefallonia, politician and general between 1936-1941. Famous for saying simply 'no' to the Italian ultimatum for Greece to capitulate during WWII.

Νίκος Καζαντζάκης **Nikos Kazantzakis (1883-1957)** – author and poet from Crete. Amongst his works are *The Last Temptation of Christ*, *Zorbas* and *Christ Recrucified*.

Κωνσταντίνος Καβάφης **Konstandinos Kavafis (1863-1933)** – Greek poet from Alexandria. The poem 'Ithaki' is one of his best known works.

Βύρων **Viron** – Greek rendering of the name of Lord Byron, whose romantic poetry was deeply inspired by the Greek war of Independence

ACCOMMODATION

CHECKING OUT

Η ΑΝΑΧΩΡΗΣΗ

Can I have the bill?
   boro na echo ton
   loghariasmo?

Μπορώ να έχω τον
λογαριασμό;

There is a mistake.
   iparchi kapio lathos

Υπάρχει κάποιο λάθος.

What is this charge for?
   yiati chreothika yiafto?

Γιατί χρεώθηκα γι' αυτό;

Can I leave my luggage here ...?	boro nafiso edho tis aposkeves mu ...?	Μπορώ ν' αφήσω εδώ τις αποσκευές μου ...;
until later	os arghotera	ως αργότερα
until tonight	os apopse	ως απόψε
for (three) hours	ya (tris) ores	για (τρεις) ώρες

ΣΤΗΝ ΠΟΛΗ

AROUND TOWN

LOOKING FOR ...

ΨΑΧΝΩ ΓΙΑ ...

Where is the/a ...?	pu ine ...?	Πού είναι ...;
bank	i trapeza	η τράπεζα
beach	i paralia	η παραλία
city centre	to kendro tis polis	το κέντρο της πόλης
embassy of ...	i presvia tis ...	η πρεσβεία της ...
hotel	to ksenodhochio	το ξενοδοχείο
main square	i kendriki platia	η κεντρική πλατεία
market	i aghora	η αγορά
museum	to musio	το μουσείο
post office	to tachidhromio	το ταχυδρομείο
phone box	enas tilefonikos thalamos	ένας τηλεφωνικός θάλαμος
police station	to astinomiko tmima	το αστυνομικό τμήμα
tourist information	to ghrafio turismu	το γραφείο τουρισμού

WELL IS THERE?

To say 'Is there a ... here?' use Υπάρχει ... εδώ; iparchi ... edho?. For example:

> Υπάρχει μια τράπεζα εδώ;
> iparchi mia trapeza edho?
> Is there a bank here?

For the plural 'Are there ...' use Υπάρχουν iparchun.

AT THE BANK   ΣΤΗΝ ΤΡΑΠΕΖΑ

The main reason for going into a bank as a traveller is exchanging money. The process has been much simplified in recent years, with no forms to fill and very little bureaucracy involved. Your passport should suffice. Don't be put off by the frequent long queues, you'll usually find a separate window which is marked ΣΥΝΑΛΛΑΓΜΑ/EXCHANGE, used only for this purpose.

What time does the bank open/close?
 ti ora aniyi/klini i trapeza?   Τι ώρα ανοίγει/κλείνει η τράπεζα;

Can I change money/travellers cheques?
 boro nalakso chrimata/ taksidhiotikes epitayes?   Μπορώ ν' αλλάξω χρήματα/ ταξιδιωτικές επιταγές;

How much is the commission?
 poso ine i promiithia?   Πόσο είναι η προμήθεια;

Smaller notes please.
 echete psilotera parakalo?   Έχετε ψιλότερα, παρακαλώ;

Can I withdraw money with my credit card?
 boro na kano analipsi me tin pistotiki mu karta?   Μπορώ να κάνω ανάληψη με την πιστωτική μου κάρτα;

Can I use this card in the ATM?
 boro na chrisimopi-iso afti tin karta ston aftomato?   Μπορώ να χρησιμοποιήσω αυτή την κάρτα στον αυτόματο;

The ATM has eaten my card.
 o aftomatos katapie tin karta mu   Ο αυτόματος κατάπιε την κάρτα μου.

Can I have money transferred from my bank?
 boro na metafero chrimata apo tin trapeza mu?   Μπορώ να μεταφέρω χρήματα από την τράπεζα μου;

How long do I have to wait?
   poso kero prepi na   Πόσο καιρό πρέπει να
   perimeno?   περιμένω;

Has my money arrived?
   echun ftasi ta chrimata mu   Έχουν φτάσει τα χρήματα μου;

money	ta chrimata/lefta	τα χρήματα/λεφτά
banknotes	chartonomismata	χαρτονομίσματα
coins	kermata	κέρματα

AT THE POST OFFICE   ΣΤΟ ΤΑΧΥΔΡΟΜΕΙΟ

Greek post offices are the focus of most mailing activity in any
town. This is because most Greeks don't seem to like using
mailboxes and always go the post office to mail their letters.
The Greek Postal Service is generally reliable and economical
for domestic mail, but mail to and from overseas has sometimes suffered from a bad reputation – delays, losses and strikes.
If you are sending parcels overseas, take them in unsealed, so
that they can be checked. You can usually change travellers cheques
at post offices – useful on weekends, or when banks are closed.
You can often send faxes from post offices too. Stamps can be
bought from most kiosks and souvenir shops.

I'd like to send a ...   thathela na stilo ...   Θα 'θελα να
                                     στείλω ...

fax	ena faks	ένα φαξ
letter	ena ghrama	ένα γράμμα
postcard	mia karta	μια κάρτα
parcel	ena dhema	ένα δέμα
telegram	ena tileghrafima	ένα τηλεγράφημα

I'd like some stamps for ...
   thathela merika   Θα 'θελα μερικά
   ghramatosima ya ...   γραμματόσημα για ...

AROUND TOWN

How much is it to send
this to ...?

  poso kani ya na stilo   Πόσο κάνει για να στείλω
  afto stin ...?   αυτό στην ...;

air mail	aeroporikos	αεροπορικός
express mail	ekspres	εξπρές
registered mail	sistimeno	συστημένο
post code	o tachidhromikos	ο ταχυδρομικός
	kodhikas	κώδικας (Τ.Κ.)

TELECOMMUNICATIONS ΤΗΛΕΠΙΚΟΙΝΩΝΙΕΣ

With OTE (Οργανισμός Τηλεποικοινωνιών Ελλάδος – Greek
Telecommunications Company) you can make both national and
international phone calls from the designated booths
(ΤΗΛΕΦΩΝΙΚΕΣ ΘΥΡΙΔΕΣ) – you don't need coins or
phonecards for these, as you get charged after you've made the
phone call. You'll also most likely find a fax (ΦΑΞ) and telegram
(ΤΗΛΕΓΡΑΦΗΜΑΤΑ) service. The more central OTE offices will
also have online services. If you'd rather send emails in a more
informal environment, Internet cafes are springing up everywhere,
so you'll certainly find one.

Where is the OTE office?

  pu ine o ote?   Πού είναι ο Ο.Τ.Ε.;

I want to make a phone call
to (Australia).

  thelo na kano ena   Θέλω να κάνω ένα
  tilefonima (stin Afstralia)   τηλεφώνημα (στην Αυστραλία).

How much does a five-minute
call cost to ...?

  poso kani ena tilefonima   Πόσο κάνει ένα τηλεφώνημα
  pende lepton stin ...?   πέντε λεπτών στην ...;

How much is it per minute?
  poso ine to lepto?

Πόσο είναι το λεπτό;

I want to make a collect call.
  thelo na kano ena
  tilefonima me chreosi tu
  kalumenu

Θέλω να κάνω ένα
τηλεφώνημα με χρέωση του
καλούμενου.

What is the area code for ...?
  pios ine o tilefonikos
  kodhikas ya ...?

Ποιος είναι ο τηλεφωνικός
κώδικας για ...;

It's engaged.
  vuizi

Βουΐζει.

It's been cut off.
  kopike i ghrami

Κόπηκε η γραμμή.

I'll try again.
  tha ksanaprospathiso

Θα ξαναπροσπαθήσω.

It's urgent!
  ine epighon!

Είναι επείγον!

I want to send a fax.
  thelo na stilo ena faks

Θέλω να στείλω ένα φαξ.

How much is a fax per page?
  poso kani i selidha ya faks?

Πόσο κάνει η σελίδα για φαξ;

Where can I email from?
  apo pu boro na stilo
  email?

Από πού μπορώ να στείλω
email;

Is there an Internet cafe near here?
  iparchi ena internet cafe
  edho konda?

Υπάρχει ένα Internet cafe
εδώ κοντά;

AROUND TOWN

phone card	i tilekarta	η τηλεκάρτα
phone book	o tilefonikos odhighos	ο τηλεφωνικός οδηγός
phone box	o tilefonikos thalamos	ο τηλεφωνικός θάλαμος

USING A GREEK COMPUTER

Most computers in Greece will allow you to type both Greek and Latin characters. There is usually a small flag sign at the top of the screen indicating whether the keyboard is set for Greek or English – click on it to change it, accordingly. Keyboards are usually bilingual – both Greek and Latin characters are marked on the keys. Some computers may have a Greek version of Microsoft Windows loaded; this looks exactly like what you are used to back home, except all the prompts are in Greek. If you're already familiar with various packages they are much the same in Greek and you should be able to find your way around without much difficulty. Here are some of the basic Greek prompts and commands, in case it all begins to look a bit daunting:

File	Φάκελλος
Save (as)	Σώζω (ως)
Open	Ανοίγω
Close	Κλείνω
Yes	Ναι
No	Όχι
Cancel	Ακύρωση
Table	Πίνακας
Edit	Επεξεργασία
Window	Παράθυρο
Help	Βοήθεια
Font	Γραμματοσειρά
Cut	Κόβω
Copy	Αντιγράφω
Paste	Κολλάω
Column	Στήλη
Row	Γραμμή
Print	Εκτύπωση

USING A GREEK COMPUTER

Computer Parts

computer	to compiuter,	το κομπιούτερ,
	o ipologhistis	ο υπολογιστής
screen	i othoni	η οθόνη
keyboard	to pliktrologhio	το πληκτρολόγιο
mouse	to pondiki	το ποντίκι
hard drive	o skliros (dhiskos)	ο σκληρός (δίσκος)
diskette	i dhisketa	η δισκέτα
software	to loghismiko	το λογισμικό

Most computing terms, such as email, website, Internet etc, will be widely understood in English.

Making a Call   Κάνω Τηλεφώνημα

Hello?
   embros?   Εμπρός;

Do you speak English?
   milate anglika?   Μιλάτε Αγγλικά;

Is ... there?
   ine o/i ... eki?   Είναι ο/η ... εκεί;

This is ... speaking.
   ime o/i ...   Είμαι ο/η ...

Can I leave a message?
   boro nafiso ena minima?   Μπορώ ν'αφήσω ένα μήνυμα;

I'll call back later.
   tha ksanaparo arghotera   Θα ξαναπάρω αργότερα.

Could you ask him/her
to call me?
   borite na tu/tis pite na   Μπορείτε να του/της πείτε να
   me pari tilefono?   με πάρει τηλέφωνο;

My number is ...
   o arithmos mu ine ...   Ο αριθμός μου είναι ...

Good-bye.
   cherete/andio   Χαίρετε/Αντίο.

AROUND TOWN

SIGHTSEEING

ΠΗΓΑΙΝΟΝΤΑΣ ΣΤΑ ΑΞΙΟΘΕΑΤΑ

Look out for the sign EOT (Ελληνικός Οργανισμός Τουρισμού) the Greek Tourist Organization, which runs several tourist offices in airports, major cities and areas of interest. They will be able to give you leaflets with places to visit, opening times, bus timetables and other useful information.

Where is the EOT office?
  pu ine to ghrafio eot?   Πού είναι το γραφείο ΕΟΤ;
Do you have a map of the area/the city?
  echete ena charti tis
  periochis/polis?   Έχετε ένα χάρτη της περιοχής/πόλης;
What time does it open/close?
  ti ora aniyi/klini?   Τι ώρα ανοίγει/κλείνει;

SIGNS	
ΑΝΟΙΧΤΟ	OPEN
ΚΛΕΙΣΤΟ	CLOSED
ΕΙΣΟΔΟΣ	ENTRANCE
ΕΞΟΔΟΣ	EXIT
ΑΠΟΧΩΡΗΤΗΡΙΑ/ ΤΟΥΑΛΕΤΕΣ	TOILETS
ΑΝΔΡΩΝ	MEN'S
ΓΥΝΑΙΚΩΝ	WOMEN'S
ΑΠΑΓΟΡΕΥΕΤΑΙ Η ΕΙΣΟΔΟΣ	NO ENTRY
ΙΔΙΩΤΙΚΟΣ ΧΩΡΟΣ	PRIVATE AREA
ΜΗΝ ΑΓΓΙΖΕΤΕ	DO NOT TOUCH
ΑΠΑΓΟΡΕΥΕΤΑΙ Η ΦΩΤΟΓΡΑΦΗΣΗ	NO PHOTOGRAPHY
Ο ΣΚΥΛΟΣ ΔΑΓΚΩΝΕΙ	BEWARE OF DOG (lit: the dog bites)

AROUND TOWN

Is it open every day?
ine anichta kathe mera?   Είναι ανοιχτά κάθε μέρα;

Is there an admission charge?
prepi na pliroso isodho?   Πρέπει να πληρώσω είσοδο;

One adult/student/child's ticket.
ena kanoniko/fititiko/   Ένα κανονικό/φοιτητικό/
pedhiko isitirio   παιδικό εισιτήριο.

What's that building?
ti ktirio ine afto?   Τι κτίριο είναι αυτό;

Can I take a photograph?
boro na vghalo fotoghrafia?   Μπορώ να βγάλω φωτογραφία;

Can I go in with these clothes?
boro na bo mafta ta   Μπορώ να μπω μ' αυτά τα
rucha?   ρούχα;

ancient	archeos/archea/ archeo	αρχαίος/αρχαία/ αρχαίο
archaeological site	o archeoloyikos choros	ο αρχαιολογικός χώρος
castle	to kastro	το κάστρο
city walls	ta tichi	τα τείχη
fresco	i tichoghrafia	η τοιχογραφία

THEY MAY SAY ...

embros!	Hello?
dhen ine edho.	He/She isn't here.
pios ton/tin zita?	Who's speaking?
miso lepto, parakalo.	Just a minute, please.
thelete nafisete ena minima?	Would you like to leave a message?

main square	i kendriki platia	η κεντρική πλατεία
market place	i aghora	η αγορά
mosaic	to psifidhoto	το ψηφιδωτό
museum	to musio	το μουσείο
mosque	to tzami	το τζαμί
old quarter	i palia poli	η παλιά πόλη

ABBREVIATIONS

Some commonly used abbreviations that you might see around town are:

Abbreviation	In Full	Stands For
1ος, 2ος	πρώτος/δεύτερος protos/ dhefteros	first/second
Αγ.	Άγιος/Αγία aghios/aghia	Saint
Οσ.	Όσιος/Οσία osios/osia	Saint
δρχ.	δραχμές dhrachmes	drachmas
Οδ.	Οδός odhos	street
Λεωφ.	Λεωφόρος leoforos	avenue
Δημ.	Δήμος dhimos	borough
αρ.	αριθμός arithmos	number
ΕΛΤΑ	Ελληνικά Ταχυδρομεία elinika tachidhromia	Greek Post Office (on post boxes)

orthodox church	i orthodhoksi eklisia	η ορθόδοξη εκκλησία
palace	ta anaktora	τα ανάκτορα
ruins	ta eripia	τα ερείπια
statue	to aghalma	το άγαλμα

For a more detailed list of archaeological terms see page 117.

EXCUSE ME?

If you'd like something to be repeated ask Ορίστε; oriste meaning Excuse me?/I beg your pardon?

ΒΡΑΔΙΝΗ ΕΞΟΔΟΣ

Like all their Mediterranean neighbours, Greeks love going out in the evenings and partying, and they do so regularly, even mid-week. Plentiful food, wine, music and dance are usually all included in a typical evening outing, and this is what you can expect from a night out at the buzukia (restaurants with live Greek music).

Having spent the early evening resting, Greeks start their evening outings rather late – they tend to meet up at nine or 10 o'clock, then have a meal that may last until midnight. If there is live music at the restaurant, which is usually the case, they will stay there and dance. In the early 90s, new legislation came in specifying opening hours for clubs and restaurants (they were unlimited prior to that). Officially, most clubs and restaurants shut at 2am during the week and 4am on Fridays and Saturdays. Unofficially, and following the unpopularity of these laws that sent the party-loving population into near riot-mode, most places will stay open until the dancing stops and the kefi (party mood) runs out – usually at dawn.

There are two English publications *Athens News* and *Greek News* which include a section onz what's on. Also, *EOT* (pronounced eot), the Greek Tourist Organization produces a free quarterly entertainment and sight-seeing guide, called *Athina*. Also see Festivals page 197.

DON'T BE AN EMPTY HANDED GUEST

When you visit someone's house, it's important not to turn up empty handed. It is customary to bring ένα κουτί γλυκά ena kuti ghlika 'a box of sweets' or μια ανθοδέσμη mia anthodhesmi, 'a bunch of flowers'.

WHERE TO GO   ΠΟΥ ΘΑ ΠΑΜΕ;

What can we do this evening?
    ti borume na kanume   Τι μπορούμε να κάνουμε
    apopse?   απόψε;
Where can I find out what's on?
    pu boro na matho ti   Πού μπορώ να μάθω τι
    pezete apopse?   παίζεται απόψε;
What's on tonight at the
theatre/cinema?
    ti pezete apopse sto   Τι παίζεται απόψε στο
    theatro/sinema?   θέατρο/σινεμά;

I'd like to go to a/the ...	thathela na pao ...	Θα 'θελα να πάω ...
theatre	sto theatro	στο θέατρο
cinema	sto sinema	στο σινεμά
concert	se sinavlia	σε συναυλία
restaurant	se estiatorio	σε εστιατόριο
disco	sti diskotek	στη ντισκοτέκ
bouzouki place (restaurant with Greek music)	sta buzukia	στα μπουζούκια

INVITES   ΠΡΟΣΚΛΗΣΕΙΣ

If you are ever invited to someone's house, it is customary to present
the hostess with a box of sweets from a pastry shop. Punctuality,
for social engagements at least (not for business meetings), is not
taken as seriously as you might be used to. An invitation for 9pm,
means that most people won't turn up before 9.30. An invitation
to evening coffee can sometimes be extended to dinner, and not
end until after midnight. Such a long visit is known in Greek as
αρμένικη βίζιτα armeniki visita 'an Armenian visit'. Just try to get
used to a different concept of the word 'time'.

What are you doing tonight?
    ti kanis (inf)/kanete (pol)   Τι κάνεις/κάνετε απόψε;
    apopse?

Let's go to the theatre/cinema.
    pame sto sinema/theatro?   Πάμε στο σινεμά/θέατρο;

Do you want to go dancing?
    thelis na pame na
    chorepsume?   Θέλεις να πάμε να
               χορέψουμε;

Yes, I'd love to (come).
    ne, (tha ertho) efcharistos   Ναι, (θα έρθω) ευχαρίστως.

NIGHTCLUBS & BARS
ΝΥΧΤΕΡΙΝΑ ΚΕΝΤΡΑ & ΜΠΑΡ

Are there any discos/clubs here?
    iparchun edho diskotek/
    klab?   Υπάρχουν εδώ ντισκοτέκ/
             κλαμπ;

Do you have live music?
    echete zondani musiki?   Έχετε ζωντανή μουσική;

How much is it to get in?
    poso kani i isodhos?   Πόσο κάνει η είσοδος;

What time shall we meet?
    ti ora na vrethume?   Τι ώρα να βρεθούμε;

What shall I wear?
    ti na foreso?   Τι να φορέσω;

What type of music do they play?
    ti idhos musikis pezun?   Τι είδος μουσικής παίζουν;

When is the best night?
    pote ine i kaliteri vradhia?   Πότε είναι η καλύτερη βραδιά;

Who's playing tonight?
    pios pezi apopse?   Ποιος παίζει απόψε;

What time does it open/shut?
    ti ora aniyi/klini?   Τι ώρα ανοίγει/κλείνει;

GOING OUT

See page 166 for types of drinking and eating establishments.

ARRANGING TO MEET

ΚΑΝΟΝΙΖΩ ΤΗΝ ΣΥΝΑΝΤΗΣΗ

What time shall we meet?
  ti ora na vrethume?

Τι ώρα να βρεθούμε;

Where shall we meet?
  pu na vrethume?

Πού να βρεθούμε;

Let's meet at (nine o'clock).
  na vrethume stis (enia)

Να βρεθούμε στις (εννιά)

Outside ...
  ekso apo ...

Έξω από ...

I'll be there at (seven).
  tha ime eki stis (epta)

Θα είμαι εκεί στις (επτά).

I'll come later.
  tha ertho arghotera

Θα έρθω αργότερα.

AFTERWARDS

ΚΑΤΟΠΙΝ

It was nice talking to you.
  charika pu ta ipame

Χάρηκα που τα είπαμε.

It was nice to meet you. (pol)
  charika ya tin ghnorimia

Χάρηκα για την γνωριμία.

I must be going now.
  prepi na piyeno

Πρέπει να πηγαίνω.

It was a great day/evening.
  itan mia thavmasia imera/
  vradhia

Ήταν μια θαυμάσια ημέρα/
βραδιά.

I'll call you.
  tha se paro tilefono

Θα σε πάρω τηλέφωνο.

Let's meet up again.
  na ksanavrethume

Να ξαναβρεθούμε.

DATING & ROMANCE

ΤΟ ΡΑΝΤΕΒΟΥ & ΤΟ ΕΙΔΥΛΛΙΟ

The feminine form of adjectives appears first for the rest of this section.

Breaking the Ice

Κάνω την Αρχή

Can I sit here?
  boro na kathiso edho?

Μπορώ να καθήσω εδώ;

Can I get you something?
  ti na se keraso?

Τι να σε κεράσω;

Do you want to dance?
  thelis na chorepsume?

Θέλεις να χορέψουμε;

Shall we get some fresh air?
  na parume ligho aera?

Να πάρουμε λίγο αέρα;

Do you have a boyfriend/
girlfriend?
  echis filo/fili?

Έχεις φίλο/φίλη;

Can I call you?
  na se paro tilefono?

Να σε πάρω τηλέφωνο;

Can I take you home?
  na se pao spiti?

Να σε πάω σπίτι;

DID YOU KNOW ...

Κερνάω kernao means 'It's my treat'. Τι να σε κεράσω; ti na se keraso 'What shall I get you?', implies that the other person is going to pay, while Κερνάει το μαγαζί kernai to maghazi means 'Drinks are on the house'. Greeks don't often 'go Dutch' – usually one person pays for one outing and the κέρασμα kerasma 'treat' is returned at a future occasion.

GOING OUT

Rejections   Απόρριψη

You have no doubt heard of Greek men who enjoy picking up foreign girls and showing them a good time. They are locally known as καμάκι kamaki 'a fishing spear', and what they do is κάνω καμάκι kano kamaki 'spearing'. Their main area of activity is the beach.

No, thank you.
  ochi efcharisto   Όχι, ευχαριστώ.
I'm waiting for someone.
  perimeno kapion   Περιμένω κάποιον.
I'm OK on my own.
  ime endaksi moni/   Είμαι εντάξει μόνη/
  monos mu   μόνος μου.
Leave me alone!
  ase me/(parata me)!   Άσε με/(Παράτα με)!
I don't find you attractive.
  dhen se vrisko ghoiteftiko/   Δεν σε βρίσκω γοητευτικό/
  ghoiteftiki   γοητευτική.
Don't touch me!
  mi mangizis!   Μη μ'αγγίζεις!

CLASSIC PICK-UP LINES

Do I know you from somewhere?	se ksero apo kapu?
Have we met before?	echume idhothi paleotera
Do you smoke?	kapnizis?
Are you here alone?	ise edho moni su/ monos su
Would you like company?	thelis parea?

The Date   Το Ραντεβού

Would you like to go
out somewhere?
   thelis na pame kapu?   Θέλεις να πάμε κάπου;
Can you take me home?
   me pas sto spiti?   Με πας στο σπίτι;
Do you want to come back to
my place?
   thelis narthis sto spiti mu?   Θέλεις ν' ρθεις στο σπίτι μου;
I'd like to be going now.
   thathela na piyenume tora   Θα' θελα να πηγαίνουμε τώρα.
I'd like to go back to your place.
   thathela nartho sto   Θα' θελα να' ρθω στο
   spiti su   σπίτι σου.
Can you call me a taxi?
   mu kalis ena taksi?   Μου καλείς ένα ταξί;
Thanks for a lovely evening.
   sefcharisto ya mia omorfi   Σ'ευχαριστώ για μια όμορφη
   vradhia   βραδιά.
Can I see you again tomorrow?
   boro na se ksanadho avrio?   Μπορώ να σε ξαναδώ αύριο;
Do you want to come inside
for a while?
   thelis narthis mesa ya ligho? Θέλεις να' ρθεις μέσα για λίγο;

relationship/affair	i schesi	η σχέση
a date	to randevu	το ραντεβού
single	eleftheros/eleftheri	ελεύθερος/ελεύθερη
to be engaged	ime	είμαι
	aravoniazmenos/	αρραβωνιασμένος/
	aravoniazmeni	αρραβωνιασμένη
to flirt	flertaro	φλερτάρω
to fall in love	erotevome	ερωτεύομαι
to get engaged	aravoniazome	αρραβωνιάζομαι
to go out with ...	ta ftiachno me ...	τα φτιάχνω με ...
to split up with ...	ta chalao me ...	τα χαλάω με ...

GOING OUT

In the Bedroom · Στην Κρεβατοκάμαρα

I want you.
se thelo
Σε θέλω.

I want to make love to you.
thelo na kanume erota
Θέλω να κάνουμε έρωτα.

I want you to use a condom.
thelo na chrisimopi-isis
profilaktiko
Θέλω να χρησιμοποιήσεις
προφυλακτικό.

Please stop now.
stamata tora
Σταμάτα τώρα.

I like your ...	maresi ... su	Μ'αρέσει ... σου.
body	to soma	το σώμα
breasts	to stithos	το στήθος
bum	o kolos	ο κώλος
eyes	ta matia	τα μάτια
hair	ta malia	τα μαλλιά
lips	ta chili	τα χείλη
mouth	to stoma	το στόμα
skin	to dherma	το δέρμα

Intimate Greek · Ερωτικά Ελληνικά

Do you like this?
saresi afto?
Σ'αρέσει αυτό;

Don't do that.
min to kanis afto
Μην το κάνεις αυτό.

Kiss me.
filise me
Φίλησε με.

GOING OUT

A PLATONIC FRIEND?

Ο φίλος μου/η φίλη μου ο filos mu/i fili mu can mean my boyfriend/my girlfriend, but it can also mean just a friend. To avoid confusion you can say ένας φίλος μου/μια φίλη μου enas filos mu/mia fili mu, which can only mean a friend.

Embrace me.
   angaliase me   Αγκάλιασέ με.
Caress me.
   cha-idhepse me   Χάιδεψέ με.
Don't stop!
   mi stamatas!   Μη σταματάς!
Touch me here.
   angikse me edho   Άγγιξέ με εδώ.
Tie me.
   dhese me   Δέσε με.
You're the best. (m, slang)
   ise o protos   Είσαι ο πρώτος.
You're fantastic!
   ise foveros!   Είσαι φοβερός!

erection	i stisi	η στύση
penis	to peos	το πέος
condom (slang)	i kapota	η καπότα
orgasm	o orghasmos	ο οργασμός
to fuck	ghamizo/pidhao	γαμίζω/πηδάω
lover	o erastis	ο εραστής
to kiss	filo	φιλώ
a kiss	to fili	το φιλί

Afterwards   Κατόπιν

It was great!
   itan fandastika!   Ήταν φανταστικά!
You are a great lover!
   ise foveros erastis!   Είσαι φοβερός εραστής!
Let's do it again.
   na to ksanakanume   Να το ξανακάνουμε.
I'm knackered/wiped out.
   ime ksetheomeni/   Είμαι ξεθεωμένη/
   ksetheomenos   ξεθεωμένος.
Do you want a cigarette?
   thelis ena tsigharo?   Θέλεις ένα τσιγάρο;

GOING OUT

SWEARING

Considering how graphic some of the Greek swear words are, they are used at a surprising frequency and at situations where, perhaps an English speaker would use something tamer. These are some of the more common swear words, and by no means the worst you'll hear.

Μαλάκα!   malaka!   Wanker/jerk off!
– also used as a term of camaraderie among young men, a bit like 'mate'.

Πούστη!   pusti!   slang for a gay man
– again, it can be used in a friendly way.

Αλήτη!   aliti!   Bastard!

Άει   ai sta   Get lost/Damn!
    στα κομμάτια!   komatia!

Άντε χάσου!   ande chasu!   Get lost!

Άει στο διάολο!   ai sto   Go to hell!
                    dhiaolo!

Χέστα!   chesta!   Shit!

Άντε γαμίσου!   ande   Go fuck yourself!
                    ghamisu!

Γαμώτο!   ghamoto!   Fuck!

Στ' αρχίδια μου.   starchidhia   (I write it) on my
                    mu   balls.
– means something like 'I don't care about what you say'. This is often very graphically reduced to just pointing towards the relevant part of the body.

Can I stay here tonight?
    boro na mino edho apopse?   Μπορώ να μείνω εδώ απόψε;
You can't stay here tonight.
    dhen boris na minis edho   Δεν μπορείς να μείνεις εδώ
    apopse   απόψε.
Do you want to keep on
seeing each other?
    thelis na sinechisume na   Θέλεις να συνεχίσουμε να
    vriskomaste?   βρισκόμαστε;
It was a good night, but ...
    itan kali vrathia, ala ...   Ήταν καλή βραδιά, αλλά ...

Love   Έρωτας

I think I've fallen in
love with you.
    nomizo oti seroteftika   Νομίζω ότι σ'ερωτεύτηκα.
I love you.
    saghapo   Σ'αγαπώ.
My love.
    aghapi mu   Αγάπη μου.
I'll never forget you.
    dhen tha se ksechaso pote   Δεν θα σε ξεχάσω ποτέ.
It's love at first sight.
    ine keravnovolos erotas   Είναι κεραυνοβόλος έρωτας.
Do you love me?
    maghapas?   Μ'αγαπάς;
Do you want to go out with me?
    thelis na ta ftiaksume?   Θέλεις να τα φτιάξουμε;
Do you want to marry me?
    thelis na me pandreftis?   Θέλεις να με παντρευτείς;

GOING OUT

Leaving & Breaking Up

Η Αναχώρηση και ο Χωρισμός

I have to go tomorrow.
  prepi na figho avrio

Πρέπει να φύγω αύριο.

I'll miss you.
  tha mu lipsis

Θα μου λείψεις.

I'll come to visit you.
  tha sepiskefto

Θα σ'επισκεφτώ.

Can you give me your phone number/your address?
  mu dhinis to tilefono su/ ti dhiefthinsi su?

Μου δίνεις το τηλέφωνό σου/ τη διεύθυνσή σου;

Come with me.
  ela mazi mu

Έλα μαζί μου.

I want to keep in touch.
  thelo na kratisume epafi

Θέλω να κρατήσουμε επαφή.

Don't forget me!
  mi me ksechasis

Μη με ξεχάσεις!

I don't think we're compatible.
  dhen nomizo oti teriazume

Δεν νομίζω ότι ταιριάζουμε.

I want to stay friends.
  thelo na minume fili

Θέλω να μείνουμε φίλοι.

I don't love you (anymore).
  dhen saghapo (pia)

Δεν σ'αγαπώ (πια).

Is there someone else?
  iparchi kapios alos/ kapia ali?

Υπάρχει κάποιος άλλος/ κάποια άλλη;

Η ΟΙΚΟΓΕΝΕΙΑ THE FAMILY

The family still forms a very important part of the social structure in Greece. Families, and that includes members of the extended family (aunts, uncles, in-laws, cousins, etc) tend to be very close. On feast days like Christmas, Easter Day, name days (see Festivals section), families usually spend the day together. It is not uncommon for the sons and daughters of the family to continue living at home until they are engaged or married, although this is now beginning to change.

The concepts of 'protecting the family honour' and 'disgracing the family name' are still widely upheld all over Greece. If you happen to be from Mani or Crete, this would be taken a step further – a Sicilian-style vendetta system is still practised in the more remote areas and differences between families can take generations to resolve.

Greeks are known for their hospitality, η φιλοξενία i filoksenia. Don't be surprised, therefore, if you are invited into somebody's home for no particular reason other than being a foreigner in Greece. This is the best way to get to meet some of the local people.

QUESTIONS   ΕΡΩΤΗΣΕΙΣ

Are you married?
    ise (inf)/iste (pol)   Είσαι/Είστε παντρεμένος/
    pandremenos (m)/   παντρεμένη;
    pandremeni(f)?
Do you have any children?
    echis (inf)/echete (pol)   Έχεις/Έχετε παιδιά;
    pedhia?
Do you live alone?
    menis monos su/   Μένεις μόνος σου/
    moni su? (inf)   μόνη σου;
    menete monos sas/   Μένετε μόνος σας/
    moni sas? (pol)   μόνη σας;
Do you have any siblings?
    echis (inf)/echete (pol) adhelfia?   Έχεις/Έχετε αδέλφια;

FAMILY

I'm single.
   ime eleftheros/eleftheri   Είμαι ελεύθερος/ελεύθερη.
I'm engaged.
   ime aravoniasmenos/   Είμαι αρραβωνιασμένος/
   aravoniasmeni   αρραβωνιασμένη.
I'm married.
   ime pandremenos/   Είμαι παντρεμένος/
   pandremeni   παντρεμένη.
I/We don't have any children.
   dhen echo/echume pedhia   Δεν έχω/έχουμε παιδιά.
I have a daughter/son.
   echo mia kori/ena yio   Έχω μια κόρη/ένα γιο.
I have a boyfriend/girlfriend.
   echo filo/fili   Έχω φίλο/φίλη.

MEMBERS OF THE FAMILY
ΤΑ ΜΕΛΗ ΤΗΣ ΟΙΚΟΓΕΝΕΙΑΣ

The concept of the 'extended' family through blood and marital ties is still very much alive in Greece, with second cousins or aunts twice removed being seen as part of the family. Here is a list, by no means exhaustive, of the names you may need.

relatives	i singenis	οι συγγενείς
parents	i ghonis	οι γονείς
father	o pateras	ο πατέρας
mother	i mitera	η μητέρα
brother	o adhelfos	ο αδελφός
sister	i adhelfi	η αδελφή
husband	o andhras/o sizighos	ο άνδρας/ο σύζυγος
wife	i yineka/i sizighos	η γυναίκα/η σύζυγος
son	o yios	ο γιος
daughter	i kori	η κόρη
child (affectionate)	to pedhi/pedhaki	το παιδί/παιδάκι
grandfather	o papus	ο παππούς
grandmother	i yiayia	η γιαγιά
grandchild	to engoni	το εγγόνι
grandson	o engonos	ο εγγονός

FAMILY

granddaughter	i engoni	η εγγονή
uncle	o thios	ο θείος
aunt	i thia	η θεία
cousin	o ksadhelfos (m)/	ο ξάδελφος/η
	i ksadhelfi (f)	ξαδέλφη
nephew	o anipsios	ο ανηψιός
niece	i anipsia	η ανηψιά

father-in-law	o petheros	ο πεθερός
mother-in-law	i pethera	η πεθερά
parents-in-law	i simbetheri	οι συμπέθεροι
(relationship of		
the two sets of		
parents to each		
other)		
sisters-in-law	i sinifadhes	οι συννυφάδες
(two women		
whose husbands		
are brothers)		
brothers-in-law	i sigambri	οι συγαμπροί
(two men whose		
wives are sisters)		
sister-in-law	i kuniadha	η κουνιάδα
(husband's/wife's		
sister)		
brother-in-law	o kuniadhos	ο κουνιάδος
(husband's/wife's		
brother)		
son-in-law	o gambros	ο γαμπρός
daughter-in-law	i nifi	η νύφη
family	i ikoyenia	η οικογένεια

FAMILY

TALKING TO CHILDREN

ΜΙΛΑΩ ΣΤΑ ΠΑΙΔΙΑ

What's your name?
    pos se lene?   Πώς σε λένε;

Do you go to school?
    pas scholio?   Πας σχολείο;

Do you like school?
    saresi to scholio?   Σ'αρέσει το σχολείο;

What grade are you in?
    ti taksi pas?   Τι τάξη πας;

What will you be when you grow up?
    ti tha yinis otan meghalosis?   Τι θα γίνεις όταν μεγαλώσεις;

What's your favourite subject?
    pio ine to aghapimeno su mathima?   Ποιο είναι το αγαπημένο σου μάθημα;

Are you learning English?
    mathenis anglika?   Μαθαίνεις αγγλικά;

Mum!	mama!	Μαμά!
Dad!	baba!	Μπαμπά!
Don't! (don't do that)	mi!	Μη!

CHILDREN'S TALK

Greeks may add the ending -ακι to a noun or a name: this either means that something is small, or that the word is being used as a term of affection. For example, το σκυλάκι to skilaki is a 'small dog', το σπιτάκι to spitaki is a 'small house', but you may hear adults calling each other Κωστάκη, Ελενάκι kostaki, elenaki, 'little Kosta, little Helen' as a term of affection.

Note that when you add -ακι to a word, the gender always changes to neuter.

'MY CHILD'

Το παιδί/παιδάκι μου to pedhi/pedhaki mu means 'my child', but you will almost certainly hear people of all ages address each other this way as a term of endearment.

TALKING TO PARENTS

ΜΙΛΑΩ ΣΤΟΥΣ ΓΟΝΕΙΣ

You'll notice that Greek parents tend to take their kids with them almost everywhere, even quite late at night, and seem quite laid back about letting them socialize with people. Talking about your children is a good ice-breaker. Here's a few phrases to help you:

What a pretty child!		
	ti omorfo pedhaki!	Τι όμορφο παιδάκι!
How old is he/she?		
	poson chronon ine?	Πόσων χρονών είναι;
What's his/her name?		
	pos to lene?	Πώς το λένε;
Does he/she go to school/kindergarten?		
	pai scholio/nipiaghoyio?	Πάει σχολείο/νηπιαγωγείο;
Is this your dog?		
	aftos o skilos ine dhikos sas?	Αυτός ο σκύλος είναι δικός σας;
Is this your cat?		
	afti i ghata ine dhiki sas?	Αυτή η γάτα είναι δική σας;
Do you have any pets?		
	echete zoa tu spitiu?	Έχετε ζώα του σπιτιού;
Does it bite?		
	dhangoni?	Δαγκώνει;

GREEK NAMES

ΕΛΛΗΝΙΚΑ ΟΝΟΜΑΤΑ

Greek names can be quite different from Western European ones. As they can be quite long, they are often shortened to another unrecognizable form. Here are some of the more common names that you may hear:

FAMILY

Men's names

Name	Shortened form(s)	English equivalent
aleksandhros	alekos	Alexander
emanuil	manolis	Emmanuel
ioanis	yianis	John
konstandinos	kostas	Constantine
nikolaos	nikos	Nicholas
sokratis	takis	Socrates

Women's Names

Name	Shortened form(s)	English equivalent
angeliki	kula	Angela
ekaterini	katerina/katia	Catherine
artemis	mitsa	Diana
irini	rena	Irene
eleni	lena	Helen
ioana	yiana	Joanna

ΕΝΔΙΑΦΕΡΟΝΤΑ INTERESTS

Sportswise most Greeks are football and/or basketball fans (see page 131-32). They love discussing politics and current affairs, and they are avid newspaper readers. Generally, it's quite easy to strike up a conversation with a local about almost anything.

What do you do in your spare time?		
ti kanis ton elefthero su chrono?		Τι κάνεις τονελεύθερο σου χρόνο;
Do you like ...?	saresi (inf)/ (sas aresi) (pol) ...?	Σ'αρέσει/(Σας αρέσει) ...;
I (don't) like ... (sg)	(dhen) maresi (sg)/ maresun (pl) ...	(Δεν) Μ' αρέσει/ Μ' αρέσουν ...
cooking	i mayiriki	η μαγειρική
films	i tenies	οι ταινίες
listening to music	nakuo musiki	ν' ακούω μουσική
going to the cinema	na piyeno sto sinema	να πηγαίνω στο σινεμά
going to the theatre	na piyeno sto theatro	να πηγαίνω στο θέατρο
reading	to dhiavazma	το διάβασμα
travelling	na taksidevo	να ταξιδεύω
walking (in the country)	na perpatao (stin eksochi)	να περπατάω (στην εξοχή)

IS IT PLEASING TO YOU?

The verb 'to like' is a bit unusual in Greek – μου αρέσει mu aresi or μ'αρέσει maresi translates as 'it is pleasing to me'. To say 'I like Greece', you are literally saying 'Greece is pleasing to me' as in μ'αρέσει η Ελλάδα maresi i eladha.

ART   ΤΕΧΝΗ

It is likely that one of the reasons for your visiting Greece, is to indulge in the hundreds of historical sights around the country. Of course, as a first-time visitor you will want to see the Acropolis and the oracle of Delphi – but Greece has a lot more to offer. For example, it would take months to explore historical Athens, representing 3000 years of history. Try to leave some time to visit something off the beaten track like the temple of Apollon at Vassai; Pella the ancient capital of Macedon; the medieval town of Monemvasia; the exquisite Byzantine frescoes at Mistras or dozens of temples buried in the countryside that are as evocative as they are architecturally beautiful.

Wherever you go, try to avoid the midday heat (and crowds). Also, unlike some cretinous tourists, don't attempt to take any bits of marble home as a souvenir. It's not worth the risk, and you are spoiling everyone else's fun.

INTERESTS

What type of art do you like?
    ti idhos technis saresi?   Τι είδος τέχνης σ'αρέσει;
I'd like to see ...
    tha ithela na dho ...   Θα ήθελα να δω ...
I am interested in art from
(5th century BC).
    mendhiaferi i techni tu   Μ' ενδιαφέρει η τέχνη του
    (pemptu eona pro christu)   (5ου αιώνα π.Χ.)
Is this piece of work by
(Praxitelis)?
    afto ine ergho tu   Αυτό είναι έργο του
    (praksiteli)?   (Πραξιτέλη);
Where are the exhibits
from (Knossos)?
    pu ine ta ekthemata apo   Πού είναι τα εκθέματα από
    (tin knoso)?   (την Κνωσό);
When were the excavations done?
    pote eyinan i anaskafes?   Πότε έγιναν οι ανασκαφές;
When was this discovered?
    pote anakalifthike afto?   Πότε ανακαλύφθηκε αυτό;

What style is this?
  ti rithmos inaftos?   Τι ρυθμός είν' αυτός;
Is it an original or a copy?
  ine prototipo i andighrafi?   Είναι πρωτότυπο ή αντιγραφή;

Is it ...?	ine ...?	Είναι ...;
bronze	orichalkino	ορειχάλκινο
clay	pilino	πήλινο
copper	chalkino	χάλκινο
gold	chriso	χρυσό
ivory	apo elefandosto	από ελεφαντοστό
marble	marmarino	μαρμάρινο
silver	asimenio	ασημένιο

ARCHAEOLOGICAL TERMS
Historical Periods

ΑΡΧΑΙΟΛΟΓΙΚΩΝ ΟΡΩΝ
Ιστορικές Περίοδοι

neolithiki Νεολιθική
  neolithic, c.7000-3000 BC
epochi tu chalku η εποχή του Χαλκού
  the Bronze Age (lit: the Copper Age), c.3000-1050 BC
yeometriki Γεωμετρική
  Geometric, 1000-700 BC
archaiki Αρχαϊκή
  Archaic, 700-475 BC
klasiki Κλασσική
  Classical, 475-325 BC
elinistiki Ελληνιστική
  Hellenistic 325-27 BC
romaiki Ρωμαϊκή
  Roman 27 BC-330 AD
vizandini Βυζαντινή
  Byzantine 330 AD - 1453 AD
i epochi tis turkokratias η εποχή της Τουρκοκρατίας
  Occupation by Ottoman Turks, 1453 AD-1821 AD
neoeliniki Νεοελληνική
  Modern Greece 1832-present

Civilizations   Πολιτισμοί

kikladhikos politismos κυκλαδικός πολιτισμός
    Cycladic civilization. Flourished in Κυκλάδες kiklades, the
    Cycladic islands, 3200-1100 BC
minoikos politismos μινωικός πολιτισμός
    Minoan civilization, flourished on Crete, especially Κνωσσός
    Knossos, Φαιστός Festos and Μάλια Malia, 3000-1100 BC
mikinaikos politismos μυκηναϊκός πολιτισμός
    Mycenean civilization, flourished in Μυκήνες Mikines
    (Mycenae), Τίρυνθα Tiryntha and Πύλος Pilos, 1600-1100 BC

Ancient Politics   Αρχαία Πολιτική

tirania τυραννία
    tyranny
monarchia μοναρχία
    monarchy
oligharchia ολιγαρχία
    oligarchy
aristokratia αριστοκρατία
    aristocracy
dhimokratia δημοκρατία
    democracy
i vuli η βουλή
    parliament
o troikos polemos ο Τρωικός Πόλεμος
    the Trojan War
i persiki polemi οι Περσικοί πόλεμοι
    the wars against the Persians (6th-5th BC)
i machi tu marathona η μάχη του Μαραθώνα
    the battle of Marathon (490 BC)
i peloponisiaki polemi οι Πελοποννησιακοί πόλεμοι
    the Peloponnesian wars (5th BC)
i stavrofories οι Σταυροφορίες
    the Crusades

to aghalma το άγαλμα
a statue

to angio το αγγείο
a vessel

i aghora η αγορά
the market place

to akondio το ακόντιο
javelin

i akropolis η ακρόπολις
a fortified hilltop

to amfitheatro το αμφιθέατρο
amphitheatre

to anaghlifo το ανάγλυφο
relief

ta anaktora τα ανάκτορα
palace

i aspidha η ασπίδα
shield

o tholos ο θόλος
a vaulted roof, or a circular
temple

o tholotos tafos
ο θολωτός τάφος
a vaulted tomb (especially
mycaenian)

to klimakostasio
το κλιμακοστάσιο
staircase

i kori η κόρη
statue of a young woman
typical of the Archaic period

o kuros ο κούρος
statue of a young man typical of the Archaic period

to kranos το κράνος
helmet

i lonchi η λόγχη
spear

ta lutra τα λουτρά
baths

to mandio το μαντείο
oracle

to ksifos το ξίφος
sword

i palestra η παλαίστρα
a wrestling ring

i pili η πύλη
gate

i (epitimvia) stili
η (επιτύμβια) στήλη
funerary upright stone slab,
decorated with figures, usually
including that of the deceased

i stoa η στοά
covered walk with colon-
nade on one or both sides

o timvos ο τύμβος
grave, usually with a tumulus

o chiton ο χυτών
tunic, typical dress of the
ancient Greeks

to odhio το ωδείο
music school

THE TWELVE GODS OF OLYMBOS

The 12 Greek Gods were believed to live on Mt. Olymbos. They were not portrayed as perfect, but with many human traits instead. They were playful, mischievous, jealous, quarrelsome, lustful. They frolicked a lot with other gods and humans and played nasty tricks on human lives.

zefs/dhias Ζευς/Δίας
  sovereign god, his symbol of power is the thunderbolt, which he uses to show his displeasure. Roman equivalent: Jupiter

ira Ήρα
  sister and wife of Zeus – goddess of marriage and maternity. Roman equivalent: Juno

estia Εστία
  goddess of the sacred hearth – protectress of the home. Roman equivalent: Vesta

athina Αθηνά
  daughter of Zeus – goddess of wisdom and courage Usually shown wearing a helmet. The city of Athens and the sacred buildings of its Akropolis were dedicated to her. Roman equivalent: Minerva

artemis Άρτεμις
  daughter of Zeus and twin sister of Apollo. Goddess of fertility and childbirth. Often portrayed as the hunter. Roman equivalent: Diana

apolon Απόλλων
  son of Zeus and twin brother of Artemis. God of reason and high moral principles. Protector of music and poetry. Bringer of plague. Roman equivalent: Apollo

afrodhiti Αφροδίτη
  daughter of Zeus -- goddess of love and beauty. Roman equivalent: Venus

aris Άρης
  son of Zeus and Ira – god of war. Roman equivalent: Mars

ifestos Ήφαιστος
  son of Zeus and Ira – the craftsman, god of metalwork. Roman equivalent: Vulcan

THE TWELVE GODS OF OLYMBOS

posidhon Ποσειδών
   brother of Zeus – god of the sea. He causes storms and
   earthquakes and is usually portrayed holding a trident.
   Roman equivalent: Neptune
ermis Ερμής
   son of Zeus – the messenger god often portrayed with
   wings on his feet. Protector of shepherds and travellers.
   Roman equivalent: Mercury
dhimitra Δήμητρα
   goddess of agriculture, and especially wheat. Roman
   equivalent: Ceres

Apart from the 12 main Gods, the dodecatheon, there were
several other gods, semi-gods and heroes, also prominent in the religious lives of Greeks.

adhis Άδης
   Hades, god of the underworld, brother of Zeus. Roman
   equivalent: Pluto
persefoni Περσεφόνη
   wife of Hades goddess of the underworld. Roman
   equivalent: Proserpina
dhionisos/vakhos Διόνυσος/Βάκχος
   god of wine and revelry. Many theatrical festivals were
   dedicated to him. Roman equivalent: Bacchus
iraklis Ηρακλής
   half-human, half-god, son of Zeus. Known for the 12
   labours οι δώδεκα άθλοι i dhodeka athli. Roman equivalent: Hercules
thiseas Θησέας
   a hero of Greek mythology, known for slaying the
   Minotaur.
eros Έρως
   god of Love. Roman equivalent: Cupid
pan Παν
   half human, half beast. Lives in forests, often portrayed
   with 'pan pipes'. Roman equivalent: Faunus
io Ιώ
   dawn – one of the Titans. Roman equivalent: Aurora

Styles   Ρυθμοί

ionikos rithmos ιωνικός ρυθμός Ioanian style.
Slender tapering columns, capital decorated with symmetrical spirals

dhorikos rithmos δωρικός ρυθμός Doric style.
Robust columns often fluted, plain capital

korinthiakos rithmos κορινθιακός ρυθμός Corinthian style.
Capitals decorated with acanthus leaves

Parts of a Temple   Τα μέρη του ναού

to aetoma το αέτωμα
the pediment, a triangular gable often decorated with reliefs

to yiso το γείσο
frieze, a row of stone blocks above the architrave, often decorated with triglyphs and metopes

to epistilio το επιστύλιο
architrave, the row of stone blocks above the columns

o kionas ο κίονας
a column

to kionokrano το κιονόκρανο
capital of a column

i korniza η κορνίζα
cornice, the moulding around the pediment

i metopi η μετόπη
metope, the square space between triglyphs, sometimes decorated with reliefs

o naos ο ναός
temple, but also a christian church

o pronaos ο πρόναος
the entrance to the temple

o stilovatis ο στυλοβάτης
the steps leading up to the temple

to trighlifo το τρίγλυφο
triglyph, part of the frieze with three vertical channels

POTTERY ΑΓΓΕΙΟΠΛΑΣΤΙΚΗΣ

Local workshops, especially the Athenian ones, produced a stunning variety of jars, jugs, cups and other vessels. Μελανόμορφοι melanomorfi are vessels with black figures on an earth-coloured background, while ερυθρόμορφοι erithromorfi are ones with earth-coloured figures on a black background. Some vessels are of such exquisite quality and condition, you will be left wondering whether they were really made 2500 years ago.

inochoi οινοχόη
tall jug with a slender neck and a spout for serving wine

olpi όλπη
jug with a short neck

chus χους
pouring jug with smooth sides

idhria υδρία
water jug with three handles to facilitate carrying and pouring

kratir κρατήρ
vessel for mixing wine and water (Greeks always drank their wine diluted)

dhinos δίνος
wine bowl, usually on a slender stand

nestoris νεστορίς
jar, its shape varied locally

kratiriskos κρατηρίσκος
jug

kantharos κάνθαρος
cup with a narrow neck

kiliks κύληξ
stemmed drinking cup

riton ρύτων
drinking horn in the shape of an animal's head, usually bull's

amfora αμφορά
storage jar, used for wine, oil, grain, fish sauce. Usually slender vessels, sometimes with a spiked end for a better grip.

pithos πίθος
large barrel-like storage jar

INTERESTS

arivalos αρύβαλλος
   oil bottle with a very narrow neck
likithos λήκυθος
   oil bottle with a long slender neck
alavastron αλάβαστρον
   perfume bottle, slender usually without handles
piksis πυξίς
   cosmetic box
ghamikos γαμικός
   very ornate vase, usually with an exceptionally elaborate lid.
   Used at weddings.
podhaniptir ποδανιπτήρ
   footbath
lutroforos λουτροφόρος
   elaborate water carrier used in ceremonies, especially weddings
   and funerals. Placed on the tomb of an unmarried person.
askos ασκός
   jar in the shape of an oil skin
lekanis λεκανίς
   bowl
ghutus γουτούς
   baby bottle
larnaks λάρναξ
   bath-shaped trough (mainly Minoan/Mycenean)

CINEMA & THEATRE

ΚΙΝΗΜΑΤΟΓΡΑΦΟΣ & ΘΕΑΤΡΟ

All films have Greek subtitles, except some afternoon showings
of children's films. ΚΑΤΑΛΛΗΛΟ is suitable for all ages,
ΑΚΑΤΑΛΛΗΛΟ is suitable for those over 18. If you're in Greece
in the summer, it's worth going to a θερινός κινηματογράφος
therinos kinimatoghrafos, 'an open-air cinema'. If the film is bad,
you can at least look at the stars.

What's on tonight?
   ti pezete apopse?   Τι παίζεται απόψε;
I feel like seeing ... tonight.
   echo oreksi na dho ... apopse   Έχω όρεξη να δω ... απόψε.
What time does the film/
play start?
   ti ora archizi to ergho/i   Τι ώρα αρχίζει το έργο/η
   parastasi?   παράσταση;
Is it in English?
   ine stanglika?   Είναι στ'Αγγλικά;
Is it in Ancient Greek?
   ine starchea elinika?   Είναι στ'αρχαία Ελληνικά;
Is it subtitled or dubbed?
   ine me ipotitlus i   Είναι με υποτίτλους ή
   dublarismeno?   ντουμπλαρισμένο;

film	to film/(i tenia)	το φιλμ/(η ταινία)
tragic play (classical)	i traghodhia	η τραγωδία
comedy	i komodhia	η κωμωδία
action film	tenia dhrasis	ταινία δράσης
animation	kinumena schedhia	κινούμενα σχέδια
horror film	tenia tromu	ταινία τρόμου
science fiction film	tenia epistimonikis fantasias	ταινία επιστημονικής φαντασίας
thriller	thriler	θρίλλερ
documentary	dokimanter	ντοκιμαντέρ

INTERESTS

EVERYONE'S A CRITIC   ΟΛΟΙ ΕΙΝΑΙ ΚΡΙΤΙΚΟΙ

Did you like it?
   sarese?   Σ' άρεσε;
Yes, I liked it (a lot).
   ne, marese (poli)   Ναι, μ' άρεσε (πολύ).
No, I didn't like it (at all).
   ochi, dhen marese (katholu) Όχι, δεν μ'άρεσε (καθόλου).

It was ...	itan ...	Ήταν ...
excellent	katapliktiko	καταπληκτικό
good/OK	kalo	καλό
average	metrio	μέτριο
so-so	etsi kietsi	έτσι κι έτσι
boring	vareto	βαρετό
rubbish	eschos	αίσχος

MUSIC & DANCE ΜΟΥΣΙΚΗ & ΧΟΡΟΣ

Greeks love music and dance, especially their own. In a disco, the evening will usually start with western style pop music, and end with Greek dancing in the small hours of the morning.

You will see Greeks dancing at any occasion – religious feasts in particular, weddings, get-togethers with friends and any other happy occasion.

Do you like music?
saresi i musiki? Σ'αρέσει η μουσική;

What type of music do you like?
ti idhos musikis saresi? Τι είδος μουσικής σ'αρέσει;

Have you heard of (Hatzidakis)?
echis akusta ton Έχεις ακουστά τον
(chadzidhaki)? (Χατζηδάκη);

Where can I see traditional
Greek dancing?
pu boro na dho Πού μπορώ να δω
paradhosiako eliniko choro? παραδοσιακό ελληνικό χορό;

Where can I hear ... music?	pu boro nakuso ... musiki?	Πού μπορώ ν'ακούσω ... μουσική;
classical	klasiki	κλασσική
rock	rok	ροκ
Greek folk	laiki eliniki	λαϊκή Ελληνική

INTERESTS

Types of Popular Greek Dance

Είδη Ελληνικού Λαϊκού Χορού

Most Greek dancing is done in the form of small steps round a circle or a line, holding hands. Just shed your inhibitions and give it a go!

kalamatianos καλαματιανός
originally from Καλαμάτα kalamata, is the most popular folk dance and danced at every feast.

pendozali πεντοζάλη
pendozali means 'five times dizziness', because of the speed of the steps. It comes from Crete, and men often compete as to how fast they can do the steps.

sirtos συρτός from the Aegean islands.

zembekikos ζεμπέκικος
popular dance from Asia Minor. This is the one for showing off and is often accompanied by the legendary Greek plate smashing.

chasapikos χασάπικος
this is the archetypal Greek dance, performed with men and women in a straight line with arms on each other's shoulders.

sirtaki συρτάκι
think Zorba the Greek.

tsifteteli τσιφτετέλι
oriental style dance with a lot of hip and arm swaying. Often danced on tables.

INTERESTS

TRAVEL

ΤΑΞΙΔΙΑ

Most of your fellow travellers are likely to speak English. It is very unlikely that you will meet any Greek backpackers, as Greeks don't generally backpack in their own country. However, you may like to ask some of the locals to recommend some places.

Is it worth going to (Siros)?
aksizi na pao (stin siro)?　　Αξίζει να πάω (στην Σύρο);
Are there many tourists there?
iparchun poli turistes eki?　　Υπάρχουν πολλοί τουρίστες
　　　　　　　　　　　　　　εκεί;

When is the best time to go?
    pote ine i kaliteri epochi   Πότε είναι η καλύτερη εποχή
    ya na pao?   για να πάω;
Do you know a place I can stay?
    kseris (inf)/kserete (pol) pu   Ξέρεις/Ξέρετε πού μπορώ
    boro na mino?   να μείνω;

THEY MAY SAY ...

ine oreo meros	It's a nice place.
echi kala estiatoria	It has good restaurants.
echi orea paralia	It has a nice beach.
ine yemato turistes	It's full of tourists.
dhen echi tipota na kanis	There's nothing to do.
ine chalia	It's awful.
na pas!	Go!
min pas!	Don't go!

INTERESTS

ASTROLOGY   ΑΣΤΡΟΛΟΓΙΑ

What star sign   ti zodhio ise?   Τι ζώδιο είσαι;
  are you?

I'm ...   ime ...   Είμαι ...

Capricorn	eghokeros	Αιγόκερως
Aquarius	idhrocho-os	Υδροχόος
Pisces	ichthis	Ιχθύς
Aries	krios	Κριός
Taurus	tavros	Ταύρος
Gemini	dhidhimi	Δίδυμοι
Cancer	karkinos	Καρκίνος
Leo	leon	Λέων
Virgo	parthenos	Παρθένος
Libra	zighos	Ζυγός
Scorpio	skorpios	Σκορπιός
Sagittarius	toksotis	Τοξότης

SPORT

О АΘΛΗΤΙΣΜΟΣ

Do you play ...?
    pezis (inf)/pezete (pol) ...?   Παίζεις/Παίζετε ...;

Where can I play ... ?	pu boro na pekso ...?	Πού μπορώ να παίζω ...;
sport	to spor/athlima/ aghonisma	το σπορ/άθλημα/ αγώνισμα
sports event	o aghonas	ο αγώνας
aerobics	i aeroviki ghimnastiki	η αεροβική γυμναστική
boxing	to boks	το μποξ
cycling	i podhilasia	η ποδηλασία
gymnastics	i rithmiki ghimnastiki	η ρυθμική γυμναστική
rowing	i kopilasia	η κωπηλασία
sailing	i istioplo-ia	η ιστιοπλοΐα
swimming	to kolimbi	το κολύμπι
waterskiing	to thalasio ski	το θαλάσσιο σκι
weightlifting	i arsi varon	η άρση βαρών
windsurf	to ghuind serfing	το γουίντ σέρφινγκ
wrestling	i pali	η πάλη

INTERESTS

Talking About Sport

Μιλάω Για Τον Αθλητισμό

Do you like playing sports?
    saresi o athlitismos?   Σ'αρέσει ο αθλητισμός;
What sports do you play?
    ti spor pezis?   Τι σπορ παίζεις;
What's your favourite sport?
    pio ine to aghapimeno su
    spor?   Ποιο είναι το αγαπημένο σου
                                       σπορ;
I like watching sports.
    maresi na parakolutho
    spor   Μ' αρέσει να παρακολουθώ
                                       σπορ.

INTERESTS

I follow ...
  parakolutho ...   Παρακολουθώ ...
Which team do you support?
  ti omadha ise?   Τι ομάδα είσαι;
I'm a fan of (Panathinaikos).
  ime (panathina-ikos)   Είμαι (Παναθηναϊκός).

Going to the Match   Πηδαίνω Στον Αγώνα

You shouldn't have many problems following a sports game, as
many of the terms used are borrowed from English.

I'd like to go to a
(basketball) game.
  thathela na dho ena aghona   Θα'θελα να δω ένα αγώνα
  (basket)   (μπάσκετ).
How much is the ticket?
  poso kani to isitirio?   Πόσο κάνει το εισιτήριο;

What time does it start?	
ti ora archizi?	Τι ώρα αρχίζει;
Who's playing?	
pios pezi?	Ποιος παίζει;
Who's winning?	
pios kerdhizi?	Ποιος κερδίζει;
Who are you supporting?	
pion ipostirizis?	Ποιον υποστηρίζεις;
What's the score?	
ti ine to skor?	Τι είναι το σκορ;
What was the final score?	
ti itan to teliko skor?	Τι ήταν το τελικό σκορ;
A draw.	
isopalia	Ισοπαλία.
(Aris) won 1-0.	
kerdhise o (aris)(ena-midhen)	Κέρδισε ο (Άρης) 1-0 (ένα μηδέν).
Good game.	
kalo pechnidhi	Καλό παιχνίδι.
Very boring.	
poli vareto	Πολύ βαρετό.
They played terribly.	
epeksan chalia	Έπαιξαν χάλια.
They played really well.	
epeksan poli kala	Έπαιξαν πολύ καλά.

Soccer   Ποδόσφαιρο

Soccer (football) is equal in popularity with basketball. There is a national league το πρωτάθλημα to protathlima and a national cup το κύπελλο to kipelo. The teams that have recently monopolized the international scene are Panathinaikos Παναθηναϊκός, Olymbiakos Ολυμπιακός and AEK (pronounced a-ek). The very popular ΠΡΟ-ΠΟ propo is the equivalent of the football pools.

Olimbiakos is playing
Panathinaikos tonight.

o olimbiakos pezi ton Panathina-iko apopse	Ο Ολυμπιακός παίζει τον Παναθηναϊκό απόψε.

ball	i bala	η μπάλα
match/game	to mats/o aghonas	το ματς/ο αγώνας
goal keeper	o termatofilakas	ο τερματοφύλακας
halftime	to imichrono	το ημίχρονο
to score	skoraro	σκοράρω
shoot	to sut	το σουτ
hooligan	o chuligan	ο χούλιγκαν

Basketball

Μπάσκετ

basketball	to basket	το μπάσκετ
basketball match (pol)	o aghonas kalathosferisis	ο αγώνας καλαθοσφαίρησης
foul	to faul	το φάουλ
referee	o dhietitis	ο διαιτητής
to score	vazo kalathi	βάζω καλάθι
three points	to tripondo	το τρίποντο
two points	to dhipondo	το δίποντο

INTERESTS

SKIING

ΣΚΙ

If you do find yourself in Greece during the winter months, you can try one of the ski resorts that have sprung up in the last 20 years. Because skiing is a relatively recent introduction, several skiing terms are English/French.

Is there any fresh snow at the top?
  echi fresko chioni stin korifi?

Έχει φρέσκο χιόνι στην κορυφή;

Are the weather conditions good for skiing?
  ine kales i kerikes sinthikes ya ski?

Είναι καλές οι καιρικές συνθήκες για σκι;

Which is the easiest/hardest piste?
  pia ine i pio efkoli/ dhiskoli pista?

Ποια είναι η πιο εύκολη/ δύσκολη πίστα;

At what level are the ski pistes?
  se ti ipsos vriskonde i pistes tu ski?

Σε τι ύψος βρίσκονται οι πίστες του σκι;

skiing	to ski	το σκι
skis	ta ski	τα σκι
cable car	to teleferik	το τελεφερίκ
skiing instructor	o ekpedheftis tu ski	ο εκπαιδευτής του σκι
ski boots	i botes tu ski	οι μπότες του σκι
slope	i playia	η πλαγιά
top	i korifi	η κορυφή

SNORKELLING/ SCUBA DIVING
ΚΟΛΥΜΠΙ ΜΕ ΜΑΣΚΑ/ ΥΠΟΒΡΥΧΙΕΣ ΚΑΤΑΔΥΣΕΙΣ

INTERESTS

On the larger islands and coastal towns, you will be able to find a scuba diving school ΣΧΟΛΗ ΚΑΤΑΔΥΣΕΩΝ. During the summer, some diving courses are conducted in English, and there are frequent diving excursions (usually bilingual) to the best diving sites. The clarity of the water, the number of shipwrecks and the rich marine life make Greece an excellent place for scuba diving. However, diving restrictions are quite severe: diving without the appropriate certification, diving at night, using a speargun, or diving at non-designated sites, are all strictly forbidden. Most of the coastline is out of bounds where diving is concerned. To avoid getting into trouble, you are strongly advised to liaise with the local diving school before going diving.

Is there a diving school here?
　　iparchi scholi katadhiseon edho?　　Υπάρχει σχολή καταδύσεων εδώ;

Is diving allowed from this beach?
　　epitrepete i katadhisi apafti tin paralia?　　Επιτρέπεται η κατάδυση απ' αυτή την παραλία;

Can I refill my tank here?
　　boro na yemiso ti bukala mu edho?　　Μπορώ να γεμίσω τη μπουκάλα μου εδώ;

Do you organise dives?
　　orghanonete katadhisis?　　Οργανώνετε καταδύσεις;

INTERESTS

How deep are the waters?
poso vathia ine ta nera?   Πόσο βαθιά είναι τα νερά;

Are there any dangerous currents here?
iparchun epikindhina   Υπάρχουν επικίνδυνα
revmata edho?   ρεύματα εδώ;

CMAS	kmas	CMAS (European equivalent to PADI)
console	i konsola	η κονσόλα
depth gauge	to vathimetro	το βαθύμετρο
wetsuit	i stoli dhiti	η στολή δύτη
flippers	ta vatrachopedhila	τα βατραχοπέδιλα
knife	to macheri	το μαχαίρι
manometer	to manometro	το μανόμετρο
mask	i maska	η μάσκα
octopus (diving)	to chtapodhi	το χταπόδι
regulator	o rithmistis	ο ρυθμιστής
shipwreck	to navayio	το ναυάγιο
snorkel	o anapnefstiras	ο αναπνευστήρας
tank	i bukala	η μπουκάλα
weights	ta vari	τα βάρη

AQUATIC SPORTS   ΘΑΛΑΣΣΙΑ ΣΠΟΡ

Can I learn water skiing/sailing?
boro na matho thalasio   Μπορώ να μάθω θαλάσσιο
ski/istioplo-ia?   σκι/ιστιοπλοΐα;

I've never done it before.
dhen to echo ksanakani   Δεν το έχω ξανακάνει.

sailing boat	to istioplo-iko	το ιστιοπλοϊκό
water skiing	to thalasio ski	το θαλάσσιο σκι
windsurf	to ghuind serfing	το γουίντ σέρφινγκ

GAMES   ΠΑΙΧΝΙΔΙΑ

Backgammon τάβλι tavli is very popular in Greece, especially among old men. They play two types of games mainly, called πόρτες portes and πλακωτό plakoto.

Do you play ... ?	pezis (inf)/ pezete (pol) ...?	Παίζεις/ Παίζετε ...;
backgammon	tavli	τάβλι
billiards	biliardho	μπιλιάρδο
cards	chartia	χαρτιά
chess	skaki	σκάκι
dominoes	domino	ντόμινο
draughts	dama	ντάμα
table soccer	podhosferaki	ποδοσφαιράκι

I don't know how to play.

dhen ksero pos na pekso   Δεν ξέρω πώς να παίξω.

bishop	o aksiomatikos	ο αξιωματικός
dice	ta zaria	τα ζάρια
king	o vasilias	ο βασιλιάς
knight	o ipos	ο ίππος (lit: horse)
pawns	i stratiotes/ta pionia	οι στρατιώτες/τα πιόνια
piece/pawn	i pulia/to pioni	η πούλια/το πιόνι
queen	i vasilisa	η βασίλισσα
rook/castle	o pirghos	ο πύργος

INTERESTS

THEY MAY SAY ...

pios echi sira?	Whose turn is it?
sira mu	My turn.

INTERESTS

Cards | | Τα Χαρατιά
Would you like to play ... ?	thelis (inf)/ thelete (pol) na peksume ... ?	Θέλεις/Θέλετε να παίζουμε ...;
gin rummy	kum kan	κουμ καν
thanasis (similar to gin rummy)	thanasi	θανάση
bridge	britz	μπριτζ
canasta	kanasta	κανάστα
thirty-one (like twenty-one)	trianda-mia	τριάντα-μία
patience/solitaire	pasietza	πασιέτζα
pack of cards	i trapula	η τράπουλα
deal the cards	mirazo	μοιράζω
shuffle the cards	anakatevo tin trapula	ανακατεύω την τράπουλα
cut the cards	kovo	κόβω
joker	o balader	ο μπαλαντέρ
jack	o vales	ο βαλές
queen	i dama	η ντάμα
king	o righas	ο ρήγας
ace	o asos	ο άσσος
clubs	bastuni	μπαστούνι
diamonds	karo	καρρό
hearts	kupa	κούπα
spades	spathi	σπαθί
ten of spades	to dheka spathi	το δέκα σπαθί
king of diamonds	o righas karo	ο ρήγας καρρό

ΚΟΙΝΩΝΙΚΑ ΘΕΜΑΤΑ

SOCIAL ISSUES

What's the goverment's policy on ...?	pia ine i politiki tis kivernisis pano ...?	Ποιά είναι η πολιτική της Κυβέρνησης πάνω ...;
unemployment	stin anerghia	στην ανεργία
education	stin ekpedhefsi	στην εκπαίδευση
defense	stin amina	στην άμυνα
green issues	sta ikologhika themata	στα οικολογικά θέματα
the economy	stin ikonomia	στην οικονομία
the EU	stin eok (evropaiki enosi)	στην ΕΟΚ (Ευρωπαϊκή Ένωση)
gay rights	sta dhikeomata ton omofilofilon	στα δικαιώματα των ομοφυλόφιλων
drugs	sta narkotika	στα ναρκωτικά
abortion	stis ektrosis	στις εκτρώσεις
immigration	stin metanastefsi	στην μετανάστευση

Because of its geographical position in the troubled Balkans, Greece receives a number of political or social refugees. These are the main groups that you are likely to encounter in Greece:

Albanian	alvanos	Αλβανός
Bosnian	vosnios	Βόσνιος
Kurd	kurdhos	Κούρδος
Palestinian	palestinios	Παλαιστίνιος
Serb	servos	Σέρβος
Romani (gypsy)	tsinganos	τσιγγάνος
Turks	turki	Τούρκοι
	pomaki	Πομάκοι

POLITICS   ΠΟΛΙΤΙΚΗ

Whether it is because of their troubled political past or as part of their heritage, Greeks – men and women alike – will discuss politics anytime, anywhere. Politics seem to be almost a national obsession. Everyone feels they have a say in it, and claim that they could do better if they were in charge. The archetypal image of a group of old men sitting in a coffee shop, criticizing the government's every move over a cup of strong Greek coffee is not far from the truth. Perhaps as a result of Greek political awareness, demonstrations and strikes are quite frequent – as a foreigner try not to get too embroiled.

What do you think of the
current government?
    pos sas fenete i torini   Πώς σας φαίνεται η τωρινή
    kivernisi?   κυβέρνηση;
Who is Prime Minister now?
    pios ine tora   Ποιος είναι τώρα
    prothipurghos?   Πρωθυπουργός;
Who is president now?
    pios ine tora proedhros?   Ποιος είναι τώρα Πρόεδρος;
Which party do you support?
    pio koma ipostirizis (inf)/   Ποιο κόμμα υποστηρίζεις/
    ipostirizete (pol)?   υποστηρίζετε;

SOCIAL ISSUES

DID YOU KNOW ... Η χούντα i chunda, a Greek rendering of the Spanish word *junta* refers to the military government of 1967-1974, which is associated with the name of the perpetrator Παπαδόπουλος papadhopulos, and the Cyprus debacle. Still a very touchy subject for most Greeks.

When are the next elections?

pote ine i epomenes
ekloyes?

Πότε είναι οι επόμενες
εκλογές;

Are they on strike?

kanun aperyia?

Κάνουν απεργία;

I support the ... party.	ipostirizo to ... koma	Υποστηρίζω το ... κόμμα.
conservative	sindiritiko	συντηρητικό
socialist	sosialistiko	το σοσιαλιστικό
communist	komunistiko	το κομμουνιστικό
green	ikoloyiko	το οικολογικό
liberal	filelefthero	το φιλελεύθερο

Major Political Parties   Τα Κύρια Πολιτικά Κόμματα

There are a couple of dozen political parties in Greece, but the main ones are listed below. Even if the initials of the party aren't there, you will know from the colour of the graffiti whose words of wisdom you are reading, as the main political parties use their own colour code.

ΔΗΚΚΙ dhiki (dhimokratiko kinoniko kinima) Democratic Socialist Movement (socialist left)

ΚΚΕ Κομμουνιστικό Κόμμα Ελλάδας komunistiko koma elladhas Greek Communist party (left) – red colour

ΝΔ Νέα Δημοκρατία nea dhimokratia New Democracy (centre right) – blue colour

ΠΑΣΟΚ Πανελλήνιο Σοσιαλιστικό Κίνημα panelinio sosialistiko kinima Greek Socialist Movement (centre left) – green colour

ΣΥΝΑΣΠΙΣΜΟΣ sinaspismos Coalition of left parties (left socialist)

ARGUING   ΔΙΑΦΩΝΩΝΤΑΣ

Watching Greeks have a discussion, especially on politics, you would think they are about to start a punch-up. People become excited and emotional, they often talk at the same time, and the discussion is accompanied by plenty of hand gestures and banging of fists on the table! You may well discover that the conversation is about something as innocuous as the choice of music band in the forthcoming village feast.

I agree with ...
    simfono me ...   Συμφωνώ με ...
I totally agree.
    simfono apolita   Συμφωνώ απόλυτα.
Absolutely.
    poli sosta   Πολύ σωστά.
Exactly!
    akrivos!   Ακριβώς!
Sure, but ...
    sighura, ala ...   Σίγουρα, αλλά ...
I am of the opinion ...
    ime tis gnomis ...   Είμαι της γνώμης ...
I would say ...
    tha elegha ...   Θα έλεγα ...
I feel/believe that ...
    pistevo oti ...   Πιστεύω ότι ...
I imagine that ...
    fandazome oti ...   Φαντάζομαι ότι ...
I would add that ...
    tha prostheta oti ...   Θα πρόσθετα ότι ...
I'd like to say something.
    tha ithela na po kati   Θα ήθελα να πω κάτι.
Don't get stressed out about it!
    mi sinchizese!   Μη συγχύζεσαι!
Enough!
    ftani pia!   Φτάνει πια!
I disagree.
    dhiafono   Διαφωνώ.

SOCIAL ISSUES

You're wrong.
    kanete lathos   Κάνετε λάθος.

I don't think it's a good idea.
    dhen ine katholu kali idhea   Δεν είναι καθόλου καλή ιδέα.

Rubbish!
    sachlamares!   Σαχλαμάρες!

No way!
    apokliete!   Αποκλείεται!

DID YOU KNOW ...

When Otto of Bavaria (Όθων othon in Greek) became King of the newly independent, post-Ottoman Greece in 1832, the new Greek flag was inspired by the 'national' colours of Bavaria - white and blue. Allegedly the five blue stripes on the flag represent the five syllables of the word Ελευθερία eleftheria 'freedom', while the 4 white stripes represent the 4 syllables of the words ή θάνατος i thanatos meaning 'or death' – 'Freedom or Death' being the rather sombre Greek motto.

On a more practical level, Otto also brought with him the recipe for Bavarian beer: the Greek brand Fix was being bottled until the 1970s, but now the factory has closed down.

ENVIRONMENT   ΤΟ ΠΕΡΙΒΑΛΛΟΝ

Road-side rubbish dumps, inadequate recycling facilities, degradation of forest land are all signs that Greece is still lagging behind its more environmentally-aware European counterparts, at least in some environmental issues. On the positive side, mainly through government initiatives, Greece has the cleanest waters in Europe, large urban areas are being pedestrianized and nature reserves are being set up throughout the country to protect the spectacularly rich fauna and flora.

Environmental concerns in Greece are centered mainly on maintaining a clean coastline, clean waters and improving the quality of air. With the year-round traffic in the Aegean and Ionian Sea it is difficult to prevent some degree of pollution in Greek waters. The Greek government undertakes a massive beach cleaning programme before the start of every summer season and Greek marine patrols monitor any signs of oil spillage or pollution. Other environmental issues that trouble Greeks from time to time are the notorious Athenian smog, the summer forest fires and reclamation of rural land for (mostly unauthorized) building.

Is there a pollution problem here?
    iparchi provlima molinsis   Υπάρχει πρόβλημα μόλυνσης
    edho?   εδώ;
Does this beach have a blue flag?
    afti i paralia echi ghalazia   Αυτή η παραλία έχει γαλάζια
    simea?   σημαία;
Is this a Nature Reserve?
    aftos ine ethnikos dhrimos?   Αυτός είναι Εθνικός Δρυμός;

DID YOU KNOW ...   Αργία ή απεργία aryia i aperyia is a favourite pun among Greeks, ridiculing their civil services. It means 'on holiday or on strike', and sometimes it feels as if this is all the public sector ever does.

Useful Words   Χρήσιμες λέξεις

Athens traffic restriction area	o dhaktilios	ο δακτύλιος
ecology	ikologhia	οικολογία
pollution	i ripansi/molinsi	η ρύπανση/μόλυνση
smog	to nefos	το νέφος
recycling	i anakiklosi	η ανακύκλωση
solar power	i iliaki eneryia	η ηλιακή ενέργεια
nuclear station	pirinikos stathmos	πυρηνικός σταθμός
threatened species	to apilomeno idhos	το απειλόμενο είδος
greenhouse effect	to fenomeno thermokipiu	το φαινόμενο θερμοκηπίου

DRUGS   ΝΑΡΚΩΤΙΚΑ

Being caught importing drugs into Greece could result in at least five years imprisonment. The choice is yours.

Do you want to smoke?
　thelis na kapnisis?　　　　　　Θέλεις να καπνίσεις;

DRUG WORDS

Here are some more common 'street' terms.

acid	acid	acid
cocaine	i kapa/aspri	η κάππα/άσπρη
hash	i mavri/to mavraki to chortari/itsika	η μαύρη/το μαυράκι το χορτάρι/η τσίκα
heroin	i aspri/alfa	η άσπρη/άλφα
speed	spid	speed
a smoking den	o tekes	ο τεκές
drug addict (slang)	o prezakias	ο πρεζάκιας

SOCIAL ISSUES

I'm stoned.
  ime masturomenos/
  masturomeni

Είμαι μαστουρωμένος/
μαστουρωμένη.

I'm addicted to drugs.
  ime toksikomanis

Είμαι τοξικομανής.

I use ... occasionally.
  perno ... pote pote

Παίρνω ... πότε πότε.

My friend has taken
  an overdose.
  o filos mu/i fili mu pire
  meghali dhosi narkotikon

Ο φίλος μου/η φίλη μου πήρε
μεγάλη δόση ναρκωτικών.

My friend has collapsed.
  o filos mu/i fili mu
  katerefse

Ο φίλος μου/η φίλη μου
κατέρρευσε.

Where can I find clean syringes?
  pu boro na vro kathares
  siringes?

Πού μπορώ να βρω καθαρές
σύριγγες;

Do you sell syringes?
  pulate siringes?

Πουλάτε σύριγγες;

I don't take drugs.
  dhen perno narkotika

Δεν παίρνω ναρκωτικά.

I'm not interested.
  dhen endhiaferome

Δεν ενδιαφέρομαι.

I don't do it any more.
  dhen perno pia narkotika

Δεν παίρνω πια ναρκωτικά.

I'm on methadone.
  perno methadhoni

Παίρνω μεθαδόνη.

ΠΗΓΑΙΝΟΝΤΑΣ **SHOPPING** ΓΙΑ ΨΩΝΙΑ

Shops in Greece are plentiful and colourful. Although superstores, selling everything from food to garden furniture, are springing up around the suburbs of big cities, there is still a strong tradition in Greece for small, family-owned, specialized stores. Once you have bought your souvenirs to bring back home, venture beyond the row of tourist shops to the noisy market streets with their colourful displays of vegetables, fresh fish, clothes, shoes, toys and just about anything else imaginable. Most goods have a fixed price, except in flea markets and also souvenir shops where you'll be able to bargain. (see page 148)

Shops tend to open early and close for lunch and siesta at about 2pm. Apart from Mondays and Wednesdays, they open again in the afternoon, at about 5pm, and close at about 9pm. Main shops are normally closed on Sundays, though you can always find local groceries open for your basic food needs.

There are two types of shops that you may not have encountered before. Firstly there is το ψιλικατζίδικο to psilikatzidhiko – a cross between a haberdashery and a stationary shop – that sells basic stationery, combs and hair accessories, buttons, threads and other sewing items, and sometimes newspapers. Secondly there are το περίπτερο to periptero – the yellow kiosks that you find on most street corners laden from top to bottom with just about any useful item imaginable.

Only the formal form of address has been given in this chapter, as this is what you will normally hear and use when shopping.

SHOPS

ΚΑΤΑΣΤΗΜΑΤΑ

Where is the nearest ...?	pu ine to kondinotero ... ?	Πού είναι το κοντινότερο ...;
shop	katastima/ maghazi	κατάστημα, μαγαζί
bookshop	vivliopolio	βιβλιοπωλείο
clothing store	katastima ruchon, butik	κατάστημα ρούχων, μπουτίκ
department store	iperkatastima	υπερκατάστημα
florist	anthopolio	ανθοπωλείο
grocery	pandopolio	παντοπωλείο
hairdresser/barber	komotirio/kurio	κομμωτήριο/ κουρείο
laundrette	katharistirio	καθαριστήριο
market	aghora	αγορά
pharmacy	farmakio	φαρμακείο
shoe shop	ipodhimatopolio	υποδηματοπωλείο
travel agency	taksidhiotiko ghrafio	ταξιδιωτικό γραφείο
toy shop	katastima me pechnidhia	κατάστημα με παιχνίδια

STREET MARKETS

Most neighbourhoods have a weekly street market known as η λαϊκή i laiki. Apart from the fact that it is quite a colourful experience, here you can get food and clothes at a much lower price than in the shops. The clothes are not always the latest fashion statement, but you can find some real bargains. The vegetables are usually of very good quality, and towards the end of the day they are practically being given away. Ask:

On which day do they hold a street market?	pote echi laiki? Πότε έχει λαϊκή;

MAKING A PURCHASE   ΚΑΝΩ ΜΙΑ ΑΓΟΡΑ

I'd like to buy ...
    tha ithela naghoraso ...   Θα ήθελα ν' αγοράσω ...
Do you have ...?
    echete ...?   Έχετε ...;
Do you sell ...?
    pulate ...?   Πουλάτε ...;
How much is it?
    poso kani?   Πόσο κάνει;
Do you have others?
    echete ala?   Έχετε άλλα;
Can I see it?
    boro na to dho?   Μπορώ να το δω;
I'm just looking.
    aplos kitazo   Απλώς κοιτάζω.
Can you write the price down?
    mu ghrafete tin timi?   Μου γράφετε την τιμή;
Do you take credit cards/
(travellers cheques)?
    dhecheste pistotiki karta/   Δέχεστε πιστωτική κάρτα/
    (taksidhiotikes epitaghes)?   (ταξιδιωτικές επιταγές);
Can I have the receipt, please?
    boro na echo tin apodiksi,   Μπορώ να έχω την απόδειξη,
    parakalo?   παρακαλώ;
Can you wrap it?
    mu to tiliyete?   Μου το τυλίγετε;

I'd like to return this.
    tha ithela na to epistrepso   Θα ήθελα να το επιστρέψω.
I'd like a refund.
    tha ithela ta chrimata mu   Θα ήθελά τα χρήματα μου
    piso   πίσω.

BARGAINING & HAGGLING
ΕΥΚΑΙΡΙΕΣ & ΠΑΖΑΡΙΑ

Stores in the city normally have fixed prices, but at the flea markets and most souvenir stores, it's customary to haggle. As a guideline, you can normally offer to pay three quarters of the stated price; buying two or more things and/or paying in a hard currency increases your chances of getting the price you want. As a last resort, try walking away.

It's a very good price.
    ine poli kali timi   Είναι πολύ καλή τιμή.
How much for (two)?
    poso mu dhinete (ta dhio)?   Πόσο μου δίνετε (τα δύο);
Can I have it for (two thousand) drachmas?
    mu to afinete ghia (dhio   Μου το αφήνετε για (δύο
    chiliadhes) dhrachmes?   χιλιάδες) δραχμές;

THEY MAY SAY ...

boro na sas eksipiretiso? /thelete voithia?   Can I help you?

Tipote alo?   Anything else?

ine ya dhoro?   Is it a present? (Shall I gift wrap it?)

ine to telefteo   It's the last one.

meyia!   roughly translates as 'with health'. You will always hear it when you buy something new.

Can you lower the price?

    mu to afinete pio ftina?   Μου το αφήνετε πιο φτηνά;

I haven't got that much money.

    dhen echo tosa chrimata   Δεν έχω τόσα χρήματα.

I can pay you in dollars/
pounds/marks.

    boro na sas pliroso se   Μπορώ να σας πληρώσω σε
    dholaria/lires/marka   δολλάρια/λίρες/μάρκα.

to haggle	kano pazari	κάνω παζάρι
sale	ekptosis	εκπτώσεις

MONEY MATTERS

COINS

taliro	τάληρο	5 drachmas
dhekariko	δεκάρικο	10 drachmas
ikosariko	εικοσάρικο	20 drachmas
penindariko	πενηντάρικο	50 drachmas
ekatostariko	εκατοστάρικο	100 drachmas

You might see a δραχμή dhrachmi one drachma coin,
or a δίδραχμο didhrachmo 2 drachmas, but they are
now out of use.

NOTES

ekatostariko	εκατοστάρικο	100 drachmas
dhiakosariko	διακοσάρικο	200 drachmas
pendakosariko	πεντακοσάρικο	500 drachmas
chiliariko	χιλιάρικο	1000 drachmas
pendochiliaro	πεντοχίλιαρο	5000 drachmas
dhekachiliaro	δεκαχίλιαρο	10000 drachmas

SHOPPING

ESSENTIAL GROCERIES

ΑΠΑΡΑΙΤΗΤΑ ΜΠΑΚΑΛΙΚΑ

batteries	i bataries	οι μπαταρίες
bottled water	to emfialomeno nero	το εμφιαλωμένο νερό
bread	to psomi	το ψωμί
chocolate	i sokolata	η σοκολάτα
coffee	o kafes	ο καφές
gas cylinder	to ighraerio	το υγραέριο
matches	ta spirta	τα σπίρτα
milk	to ghala	το γάλα
sugar	i zachari	η ζάχαρη
tea	to tsai	το τσάι
toilet paper	to charti iyias	το χαρτί υγείας
toothpaste	i odhondopasta	η οδοντόπαστα
dishwashing liquid	to sapuni piaton	το σαπούνι πιάτων
washing powder	to aporipandiko	το αποπαντικο

GIRL NUMBERS

Remember to use the feminine form of the numbers 1, 3 and 4 μία, τρεις, τέσσερις mia, tris, teseris with the word δραχμή dhrachmi drachma, and the word χιλιάδες chiliadhes 'thousands', for example διακόσιες τέσσερις δραχμές dhiakosies teseris drachmes 204 drachmas, είκοσι μία χιλιάδες ikosi mia chiliadhes 21,000.

SOUVENIRS

ΣΟΥΒΕΝΙΡ

Popular souvenirs are jewellery (gold and silver are much cheaper here than the rest of Europe), leather goods, copper and bronze tableware, backgammon boards, icons, and mass-produced copies of ancient statues and vases.

It's made of ...	ine apo ...	Είναι από ...
bronze	bruntzo	μπρούντζο
copper	chalko	χαλκό
gold	chriso	χρυσό
silver	asimi	ασήμι
backgammon board	to tavli	το τάβλι
bracelet	to vrachioli	το βραχιόλι
chain	i alisidha	η αλυσίδα
earrings	ta skularikia	τα σκουλαρίκια
evil eye (a blue eye worn to ward off evil spirits)	to mati	το μάτι
necklace	to kolie	το κολιέ
rug	to chali	το χαλί
statue	to aghalma	το άγαλμα
worry beads	to komboloi	το κομπολόι
woven shoulder bag	to taghari	το ταγάρι

CLOTHING   ΡΟΥΧΙΣΜΟΣ

blouse	i bluza	η μπλούζα
clothes	ta rucha	τα ρούχα
coat	to palto	το παλτό
dress	to forema	το φόρεμα
hat	to kapelo	το καπέλο
jumper	to pulover	το πουλόβερ
sandals	ta sandhalia/ pedhila	τα σανδάλια/ πέδιλα
shirt	to pukamiso	το πουκάμισο
shoes	ta paputsia	τα παπούτσια
socks	i kaltses	οι κάλτσες
swimsuit	to mayio	το μαγιώ
T-shirt	to bluzaki	το μπλουζάκι
trousers	to pandeloni	το παντελόνι
underwear	ta esorucha	τα εσώρουχα

Can I try it on?
boro na to dhokimaso?	Μπορώ να το δοκιμάσω;

I'm size ...
ime numero ...	Είμαι νούμερο ...

It doesn't fit.
dhen mu chorai	Δεν μου χωράει.

It doesn't suit me.
dhen mu pai	Δεν μου πάει.

It's too ...	ine poli ...	Είναι πολύ ...
big	meghalo	μεγάλο
small	mikro	μικρό
long	makri	μακρύ
short	kondo	κοντό
tight	steno	στενό
loose	fardhi	φαρδύ

SHOE REPAIRS   ΕΠΙΣΚΕΥΕΣ ΠΑΠΟΥΤΣΙΩΝ

Is there a shoe repairer near here?
iparchi paputsis edho konda?	Υπάρχει παπουτσής εδώ κοντά;

I'd like to have my shoes resoled.
chriazome kenuryies soles	Χρειάζομαι καινούργιες σόλες.

When will they be ready?
pote tha ine etima?	Πότε θα είναι έτοιμα;

heel	to takuni	το τακούνι
sole	i sola	η σόλα
shoe laces	ta kordhonia	τα κορδόνια
shoe polish	to verniki	το βερνίκι
	paputsion	παπουτσιών

I WRITE YOU ON MY OLD SHOES!

When you want to imply that you don't care about someone, you say:

> Τον γράφω στα παλιά μου τα παπούτσια.
> ton ghrafo sta palia mu ta paputsia
> (lit: I write him on my old shoes)

COLOURS   ΧΡΩΜΑΤΑ

Colours are listed in the masculine, femine and neuter.

black
    mavros/mavri/mavro   μαύρος/μαύρη/μαύρο
blue
    ble/ghalazios/ghalazia/   μπλε γαλάζιος/γαλάζια/
    ghalazio   γαλάζιο
brown
    kafe   καφέ
green
    prasinos/prasini/prasino   πράσινος/πράσινη/πράσινο
orange
    portokali   πορτοκαλί
pink
    roz   ροζ
purple
    mov   μωβ

red
    kokinos/kokini/kokino   κόκκινος/κόκκινη/κόκκινο
white
    aspros/aspri/aspro (inf)   άσπρος/άσπρη/άσπρο
    lefkos/lefki/lefko (pol)   λευκός/λευκή/λευκό
yellow
    kitrinos/kitrini/kitrino   κίτρινος/κίτρινη/κίτρινο
dark
    skuros/skuri/skuro   σκούρος/σκούρη/σκούρη
light
    anichtos/anichti/anichto   ανοιχτός/ανοιχτή/ανοιχτό

AT THE HAIRDRESSER ΣΤΟ ΚΟΜΜΩΤΗΡΙΟ

Hairdressers in Greece range from the old-fashioned barber's to outlets that specialize in designer hair cuts. The price varies accordingly. You can normally tell by the decor and clientele as to what sort of shop it is. A ΚΟΥΡΕΙΟ kurio tends to be a men's hairdresser/barber, while a ΚΟΜΜΩΤΗΡΙΟ komotirio usually caters for both sexes.

Where can I get a haircut?
    pu boro na kurefto?   Πού μπορώ να κουρευτώ;
I want it short(er).
    ta thelo (pio) konda   Τα θέλω (πιο) κοντά.
Just a trim.
    aplos ena isioma   Απλώς ένα ίσιωμα.

I'd like to have it dyed ...	thelo na ta vapso ...	Θέλω να τα βάψω ...
blonde/blonder	ksantha/pio ksantha	ξανθά/πιο ξανθά
dark/darker	skura/pio skura	σκούρα/πιο σκούρα

TOILETRIES ΚΑΛΛΥΝΤΙΚΑ

brush	i vurtsa	η βούρτσα
comb	i tsatsara/chtena	η τσατσάρα/χτένα
condoms	ta profilaktika	τα προφυλακτικά
insect repellant	apothitiko yia ta kunupia	απωθητικό για τα κουνούπια
razor blade	to ksirafaki	το ξυραφάκι
shampoo	to sampuan	το σαμπουάν
shaving cream	o afros ksirismatos	ο αφρός ξυρίσματος
soap	to sapuni	το σαπούνι
scissors	to psalidhi	το ψαλίδι
sunscreen	andiliako	αντηλιακό
tampons	ta tampon	τα ταμπόν
toilet paper	to charti iyias	το χαρτί υγείας
toothbrush	i odhondovurtsa	η οδοντόβουρτσα
toothpaste	i odhondopasta	η οδοντόπαστα

SHOPPING

FOR THE BABY
ΓΙΑ ΤΟ ΜΩΡΟ

baby chair	i karekla tu moru	η καρέκλα του μωρού
pram	to karotsi	το καρότσι
baby food	i pedhiki trofi	η παιδική τροφή
baby powder	i pudra	η πούδρα
bib	i podhia	η ποδιά
disposable nappies	i panes	οι πάνες
dummy/pacifier	i pipila	η πιπίλα
baby bottle	to bibero	το μπιμπερό

STATIONERY & PUBLICATIONS
ΧΑΡΤΙΚΑ & ΒΙΒΛΙΑ

Where can I find books in English?
    pu boro na vro vivlia stanglika?

Πού μπορώ να βρω βιβλία στ' αγγλικά;

Do you have any novels by …?
    mipos echete kapio mithistorima tu ...?

Μήπως έχετε κάποιο μυθιστόρημα του ...;

Do you have an English translation of (Kazantzakis)?
    echete ton (Kazantzaki) se angliki metafrasi?

Έχετε τον (Καζαντζάκη) σε αγγλική μετάφραση;

dictionary	to leksiko	το λεξικό
envelope	o fakelos	ο φάκελλος
magazine	to periodhiko	το περιοδικό
map	o chartis	ο χάρτης
newspaper	i efimeridha	η εφημερίδα
(in English)	(stanglika)	(στ' αγγλικά)
paper	to charti	το χαρτί
pen (ballpoint)	to stilo	το στυλό
travel guide	o taksidhiotikos odhighos	ο ταξιδιωτικός οδηγός

MUSIC   ΜΟΥΣΙΚΗ

I'm looking for a CD/
cassette by ...
  psachno yia ena CD (si-di)/   Ψάχνω για ένα CD/μια
  mia kaseta tu/tis ...   κασέτα του/της ...
Which is his/her best recording?
  pia ine i kaliteri   Ποια είναι η καλύτερη
  dhiskoghrafisi tu/tis?   δισκογράφηση του/της;

Can you   mu sistinete ... ?   Μου συστήνετε ...
recommend (a) ... ?
  good Greek singer   ena kalo elina   ένα καλό
                      traghudhisti (m)   Έλληνα
                                          τραγουδιστή
                      mia kali elinidha   μια καλή
                      traghudhistria (f) Ελληνίδα
                                          τραγουδίστρια
  traditional Greek   paradhosiaki   παραδοσιακή
    music   eliniki musiki   Ελληνική
                                          μουσική

Can I listen to it here?
  boro na to akuso edho?   Μπορώ να το ακούσω εδώ;
I want a blank tape.
  thelo mia keni kaseta   Θέλω μια κενή κασέτα.

PHOTOGRAPHY   ΦΩΤΟΓΡΑΦΙΚΑ ΕΙΔΗ

How much does it cost to
have this film developed?
  poso kani yia na mu   Πόσο κάνει για να μου
  emfanisete afto to film?   εμφανίσετε αυτό το φιλμ;
When will it be ready?
  pote tha ine etimo?   Πότε θα είναι έτοιμο;
I'd like film for this camera.
  thelo film yiafti ti michani   Θέλω φιλμ γι' αυτή τη μηχανή.

SHOPPING

Do you have (underwater)
disposable cameras?
 echete (ipovrichies)   Έχετε (υποβρύχιες)
 michanes mias chrisis?   μηχανές μιας χρήσης;
Can I have some passport
photos taken?
 boro na vghalo   Μπορώ να βγάλω
 fotoghrafies dhiavatiriu?   φωτογραφίες διαβατηρίου;

batteries	i bataries	οι μπαταρίες
black and	to aspromavro	το ασπρόμαυρο
white film	film	φιλμ
colour film	to enchromo film	το έγχρωμο φιλμ
camera	i (fotoghrafiki)	η (φωτογραφική)
	michani	μηχανή
film speed	i tachitita	η ταχύτητα
flash	to flas	το φλας
lens	o fakos	ο φακός
lightmeter	to fotometro	το φωτόμετρο
slide film	to film yia	το φιλμ για
	dhiafanies	διαφάνειες
video tape	i videotenia	η βιντεοταινία

SMOKING   ΚΑΠΝΙΣΜΑ

A packet of cigarettes, please.
 ena paketo tsighara   Ένα πακέτο τσιγάρα,
 parakalo   παρακαλώ.
Are these cigarettes
strong/light?
 afta ta tsighara ine   Αυτά τα τσιγάρα είναι
 dhinata/light?   δυνατά/light;
Do you have a light?
 echete fotia?   Έχετε φωτιά;
I don't smoke.
 dhen kapnizo   Δεν καπνίζω.

I've quit.
   ekopsa to tsigharo   Έκοψα το τσιγάρο.
I'm trying to quit.
   prospatho na to kopso   Προσπαθώ να το κόψω.
Can I smoke?
   boro na kapniso?   Μπορώ να καπνίσω;
Don't smoke, please.
   min kapnizete parakalo   Μην καπνίζετε, παρακαλώ.
May I have an ashtray?
   ena tasaki, parakalo   Ένα τασάκι, παρακαλώ.

cigarettes	ta tsighara	τα τσιγάρα
cigars	ta pura	τα πούρα
lighter	o anaptiras	ο αναπτήρας
matches	ta spirta	τα σπίρτα
tobacco	o kapnos	ο καπνός

SIZES & COMPARISONS   ΜΕΓΕΘΗ & ΣΥΓΚΡΙΣΕΙΣ

See page 30 for information on comparatives and superlatives. For more amounts see page 229.

small
   mikros/mikri/mikro   μικρός/μικρή/μικρό
smaller
   mikroteros/mikroteri/   μικρότερος/μικρότερη/
   mikrotero   μικρότερο
the smallest
   o mikroteros/i mikroteri/   ο μικρότερος/η μικρότερη/
   to mikrotero   το μικρότερο
big
   meghalos/meghali/meghalo μεγάλος/μεγάλη/μεγάλο

SHOPPING

bigger
    meghaliteros/meghaliteri/   μεγαλύτερος/μεγαλύτερη/
    meghalitero   μεγαλύτερο

biggest
    o meghaliteros/i meghaliteri/   ο μεγαλύτερος/η μεγαλύτερη/
    to meghalitero   το μεγαλύτερο

as big as ...
    toso meghalos/meghali/   τόσο μεγάλος/μεγάλη/
    meghalo oso ...   μεγάλο όσο ...

a lot/more
    poli/perisotero   πολύ/περισσότερο

a few/little/(less/fewer)
    ligho/(lighotero)   λίγο/(λιγότερο)

good/better/best
    kalos/kaliteros/o kaliteros   καλός/καλύτερος/ο καλύτερος

bad/worse/worst
    kakos/chiroteros/o   κακός/χειρότερος/ο
    chiroteros   χειρότερος

ΦΑΓΗΤΑ   FOOD

Greek cuisine relies not so much on complicated recipes, but on getting the most from the flavours of fresh, local produce: fish straight from the sea, freshly made yoghurt, locally grown vegetables and fruit and an abundance of olive oil. The combination of succulent vegetables ripened in the hot Mediterranean sun, pungent herbs, garlic and olive oil, or charcoal-grilled fish sprinkled with fresh oregano and lemon is pretty unbeatable, and perfectly suited to the sultry Greek summer evenings. To experience the best of Greek food, avoid restaurants that advertise tourist menus (especially the ones that display photographs of what you are about to eat), and go for the local ταβέρνα taverna instead.

MEALS   ΓΕΥΜΑΤΑ
Greek eating hours may be very different from what you are used to. Breakfast is frugal to non-existent, but most Greeks have a snack at about 11am. (See page 162). Lunch is eaten rather late, at 2pm but even up to 4pm. The afternoon siesta ends with a strong cup of coffee and perhaps some sweet cake in a ζαχαροπλαστείο, zacharoplastio the Greek version of a patisserie. Don't expect to be served dinner before 9pm, although most Greeks don't go out to eat before 10 or 11pm, especially on weekends.

breakfast	to proino	το πρωινό
lunch	to mesimeriano	το μεσημεριανό
dinner	to vradhino	το βραδινό

Breakfast   Πρωινό
A Greek breakfast is a rather frugal affair – usually a cup of coffee and a piece of bread. Most cafes in tourist resorts will advertise 'full English breakfast' or yoghurt and honey (the latter may sound very authentic, but Greeks never have yoghurt and honey for breakfast!). In out of the way places, do as the Greeks do, and ask for some coffee/tea and παξιμάδι paksimadhi (dried bread for dunking in your hot drink).

FOOD

bread	to psomi	το ψωμί
dried bread	to paksimadhi	το παξιμάδι
toast	i frighania	η φρυγανιά
honey	to meli	το μέλι
butter	to vutiro	το βούτυρο
milk	to ghala	το γάλα
coffee	o kafes	ο καφές
tea	to tsai	το τσάι
sugar	i zachari	η ζάχαρη
instant coffee	o neskafes	ο νεσκαφές

For ordering coffee see page 185.

Snacks   Σνακς

The Greeks make up for their lack of breakfast by the variety of tasty savoury and sweet snacks that are usually eaten at about 11 o'clock. These delights are sold in αρτοπωλείο artopolio 'bakery', γαλακτοπωλείο ghalaktopolio (lit: a milk shop), a cafeteria or any shop that says ΣΝΑΚΣ.

Is it savoury or sweet?
   ine almiro i ghliko?   Είναι αλμυρό ή γλυκό;

savoury	almiro	αλμυρό
sweet	ghliko	γλυκό
pie	pita	πίττα
cheese pie	tiropita	τυρόπιττα
spinach pie	spanakopita	σπανακόπιττα
chicken pie	kotopita	κοτόπιττα
pie with kaseri	kaseropita	κασερόπιττα
(a gruyere-like		
cheese)		
meat pie	kreatopita	κρεατόπιττα
sesame ring	kuluri	κουλούρι
sausage roll	piroski	πυροσκί
toasted sandwich	tost me tiri	τοστ με τυρί
with cheese		

toasted sandwich with ham	tost me zambon	τοστ με ζαμπόν
savoury biscuits	almira	αλμυρά
sweet scone-like biscuits (these come in a variety of shapes)	kulurakia	κουλουράκια
'custard' pie with cinnamon	bughatsa	μπουγάτσα

FOOD

Fast Food   Φαστ-φουντ

For a more substantial snack you can go to a φαστφουντάδικο fastfundadhiko fast food joint. There are the standard American chains as well as the Greek chain Goodies, serving American-style fast food with the pleasant addition of a salad bar. There are also snack bars selling pizza slices and large sandwiches.

If you'd like to taste some Greek-style fast food, why not try one of the numerous σουβλατζίδικο suvlatzidhiko. These usually look like the kebab shops that you find in most Western European cities, easily spotted by the joint of meat, γύρος yiros, that is being grilled on a spit at the front of the shop.

suvlaki σουβλάκι
    pieces of charcoal-grilled lamb wrapped in pitta bread. Ask for με απ'όλα me apola with everything, to get the full works: tomato, onion, tzatziki and sometimes chips.
kalamaki καλαμάκι
    pieces of charcoal-grilled lamb on a skewer with a slice of white bread.
yiros γύρος
    same as suvlaki, but with shavings of the joint of meat that's on the spit instead.
bifteki μπιφτέκι
    same as suvlaki but with grilled mince meat balls instead.

FOOD

VEGETARIAN & SPECIAL MEALS

ΕΙΔΙΚΑ ΓΕΥΜΑΤΑ & ΓΕΥΜΑΤΑ ΓΙΑ ΧΟΡΤΟΦΑΓΟΥΣ

The Greek diet does not contain as much meat as, say, that of Northern Europe, and perhaps for that reason the concept of strict vegetarianism can sometimes be considered rather alien. There are dozens of dishes that are vegetable or pulse-based, and these are usually suitable for vegans also, as dairy produce is rarely used in them. Food is always fried in olive or other vegetable oil, never in lard, and butter is rarely used (see also Lent food in the seasonal food section on page 170). The term 'Kosher' will not be understood.

I'm a vegetarian.
   ime chortofaghos   Είμαι χορτοφάγος.

I don't eat ...	dhen tro-o ...	Δεν τρώω ...
meat	kreas	κρέας
beef	moschari	μοσχάρι
pork	chirino	χοιρινό
lamb	arni	αρνί
seafood	ta thalasina	τα θαλασσινά

I'm allergic to ...	ime aleryikos/ aleryiki ...	Είμαι αλλεργικός/ αλλεργική ...
seafood	sta thalasina	στα θαλασσινά
flour	sto alevri	στο αλεύρι
dairy	sta ghalaktera pro-ionda	στα γαλακτερά προϊόντα

EATING OUT

ΣΤΟ ΕΣΤΙΑΤΟΡΙΟ

Is there a ... restaurant nearby?
   pu iparchi ena ... estiatorio edho konda?

Πού υπάρχει ένα ... εστιατόριο εδώ κοντά;

good	kalo	καλό
cheap	ftino	φτηνό

A table for ... please.
    ena trapezi ya ...,
    parakalo

Έγα τραπέζι για ...,
παρακαλώ.

Can I sit by the sea please?
    boro na kathiso konda sti
    thalasa, parakalo?

Μπορώ να καθήσω κοντά
στη θάλασσα, παρακαλώ.

Can I smoke?
    boro na kapniso?

Μπορώ να καπνίσω;

The menu, please.
    to menu, parakalo

Το μενού, παρακαλώ.

What's the local speciality?
    pia ine i topiki
    spesialite?

Ποια είναι η τοπική
σπεσιαλιτέ;

Is service included in the price?
    simberilamvanete to servis?

Συμπεριλαμβάνεται το σέρβις;

FOOD

FOOD

COMMON FOOD JOINTS

You'll soon notice that Greeks love eating – whether you want a light snack, a piece of cake or a hearty meal, there will usually be a place open where you can find what you want. This is a list of the most common type of food joints and what you can expect to find in each.

kafeteria καφετερία
> cafeteria, for hot and cold drinks, mid-morning snacks, toasted sandwiches, omelettes, ice creams. Unlike a snack bar, you are expected to sit at a table, rather than have a take-away meal. Cafeterias are usually located around the main square or along the harbour front.

kafenio καφενείο
> coffee shop – there are two types and it's easy to tell them apart: one is similar to a cafeteria. The second type you'll find in smaller places, and it's where men will sit for seemingly hours on end, discussing politics, swinging worry beads, playing backgammon and watching the world go by. As a female traveller, you can go in but be prepared for some unnerving stares.

suvlatzidiko σουβλατζίδικο
> a kebab shop often advertised as ΣΟΥΒΛΑΚΙ or ΓΥΡΟΣ. The Greek answer to fast food (see fast food page 163)

taverna ταβέρνα
> the most common eating place, usually family-owned and the best value for money. You will find a variety of salads, grills, local specialities. This is where Greeks eat.

COMMON FOOD JOINTS

psistaria ψησταριά
  similar to taverna, but specializes in charcoal-grilled meat, or meat roasted on a spit. Very popular.

psarotaverna ψαροταβέρνα
  same as taverna, but specializes in fish. You usually find them on harbour fronts. Look out for the ones that have the day's catch swimming in a tank.

uzeri/mezedhopolio ουζερί/μεζεδοπωλείο
  currently undergoing a revival especially with students and young people. This is where you'll find traditional drinks (ouzo, retsina, barreled wine) consumed with a selection of μεζέδες mezedhes, starter-like portions of Greek dishes.

chasapotaverna χασαποταβέρνα
  fast disappearing, this is a basic restaurant attached to a butcher's shop (χασάπης chasapis butcher). Good value meat, but the menu can be limited. Not for vegetarians.

estiatorio εστιατόριο
  restaurant – a more upmarket eating place. You usually find a mixture of Greek and European cuisine here, unless otherwise advertised.

nichterino kendro νυκτερινό κέντρο
  this is where Greeks have a night out: dine, smash plates and dance to live music. They can be expensive, depending on the calibre of the artists they attract.

zacharoplastio ζαχαροπλαστείο
  patisserie or sweet shop – there are usually tables where you can sit and enjoy a piece of cake and coffee. This is where you'll find Greeks at 5-6pm, especially on summer evenings. A real treat.

FOOD

REGIONAL SPECIALITIES   ΤΟΠΙΚΟ ΦΑΓΗΤΟ

Broadly speaking, the diet on the islands and coastal areas is more rich in fish and seafood, while in northern Greece and mountainous areas more meat is consumed. Here is a list of some regional dishes.

Northern Greece –   Βόρεια Ελλάδα –
Thessaly   Θεσσαλία

vatrachopodhara βατραχοπόδαρα
    fried frogs' legs (especially around Ioannina)

kondosuvli κοντοσούβλι
    skewered grilled pork

patsas πατσάς
    soup with tripe, garlic and vinegar (especially around the areas of Thessaloniki and north-eastern Greece)

spetzofai σπετζοφάι
    spicy sausages cooked with aubergines (Pilion)

righanokeftedhes ριγανοκεφτέδες
    fish roe rissoles with oregano (Pilion)

North Eastern Aegean   Βορειοανατολικό Αιγαίο

Many of these dishes were brought over to Greece by Greeks who emigrated from Turkey in the 1920s.

atzem pilafi ατζέμ πιλάφι
    fried rice with vegetables and olive oil

anginares ala polita αγκινάρες αλά πολίτα
    artichokes cooked with potatoes, carrots, dill and lemon

yiuslemedhes γιουσλεμέδες
    fried cheese pies (Mitilini)

yiaurtoghlu γιαουρτογλού
    grilled meat with pieces of pitta bread and yoghurt

chalvas politikos χαλβάς πολίτικος
    sweet made out of semolina, sugar, cinnamon, pine nuts, walnuts and raisins

Aegean Islands   Νησιά του Αιγαίου

frutalia φρουταλιά
  potato and spicy sausage 'omelette' (Andros)

sfugato σφουγγάτο
  baked mince and courgette omelette topped with breadcrumbs
  (Rhodes)

FOOD

Crete   Κρήτη

chochlii χοχλιοί
  snails cooked with onions and tomato

kaltsunia καλτσούνια
  cheese pies made with soft mizithra cheese

pita sfakiani πίττα σφακιανή
  thick pancake stuffed with soft cheese and eaten with honey

patudhia πατούδια
  sesame and almond turnovers flavoured with orange water

Ionian Islands   Ιόνια νησιά

pastitsadha παστιτσάδα
  veal cooked in wine and tomatoes with macaroni

sofrito σοφρίτο
  stewed steak with garlic

burdheto μπουρδέτο
  stewed fish with paprika (Corfu)

mandolato μαντολάτο
  nougat (especially Zakinthos)

Cyprus   Κύπρος

flaunes φλαούνες
  cheese tartlets made with chalumi cheese

chumus χούμους
  chick pea and garlic dip

seftalia σεφταλιά
  pork cooked with onion, parsley and cabbage

FOOD

afelia αφέλια
   pork cooked in red wine and coriander

kolokasi me chirino κολοκάσι με χοιρινό
   pork stew with colocasia

borekia μπορέκια
   small pies stuffed with cheese/mince/spinach

ghlitzista γλυτζιστά
   fried rosettes in syrup

SEASONAL FOOD   ΕΠΟΧΙΑΚΟ ΦΑΓΗΤΟ
Special dishes are prepared for religious feasts and other occasions.

'Clean Monday'   Καθαρή Δευτέρα
(beginning of Lent)
laghana λαγάνα
   flat bread with sesame

fasolia mavromatika φασόλια μαυρομάτικα
   a salad made of black-eyed beans, spring onions, oil and lemon

skordhalia σκορδαλιά
   garlic dip

patzaria πατζάρια
   beetroot salad

Lent Food   Νηστήσιμα
During the six weeks before Easter and for Holy week, religious
Greeks abstain from eating food containing meat and dairy.
These dishes are called nistisima. As Lent usually falls during the
months of March and April, the nistisima cuisine makes full use
of the glut of spring green vegetables. Nistisima are tasty enough
to be prepared even by Greeks who don't strictly follow this
period of abstinence. During Lent, most restaurants will have at
least a couple of nistisima dishes. This food is suitable for vegetarians and vegans but be aware that seafood including squid
and octopus is not on the forbidden list.

ladhera/yachni λαδερά/γιαχνί
> a method of cooking vegetables by braising them in olive oil, tomatoes and herbs. Φασόλια fasolia beans, μπιζέλι bizeli mange tout, πατάτες patates potatoes, κολοκύθια kolokithia courgettes, αρακάς arakas green peas can all be cooked in this way.

briami μπριάμι
> mixed baked vegetables with tomato sauce and herbs.

anginares ladheres αγκινάρες λαδερές
> artichokes, potatoes, carrots, peas cooked in olive oil, dill and lemon

fakes φακές
> lentils cooked with garlic, onion, herbs and vinegar. Eaten traditionally on Good Friday.

revithia ρεβύθια
> chick peas, eaten as soup or stirred into rice (ρεβυθοπίλαφο revithopilafo)

fasoladha φασολάδα
> bean stew with tomatoes, carrots and celery

rizi me supia ρύζι με σουπιά
> rice cooked with cuttle fish

chalvas χαλβάς
> sweet made with sesame and nuts

Easter Food   Πασχαλινό φαγητό

mayiritsa μαγειρίτσα
> soup made with lamb offal, dill, spring onions, eggs and lemon. Traditionally eaten at midnight on Easter Saturday.

kokina avgha κόκκινα αυγά
> hard boiled eggs dyed red

tsureki τσουρέκι
> slightly sweet egg-bread

kokoretsi κοκορέτσι
> pieces of offal twisted round a spit brushed with herbs and lemon and spit-roasted. Eaten on Easter Sunday.

arni sti suvla αρνί στη σούβλα
> whole lamb roasted on a spit, and eaten with roast potatoes on Easter Sunday.

FOOD

MENU DECODER

As a lot of the fresh food is seasonal, you won't find every item on the menu available every day. Greeks don't usually bother with the menu – they ask the waiter Τι έχετε σήμερα; ti echete simera? 'What do you have today?'. Another option is to have a look in the kitchen. This is perfectly acceptable in tavernas, but not in restaurants. You can always ask μπορώ να ρίξω μια ματιά στην κουζίνα; boro na rikso mia matia stin kuzina? 'Can I have a look in the kitchen?'

Bread and water are always brought to the table and included in the bill. Some tavernas will bring a selection of hot and cold starters on a tray for you to choose. It is customary to put starters in the middle of the table and share them.

As a main course, you can choose either something της ώρας tis oras (lit: of the hour) meaning freshly grilled, or μαγειρευτό mayirefto already cooked dishes (stews, roasts, etc). Sometimes the main courses are also shared. The meal finishes with fruit. Greeks rarely have coffee and dessert as part of a meal, but instead wait until after the afternoon siesta.

OPEKTIKA orektika **Starters/Salads**
Ντοματοσαλάτα domatosalata
   tomato salad with oil and vinegar dressing
Χωριάτικη choriatiki
   Greek salad: tomatoes, cucumber, onion, peppers, feta cheese, oregano, oil and vinegar dressing
Ρώσικη rosiki
   Russian salad: chopped boiled potatoes, carrots, peas and eggs in mayonnaise
Χόρτα chorta
   boiled dandelion and other green shoots with lemon and oil (winter to early summer only)

MENU DECODER

Πιπεριές piperies
  roast peppers with oil and vinegar
Τζατζίκι tzatziki
  yoghurt, cucumber and garlic dip
Σκορδαλιά skordhalia
  garlic dip
Ταραμοσαλάτα taramosalata
  herring roe dip
Μελιτζανοσαλάτα melitzanosalata
  aubergine and garlic dip
Τυροπιττάκια tiropitakia
  fried cheese parcels in filo pastry
Κεφτεδάκια keftedhakia
  fried mince meat balls
Τυροκεφτέδες tirokeftedhes
  fried cheese balls
Κολοκυθοκεφτέδες kolokithokeftedhes
  fried courgette balls
Γίγαντες yighandes
  dry broad beans baked in tomato sauce and celery
Ντολμαδάκια dolmadhakia
  rice or meat stuffed vine leaves with lemon
Κολοκύθια τηγανητά kolokithia tighanita
  courgettes fried in batter
Μελιτζάνες τηγανητές melitzanes tighanites
  aubergines in fried batter
Γεμιστές πιπεριές yemistes piperies
  peppers stuffed with rice or feta cheese
Μύδια/Γαρίδες σαγανάκι midhia/gharidhes saghanaki
  mussels/prawns baked in tomato sauce with a feta
  cheese topping

ΖΥΜΑΡΙΚΑ zimarika **Pasta**
Μακαρόνια με κιμά makaronia me kima
  spaghetti with mince meat sauce

FOOD

MENU DECODER

Μακαρόνια με σάλτσα ντομάτα makaronia me saltsa domata
  spaghetti with tomato sauce
Παστίτσιο pastitsio
  layers of cannelloni and tomato mince topped with a cheese sauce, a bit like lasagna

ΤΗΣ ΩΡΑΣ tis oras **Charcoal-Grilled Food**
Μπριζόλα μοσχαρίσια brizola moscharisia
  veal chop
Μπριζόλα χοιρινή brizola chirini
  pork chop
Μπριζόλα αρνίσια brizola arnisia
  lamb chop
Σουβλάκι suvlaki
  grilled skewered meat pieces
Ψαρονέφρι psaronefri
  pork steak
Παϊδάκια αρνίσια pa-idhakia arnisia
  spare ribs (lamb)
Συκώτι sikoti liver
Κοτόπουλο της σχάρας kotopulo tis scharas
  grilled chicken
Πατάτες τηγανητές patates tighanites
  chips

ΨΑΡΙΚΑ psarika **Fish**
Fresh fish is usually sold by the weight rather than by the portion. You may be asked to go to the kitchen of the taverna, to choose the pieces of fish that you'd like.

Καλαμαράκια kalamarakia
  fried baby squid
Χταπόδι chtapodhi
  boiled octopus with oil and vinegar

MENU DECODER

Γαρίδες gharidhes
  prawns
Αστακός astakos
  lobster, served boiled with mayonnaise
Μαρίδες maridhes
  fried whitebait (seasonal)
Αθερίνα atherina
  fried whitebait (a size down from maridhes)
Ψαρόσουπα psarosupa
  fish soup
Ψάρι λαδολέμονο psari ladholemono
  grilled fish of your choice with oil and lemon dressing
Γαλέος σκορδαλιά ghaleos skordhalia
  fried fish in batter with a garlic sauce
Ψάρι πλακί psari plaki
  fish baked in the oven with tomato, leeks and capers

ΜΑΓΕΙΡΕΥΤΑ mayirefta **Pre-cooked Dishes**
Μουσακάς musakas
  layers of aubergines and tomato mince topped with
  a bechamel sauce
Ντομάτες γεμιστές domates yemistes
  baked tomatoes (and sometimes peppers), stuffed
  with mince or rice and potatoes
Σουτζουκάκια σμυρνέικα sutzukakia smirneika
  garlic and cumin-flavoured mince meat balls cooked
  in a tomato and wine sauce
Γιοβαρελάκια yiovarelakia
  braised meat and rice balls with egg and lemon
  sauce (αυγολέμονο avgholemono)
Φρικασέ frikase
  lamb braised with lettuce and dill and served with
  an egg and lemon sauce (αυγολέμονο avgholemono)

FOOD

MENU DECODER

Λαχανοντολμάδες lachanodolmadhes
   cabbage leaves stuffed with mince meat and rice and
   served with an egg and lemon sauce
Στιφάδο stifadho
   traditionally hare, but now usually beef stew with
   tomato, wine and shallots (mainly a winter dish)
Γιουβέτσι yiuvetsi
   lamb pieces cooked in tomato sauce and baked with
   pasta
Κρέας ψητό kreas psito
   beef roasted in the oven with lemon
Κοτόπουλο ψητό kotopulo psito
   roast chicken
Κατσικάκι στο φούρνο katsikaki sto furno
   roast goat with lemon and oregano
Γαρδούμπα ghardhumba
   liver and offal baked in the oven with lemon and
   oregano
Φασάλκια λαδερά fasolakia ladhera
   green beans cooked in olive oil and tomato
Φασολάδα fasoladha
   bean stew with carrots, celery and tomato
Σαλιγκάρια salingaria
   snails cooked with onion, white wine and tomato
   (autumn only)
Μελιτζάνες παπουτσάκι melitzanes paputsaki
   aubergine 'shoes'. Baked aubergines stuffed with
   mince meat in tomato sauce and topped with melted
   cheese
Μελιτζάνες ιμάμ μπαϊλντί melitzanes imam baildi
   baked aubergines stuffed with chopped onion, parsley and tomato
Μελιτζανάτο melitzanato
   beef or lamb stew with baby aubergines

Christmas Food   Χριστουγεννιάτικο φαγητό

ghalopula γαλοπούλα
    roast turkey
yemisi γέμιση
    stuffing made of minced meat, tomatoes, chicken livers, chest-
    nuts, sultanas and pine nuts
ghurunopulo γουρουνόπουλο
    roast suckling pig. It used to be the traditional Christmas meal
    before the introduction of turkey.
kurambiedhes κουραμπιέδες
    shortbread-like biscuits coated with icing sugar
melomakarona μελομακάρονα
    nutty biscuits soaked in syrup
dhiples δίπλες
    fried crispy pancakes sprinkled with nuts and honey

SWEETS   ΓΛΥΚΑ

Sweets are eaten in the early evening around 6pm with a strong cup
of coffee. You will find sweets in a ζαχαροπλαστείο zacharoplastio.
Remember if you're visiting someone, always take a box of sweets.
    Filo pastry, a paper-thin sheet of flour pastry, features quite
heavily in Greek cuisine, especially sweet making.

baklavas μπακλαβάς
    layers of nuts and filo pastry dripping in syrup
kataifi καταΐφι
    nuts wrapped in vermicelli-like pastry with syrup
kopenchaghi κοπεγχάγη
    layers of nutty cake wrapped in filo pastry
ghalaktobureko γαλακτομπούρεκο
    orange flavoured custard in filo pastry
amighdhalota αμυγδαλωτά
    almond biscuits
turta amighdhalu τούρτα αμυγδάλου
    almond gateau
sokolatina σοκολατίνα
    chocolate gateau

FOOD

ghlika kutaliu γλυκά κουταλιού
    fruit preserved in syrup: pistachio, cherry, rosehip, bergamot,
    bitter orange, baby aubergine
lukumadhes λουκουμάδες
    fried balls of dough, served with cinnamon and syrup
revani ρεβανί
    sponge-like cake with walnuts and syrup
karidhopita καρυδόπιττα
    walnut cake

SELF-CATERING   ΨΩΝΙΖΩ ΤΡΟΦΙΜΑ
Bakery   Αρτοπωλείο

Bread plays a very important role in the diet of a Greek. Very few
Greeks would eat a meal without bread and it is always present on
the table. Bread is usually bought daily from the local baker.

bakery	artopolio	αρτοπωλείο
bread	to psomi	το ψωμί
long loaf	i fratzola	η φρατζόλα
round loaf	to karveli	το καρβέλι
village bread	to choriatiko	το χωριάτικο
	psomi	ψωμί
white bread	aspro psomi	άσπρο ψωμί
brown bread	mavro psomi	μαύρο ψωμί
biscuits (sweet	ta kulurakia	τα κουλουράκια
or savoury)		
cheese pie	i tiropita	η τυρόπιττα

WHAT WOULD YOU LIKE?

'I'd like ...' in Greek is θα'θελα ... thathela ..., but you can
equally say 'I want ...' θέλω ... thelo..., or use the imperative φέρτε μου ... fertemu ... 'bring me ...', and δώστε μου ... doste
mu ... 'give me ...', and add 'please' παρακαλώ parakalo.
None of those are considered impolite.

FOOD

Grocer

		Παντοπωλείο
butter	to vutiro	το βούτυρο
cheese	to tiri	το τυρί
delicatessen	alandika	αλαντικά
flour	to alevri	το αλεύρι
ham	to zambon	το ζαμπόν
honey	to meli	το μέλι
milk	to ghala	το γάλα
oil	to ladhi	το λάδι
olive oil	to eleoladho	το ελαιόλαδο
olives	i elies	οι ελιές
tin	i konserva	η κονσέρβα
sugar	i zachari	η ζάχαρη
vinegar	to ksidhi	το ξύδι

Meat & Poultry

		Κρεοπωλείο
beef	to vodhino	το βοδινό
chicken	to kotopulo	το κοτόπουλο
duck	i papia	η πάπια
goat	to katsiki	το κατσίκι
hare	o laghos	ο λαγός
lamb	to arni	το αρνί
liver	to sikoti	το συκώτι
pork	to chirino	το χοιρινό
rabbit	to kuneli	το κουνέλι
turkey	i ghalopula/ (o dhianos)	η γαλοπούλα/ (ο διάνος)
sausages	ta lukanika	τα λουκάνικα
salami	to salami	το σαλάμι
veal	to moschari	το μοσχάρι

FOOD

Fish & Seafood

Ψάρια & θαλασσινά

You will find mostly sea fish. Freshwater fish is usually imported.

baby squid	to kalamaraki	το καλαμαράκι
cod	o vakalaos	ο βακαλάος
eel	to cheli	το χέλι
grey mullet	to lithrini	το λιθρίνι
grouper	i sfiridha	η σφυρίδα
lobster	o astakos	ο αστακός
mackerel	to skumbri/	το σκουμπρί/
	o kolios	ο κολιός
mussels	ta midhia	τα μύδια
prawns	i gharidhes	οι γαρίδες
red mullet	to barbuni	το μπαρμπούνι
octopus	to chtapodhi	το χταπόδι
sardines	i sardheles	οι σαρδέλλες
scorpion fish	o skorpios	ο σκορπιός
sea bass	to lavraki	το λαβράκι
sea bream	to melanuri/	το μελανούρι/
	i sinaghridha	η συναγρίδα
smoked herring	i renga	η ρέγγα
swordfish	o ksifias	ο ξιφίας
tope	o ghaleos	ο γαλέος
trout	i pestrofa	η πέστροφα
whitebait	i maridha	η μαρίδα
whitebait	i atherina	η αθερίνα
(very small)		

CAN I HAVE?

To order food ask:

Can (I/we) have a ...?   (mu/mas) fernete ena/mia ...
                          (Μου/Μας) φέρνετε ένα/μία ...

Alternatively you can simply name the thing you want and add

parakalo!   Παρακαλώ!   Please!

FOOD

Vegetables

		Λαχανικά
green grocer	oporopolio	οπωροπωλείο
aubergine/eggplant	i melitzana	η μελιτζάνα
artichoke	i anginara	η αγκινάρα
avocado	to avokado	το αβοκάντο
beetroot	to patzari	το πατζάρι
broad beans	ta kukia	τα κουκιά
green beans	ta fasolakia	τα φασολάκια
cabbage	to lachano	το λάχανο
capsicum/pepper	i piperia,	η πιπεριά,
	to kerato	το κέρατο
carrots	ta karota	τα καρότα
celery (leaves only)	to selino	το σέλινο
celery root	i selinoriza	η σελινόριζα
corn	to kalaboki	το καλαμπόκι
courgette/zucchini	to kolokithaki	το κολοκυθάκι
cucumber	to anguri	το αγγούρι
garlic	to skordho	το σκόρδο
lettuce	to maruli	το μαρούλι
mushrooms	ta manitaria	τα μανιτάρια
onion	to kremidhi	το κρεμμύδι
parsley	o ma-indanos	ο μαϊντανός
potatoes	i patates	οι πατάτες
spinach	to spanaki	το σπανάκι
tomatoes	i domates	οι ντομάτες

Pulses

		Όσπρια
beans (dried)	ta fasolia	τα φασόλια
broad beans	ta kukia	τα κουκιά
chick peas	ta revithia	τα ρεβύθια
lentils	i fakes	οι φακές
rice	to rizi	το ρύζι
split peas/ broad beans	i fava	η φάβα

FOOD

Herbs, Spices & Condiments · Μπαχαρικά

bay leaf	i dhafni	η δάφνη
cinnamon	i kanela	η κανέλα
cloves	to gharifalo	το γαρύφαλλο
herbs	ta votana	τα βότανα
marjoram	i matzurana	η ματζουράνα
mint	o dhiosmos	ο δυόσμος
mustard	i mustardha	η μουστάρδα
nutmeg	to moschokaridho	το μοσχοκάρυδο
oregano	i righani	η ρίγανη
pepper	to piperi	το πιπέρι
rosemary	to dhendrolivano	το δενδρολίβανο
sage	to faskomilo	το φασκόμηλο
salt	to alati	το αλάτι
vinegar	to ksidhi	το ξύδι
thyme	to thimari	το θυμάρι
wild herbs (for tea)	to tsai tu vunu	το τσάι του βουνού

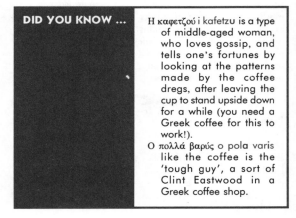

DID YOU KNOW ...

Η καφετζού i kafetzu is a type of middle-aged woman, who loves gossip, and tells one's fortunes by looking at the patterns made by the coffee dregs, after leaving the cup to stand upside down for a while (you need a Greek coffee for this to work!).

Ο πολλά βαρύς o pola varis like the coffee is the 'tough guy', a sort of Clint Eastwood in a Greek coffee shop.

FOOD

Fruit

apples	ta mila	τα μήλα
apricots	ta verikoka	τα βερίκοκα
bananas	i bananes	οι μπανάνες
cherries	ta kerasia	τα κεράσια
dates	i churmadhes	οι χουρμάδες
figs	ta sika	τα σύκα
fruit	fruta	φρούτα
grapes	ta stafilia	τα σταφύλια
lemon	to lemoni	το λεμόνι
melon	to peponi	το πεπόνι
mulberries	ta mura	τα μούρα
oranges	ta portokalia	τα πορτοκάλια
peaches	ta rodhakina	τα ροδάκινα
(yellow) peach	o yarmas	ο γιαρμάς
pear	to achladhi	το αχλάδι
pineapple	o ananas	ο ανανάς
plums (red)	ta dhamaskina	τα δαμάσκηνα
plums (yellow)	i nerambules	οι νεράμπουλες
strawberries	i fra-ules	οι φράουλες
watermelon	to karpuzi	το καρπούζι

Φρούτα

Nuts

almonds	ta amighdhala	τα αμύγδαλα
chestnuts	ta kastana	τα κάστανα
chick peas (roasted)	ta straghalia	τα στραγάλια
hazelnuts	ta fundukia	τα φουντούκια
melon seed (roasted)	ta sporakia	τα σποράκια
nuts	ksiri karpi	ξηροί καρποί
peanuts	ta fistikia	τα φυστίκια
pistachios	ta arapika fistikia	τα αράπικα φυστίκια
walnuts	ta karidhia	τα καρύδια

Ξηροί καρποί

FOOD

DRINKS
Non-alcoholic Drinks

		ΠΟΤΑ
		Μη αλκοολούχα ποτά
bottled water	to emfialomeno nero	το εμφιαλωμένο νερό
tap water	to nero tis vrisis	το νερό της βρύσης
juice	o chimos	ο χυμός
orange juice (sweetened)	i portokaladha	η πορτοκαλάδα

OLIVES

Some shops specialize in the sale of olives and olive oil only. Look out for the sign ΕΛΙΕΣ, ΛΑΔΙ. Traditional shops display their different types of olives in big barrels (you never thought there could be so many ways of pickling olives!), from where you can taste a couple before deciding which ones to buy. Greece has the highest per capita consumption of olive oil in the world – no surprise then, that when Greeks refer to λάδι ladhi oil, they always mean olive oil, although on oil bottles you will see the full label ελαιόλαδο eleoladho.

... olives	i ... elies	οι ... ελιές
green	prasines	πράσινες
black	mavres	μαύρες
cracked (green olives)	tsakistes	τσακιστές
sliced	charaktes	χαρακτές
wrinkled black olives	thrumbes	θρούμπες

ελιές Καλαμών elies kalamon olives from Kalamata are considered the finest.

olive oil	to eleoladho	το ελαιόλαδο
virgin olive oil	to partheno eleoladho	το παρθένο ελαιόλαδο
acidity	i oksitis	η οξύτης

orange juice (unsweetened)	o chimos portokali	ο χυμός πορτοκάλι
apple juice	o chimos milu	ο χυμός μήλου
morello cherry juice	i visinadha	η βυσινάδα
tea with lemon	to tsai me lemoni	το τσάι με λεμόνι
tea with milk	to tsai me ghala	το τσάι με γάλα
herbal tea	to tsai tu vunu	το τσάι του βουνού
hot chocolate	i sokolata rofima	η σοκολάτα ρόφημα

FOOD

Coffee   Καφές

Unless specified, saying έναν καφέ, παρακαλώ! enan kafe, parakalo! 'A coffee, please!' will most likely get you a nescafe in the winter and an iced coffee in the summer. Here's how to get what you want:

ena eliniko Ένα ελληνικό this will get you a Greek coffee, a strong thick brew, served in a small cup, which you have to leave for a few seconds to settle. Don't attempt to drink the dregs. You specify how you take your coffee as follows:

ena sketo Ένα σκέτο plain, no sugar

ena metrio Ένα μέτριο medium strength with a little sugar

CHEESE

Soft cheeses made from ewe's milk:
i feta η φέτα
i mizithra η μυζήθρα – a bit like ricotta
to manuri το μανούρι
i kopanisti η κοπανιστή – very mature, soured cheese. Definitely an acquired taste.

Hard cheeses:
to kaseri το κασέρι – made from ewe's milk
i ghraviera η γραβιέρα – creamy, a bit like gruyere
to kefalotiri το κεφαλοτύρι – salty, a bit like parmesan
chalumi το χαλούμι – from Cyprus, mainly used for frying

FOOD

ena pola vari Ένα πολλά βαρύ strong
ena vari ghliko Ένα βαρύ γλυκό strong and sweet
ena neskafe sketo Ένα νεσκαφέ σκέτο a plain nescafe
ena neskafe me ghala Ένα νεσκαφέ με γάλα a nescafe with milk
ena frape (me ghala) Ένα φραπέ (με γάλα) iced, shaken coffee
   (with milk)

Alcoholic Drinks   Αλκοολούχα ποτά

Most alcoholic drinks, such as vodka, gin or whisky sound similar
in Greek.

beer	i bira	η μπύρα
sweet red wine from Achaia	i mavrodhafni	η μαυροδάφνη
champagne	i sampania	η σαμπάνια
ouzo (aniseed drink)	to uzo	το ούζο
Metaxa (five) star brandy	star metaksa (pende) asteron	Μεταξά (πέντε) αστέρων
bitter orange liqueur	kum kuat	κουμ κουάτ
wine	to ... krasi	το ... κρασί
red	kokino	κόκκινο
white	aspro	άσπρο
rose	roze	ροζέ
sweet	ghliko	γλυκό
dry	ksiro	ξηρό

ΣΤΗΝ ΕΞΟΧΗ

IN THE COUNTRY

CAMPING   ΚΑΤΑΣΚΗΝΩΣΗ

Camping is very popular in Greece and you will find several campsites, especially along coastal areas. Most campsites have hot showers, a cooking/barbecue area, a washing area, and sometimes electrical sockets at every pitch.

Just setting up anywhere is not permitted in Greece. If you have to camp outside a designated campsite, please leave it clean, and please do not light fires.

Can we camp here?
    borume na kataskinosume edho?   Μπορούμε να κατασκηνώσουμε εδώ;

Is there a campsite nearby?
    iparchi kamping edho konda?   Υπάρχει κάμπινγκ εδώ κοντά;

How much is it per night?
    poso kani ti vradhia?   Πόσο κάνει τη βραδιά;

Is the electricity included?
    simberilamvanete to revma?   Συμπεριλαμβάνεται το ρεύμα;

Where are the showers?
    pu ine ta dus?   Πού είναι τα ντους;

Is this drinking water?
    pinete afto to nero?   Πίνεται αυτό το νερό;

camping	i kataskinosi/ to kamping	η κατασκήνωση/ το κάμπινγκ
campsite	o choros kataskinosis	ο χώρος κατασκήνωσης
tin opener	to anichtiri	το ανοιχτήρι
fuel	ta kafsima	τα καύσιμα
spirit	to fotistiko inopnevma	το φωτιστικό οινόπνευμα
hammock	i kremasti kunia	η κρεμαστή κούνια

IN THE COUNTRY

hammer	to sfiri	το σφυρί
mattress	to stroma	το στρώμα
mosquito net	i kunupiera	η κουνουπιέρα
penknife	o suyias	ο σουγιάς
tent	i skini	η σκηνή
rope	to skini	το σκοινί
sleeping bag	o ipnosakos	ο υπνόσακκος
tent pegs	ta palukia	τα παλούκια
torch (flashlight)	o fakos	ο φακός
waterbottle	to bukali neru	το μπουκάλι νερού

HIKING   ΟΔΟΙΠΟΡΙΑ

Greece offers excellent hiking and mountaineering country with
walks for all levels of difficulty. Footpaths are not usually
signposted, but they are frequently used by shepherds and farm-
ers, and therefore usually lead to a village. If you see a church at
the top of a mountain, you can be certain that there is a footpath
leading to it. Most hilltop churches are dedicated to Προφήτης
Ηλίας profitis ilias the Prophet Eliah who is traditionally associated with mountains.

Be prepared for what's described to you as 'an hour's walk' to turn
into a half day trek, as villagers' concept of time is somewhat erratic.

Is there a footpath to
(Profitis Ilias)?
   iparchi monopati os (ton   Υπάρχει μονοπάτι ως (τον
   profiti ilia)?   Προφήτη Ηλία);
Is it a good footpath?
   ine kalo to monopati?   Είναι καλό το μονοπάτι;
How many kilometers is it
(to the village)?
   posa chiliometra ine os   Πόσα χιλιόμετρα είναι ως
   (to chorio)?   (το χωριό);
Is it steep?
   ine apotomo?   Είναι απότομο;
Are there any rockfalls?
   yinonde katolisthisis?   Γίνονται κατολισθήσεις;

Where can we sleep?
    pu borume na kimithume?   Πού μπορούμε να κοιμηθούμε;
We're lost.
    echume chathi   Έχουμε χαθεί.

footpath	to monopati	το μονοπάτι
nature reserve	o ethnikos dhrimos	ο εθνικός δρυμός
private road	o idhiotikos dhromos	ο ιδιωτικός δρόμος
uphill road	i anifora	η ανηφόρα
downhill road	i katifora	η κατηφόρα
view	i thea	η θέα

MOUNTAINEERING   ΟΡΕΙΒΑΣΙΑ

Greece consists of 90% mountainous terrain – mountain trails
are plentiful, some better maintained than others. The Hellenic
Alpine Club or EOS (Ellinikos Orivatikos Siloghos) can give you
information regarding mountain refuges, trails, level of difficulty
and advise you on weather conditions.

Is it a difficult climb?
    ine dhiskoli anavasi?   Είναι δύσκολη ανάβαση;
Do we need ropes?
    chriazomaste skinia?   Χρειαζόμαστε σκοινιά;
Which is the easiest/
quickest way?
    pios ine o pio efkolos/   Ποιος είναι ο πιο εύκολος/
    ghrighoros dhromos?   γρήγοροσς δρόμος;
Where are you coming from?
    apo pu erchosaste?   Από πού ερχόσατε;
Which way (to Mitikas)?
    pros ta pu (ya ton Mitika)?   Προς τα πού (για τον Μύτικα);
How long did it take you?
    posi ora sas pire?   Πόση ώρα σας πήρε;
Where is the next refuge?
    pu ine to epomeno   Πού είναι το επόμενο
    katafighio?   καταφύγιο;

IN THE COUNTRY

altitude	to ipsometro	το υψόμετρο
to climb	skarfalono	σκαρφαλώνω
ascent	i anavasi	η ανάβαση
descent	i katavasi	η κατάβαση
climbing boots	i botes orivasias	οι μπότες ορειβασίας
compass	i piksidha	η πυξίδα
(climbing) equipment	o eksoplismos (orivasias)	ο εξοπλισμός (ορειβασίας)
rope	to skini	το σκοινί

GEOGRAPHICAL TERMS   ΓΕΩΓΡΑΦΙΚΟΙ ΟΡΟΙ

agriculture	i yeoryia	η γεωργία
bay	o kolpos	ο κόλπος
small bay	o ormos	ο όρμος
bridge	i yefira	η γέφυρα
cave	i spilia/to spileo	η σπηλιά/το σπήλαιο
cliff	o gremos	ο γκρεμός
forest	to dhasos/alsos	το δάσος/ άλσος
fortified hilltop	i akropoli	η ακρόπολη
gorge	to farangi	το φαράγγι
hill	o lofos	ο λόφος
island	to nisi (spoken)/ i nisos (written)	το νησί/η νήσος

THEY MAY SAY ...

Animal names are often used as insults:

ghaidhuri!	Bastard! (lit: donkey)
mulari!	Bastard! (lit: mule)
ghuruni!	Pig!
i kota	a woman with little will (lit: hen)
i alogha	an awkward, clumsy woman (lit: mare)

lake	i limni	η λίμνη
landscape	to topio	το τοπίο
mountain	to vuno (spoken)/ oros (written)	το βουνό/όρος
nature reseve	o ethnikos dhrimos	ο εθνικός δρυμός
peak	i korifi	η κορυφή
peninsula	i chersonisos	η χερσόνησος
promontory	to akrotiri	το ακρωτήρι
river	o potamos	ο ποταμός
waterfall	o katarachtis	ο καταρράχτης

IN THE COUNTRY

AT THE BEACH ΣΤΗΝ ΠΑΡΑΛΙΑ

Greece has some of the cleanest beaches in Europe. Daily tides are negligible, the water reasonably warm, and you can forget any 'Jaws' nightmare scenario – the worst thing that can happen to you is stepping on a sea urchin. Well, life could be worse.

Where is the nearest beach?
  pu ine i kondinoteri paralia? — Πού είναι η κοντινότερη παραλία;
Do I need to pay an entrance fee?
  prepi na pliroso isodho? — Πρέπει να πληρώσω είσοδο;
Can I swim here?
  boro na kolimbiso edho? — Μπορώ να κολυμπήσω εδώ;
Is the water safe (for children)?
  ine asfales to nero (yia ta pedhia)? — Είναι ασφαλές το νερό (για τα παιδιά);
How deep is the water?
  poso vathia ine ta nera? — Πόσο βαθιά είναι τα νερά;

Are there any ... ?	iparchun ... ?	Υπάρχουν ...;
jellyfish	tsuchtres	τσούχτρες
sea urchins	achini	αχινοί
rocks	vrachia	βράχια
currents	revmata	ρεύματα

IN THE COUNTRY

Where are the showers?
    pu ine ta dus?   Πού είναι τα ντους;
Is this umbrella/chair free?
    afti i ombrela/karekla ine   Αυτή η ομπρέλλα/καρέκλα
    eleftheri?   είναι ελεύθερη;

beach	i paralia	η παραλία
coast	i akti	η ακτή
sea (open sea)	to pelaghos	το πέλαγος
sea	i thalasa	η θάλασσα
rock	o vrachos	ο βράχος
sand	i amos	η άμμος
pebbles	ta votsala	τα βότσαλα
sandy beach	i amudhia	η αμμουδιά
sun	o ilios	ο ήλιος
sunscreen lotion	to andiliako	το αντηλιακό
sunglasses	ta yialia iliu	τα γυαλιά ηλίου
towel	i petseta	η πετσέτα
waves	ta kimata	τα κύματα
the Aegean	to egheo	το Αιγαίο
the Ionian	to ionio	το Ιόνιο
the Mediterranean	i mesoghios	η Μεσόγειος
sea	thalasa	θάλασσα

Sea Creatures   Τα Θαλάσσια Ζώα

crab	to kavuri	το καβούρι
cuttle fish	i supia	η σουπιά
dolphin	to dhelfini	το δελφίνι
eel	to cheli	το χέλι
fish (pl)	ta psaria	τα ψάρια
jelly fish	i tsuchtra	η τσούχτρα
lobster	o astakos	ο αστακός

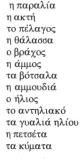

moray eel	i smerna	η σμέρνα
octopus	to chtapodi	το χταπόδι
ray	to selachi	το σελάχι
seagull	o ghlaros	ο γλάρος
seal	i fokia	η φώκια
seashell	to ostrako	το όστρακο
sea urchin	o achinos	ο αχινός
shark	o karcharias	ο καρχαρίας
shoal	to kopadhi	το κοπάδι
squid	to kalamari	το καλαμάρι
starfish	o asterias	ο αστερίας
sword fish	o ksifias	ο ξιφίας
turtle	i chelona	η χελώνα

IN THE COUNTRY

FAUNA

Η ΠΑΝΙΔΑ

Greece has a lot of countryside where animals roam freely, but, like elsewhere in the world, they are threatened by human encroachment and pollution, and are considered by many people 'fair game' for hunting. Wolves, fierce sheep dogs and the odd snake are more likely encountered in the mountains, whereas your main problems by the beach are stinging insects.

What type of animal is this?
ti idhus zo-o ine afto?   Τι είδους ζώο είναι αυτό;

animal	to zo-o	το ζώο
ant	to mirmingi	το μυρμύγκι
asp	i ochia	η οχιά
bear	i arkudha	η αρκούδα
bee	i melisa	η μέλισσα
bird	to puli	το πουλί
butterfly	i petaludha	η πεταλούδα
deer	to elafi	το ελάφι
eagle	o aetos	ο αετός
fox	i alepu	η αλεπού
frog	o vatrachos	ο βάτραχος

IN THE COUNTRY

hare	o laghos	ο λαγός
hawk	to gheraki	το γεράκι
insect	to endomo	το έντομο
mosquito	to kunupi	το κουνούπι
mouse	to pondiki	το ποντίκι
partridge	i perdhika	η πέρδικα
peacock	to paghoni	το παγώνι
pheasant	o fasianos	ο φασιανός
spider	i arachni	η αράχνη
thrush	i tsichla	η τσίχλα
wasp	i sfika	η σφήκα
wolf	o likos	ο λύκος
wild goat	to kri-kri	το κρι-κρι

Farm Animals · Τα Αγροτικά Ζώα

calf	to moschari	το μοσχάρι
cockerel	o petinos	ο πετεινός
cow	i ayeladha	η αγελάδα
donkey	o gha-idharos	ο γάιδαρος
duck	i papia	η πάπια
goat	i katsika	η κατσίκα
hen	i kota	η κότα
horse	to alogho	το άλογο
mule	to mulari	το μουλάρι
pig	to ghuruni	το γουρούνι
sheep	to provato	το πρόβατο

FLORA · Η ΧΛΩΡΙΔΑ

What type of plant is this?
ti idhus fito ine afto?   Τί είδους φυτό είναι αυτό;

basil	o vasilikos	ο βασιλικός
beech	i oksia	η οξιά
carnation	to gharifalo	το γαρύφαλλο
cypress	to kiparisi	το κυπαρίσσι
lily	o krinos	ο κρίνος

oak	i dhris	η δρυς
olive tree	i elia	η ελιά
orchid	i orchidhea	η ορχιδέα
pine tree	to pefko	το πεύκο
poplar	i lefka	η λεύκα
rose	to triandafilo	το τριαντάφυλλο
rosemary	to dhendrolivano	το δεντρολίβανο
wild tulip	i aghria tulipa	η άγρια τουλίπα

Crops   Σπαρτά

barley	to krithari	το κριθάρι
corn	o aravositos	ο αραβόσιτος
hay	to stachi	το στάχι
olive grove	o eleonas	ο ελαιώνας
orange grove	o portokaleonas	ο παρτοκαλαιώνας
orchard	to perivoli/bostani	το περιβόλι/ μποστάνι
rye	i sikali	η σίκαλη
tobacco	o kapnos	ο καπνός
vine	to ambeli	το αμπέλι
wheat	to sitari	το σιτάρι

IN THE COUNTRY

THE WEATHER   Ο ΚΑΙΡΟΣ

Greek weather is fairly predictable in the lowlands and islands, but quite unpredictable in mountainous areas. Basically, it is hot (25°C upwards) from the end of May to the end of September, with only the occasional thunderstorm in the afternoon. Frequently, but not always, mainland Greece experiences a heatwave καύσωνας kafsonas in mid July, with temperatures of around 40°C. If you're travelling in the Aegean, beware of the meltemia μελτέμια, strong northeasterly winds that peak in mid-afternoon and die down in the evening. These last for about a fortnight (approximately 1-15 August), and you could easily find yourself stranded on an island, as several sailings are cancelled during this period.

IN THE COUNTRY

The autumn is mild, but from January to mid March it can be bitterly cold especially on mainland Greece, with plenty of snow often reaching sea level. Spring starts around mid-March and it gradually warms up to 30°C by the end of May/beginning of June.

It's hot.	kani zesti	Κάνει ζέστη.
It's cold.	kani krio	Κάνει κρύο.
It's sunny.	echi liakadha	Έχει λιακάδα.
It's raining.	vrechi	Βρέχει.
It's snowing.	chionizi	Χιονίζει.
It's drizzling.	psichalizi	Ψιχαλίζει.
It's windy.	fisai	Φυσάει.

We're having a heatwave.
  echume kafsona   Έχουμε καύσωνα.
What will the weather be
like tomorrow?
  ti kero tha echume avrio?   Τι καιρό θα έχουμε αύριο;

ΓΙΟΡΤΕΣ & ΑΡΓΙΕΣ

FESTIVALS & HOLIDAYS

PUBLIC HOLIDAYS   ΑΡΓΙΕΣ

If a holiday falls on a weekend, it is not carried over and Monday remains a normal working day. A town's patron saint is a local holiday, for example St. Demetrios (26 October) in Thessaloniki, or St. Andrew (30 November) in Patras and Piraeus.

i protochronia η Πρωτοχρονιά
   1 January, New Years' Day.

ta theofania τα Θεοφάνεια
   6 January, Epiphany. On the day, the local priest throws a cross in the sea and the town's young men and women dive in to fetch it.

i ikosti pempti martiu/oevangelismos η 25η Μαρτίου/ο Ευαγγελισμός
   25th March, dual celebration of the Annunciation and the beginning of the war of Independence against the Ottoman rule in 1821.

i kathari dheftera η Καθαρή Δευτέρα
   on a Monday seven weeks before Easter. Marks the beginning of Lent.

i meghali pempti η Μεγάλη Πέμπτη
   Maundy Thursday (half day holiday)

i meghali paraskevi η Μεγάλη Παρασκευή
   Good Friday

i kiriaki tu pascha η Κυριακή του Πάσχα
   Easter Sunday

i deftera tu pascha η Δευτέρα του Πάσχα
   Easter Monday

i protomayia η Πρωτομαγιά
   1st May; May Day

tu aghiu pnevmatos του Αγίου Πνεύματος
   on a Monday 50 days after Easter, day of the Holy Spirit

o dhekapendavgustos (i kimisi tis theotoku) ο Δεκαπενταύγουστος
(η Κοίμηση της Θεοτόκου)

15 August, Dormition of the Virgin

i epetios tu ochi η επέτειος του ΟΧΙ

28 October – Celebating the day Greeks said 'no' όχι ochi to
Mussolini's ultimatum to capitulate in 1940. At this point Greece
entered WW2.

ta christughena τα Χριστούγεννα

25 December, Christmas Day.

FESTIVALS &   ΦΕΣΤΙΒΑΛ ΘΡΗΣΚΕΥΤ
RELIGIOUS FEASTS   ΙΚΕΣ ΓΙΟΡΤΕΣ

Every village in Greece has an annual feast to celebrate its patron
saint to whom its church is dedicated. Most of the feasts tend to be
during the months of June, July and August. If you happen to be
there, do join in as they're usually noisy, colourful affairs with
plenty of street markets, music and dancing. A religious feast is
known as a πανηγύρι paniyiri. Some of the bigger festivals are:

to karnavali tis Patras το καρναβάλι της Πάτρας
carnival of Patras, complete with parades and floats, on the last
Sunday before the beginning of Lent

to festival athinon το φεστιβάλ Αθηνών
Athens festival of music and dance during the summer months.
There are perfomances by international orchestras and dance
companies, which take place in the ancient amphitheatre
Herodion at the foot of the Akropolis. It's worth going just
for the stunning view.

ta epidhavria τα Επιδαύρεια
festival of ancient plays during the summer months. Staging
of ancient tragical and comical plays by Aeschylus, Sofocles,
Euripides and Aristofanes, some in the original language, at
the ancient theatre of Epidavros near Corinth.

to paniyiri tis tinu το πανηγύρι της Τήνου
15 August on the island of Tinos. Pilgrimage to the miracle-
bearing icon of the Virgin in the main church of the island.

to festival krasiu το φεστιβάλ κρασιού

wine festival, early September in Dafni, on the west side of
Athens, to celebrate the grape harvest.

BIRTHDAYS & SAINTS' DAYS
ΓΕΝΕΘΛΙΑ & ΓΙΟΡΤΕΣ

Everyone in Greece celebrates his/her birthday, but more importantly
his/her 'name' day η γιορτή i yiorti, the day dedicated to the saint
after which one has been named. It's uncommon to send greeting
cards for birthdays, or any other occasion. Greeks prefer to telephone
each other. On name days, they send flowers, cakes or a present, or
drop round in the evening for coffee and cakes. In turn, the person
celebrating takes a box of sweets to treat their colleagues.

When is your name day?	
pote yiortazis?	Πότε γιορτάζεις;
When is your birthday?	
pote ine ta yenethlia su?	Πότε είναι τα γενέθλιά σου;
My name day is on (15 August).	
yiortazo stis (dhekapende avghustu)	Γιορτάζω στις (15 Αυγούστου).
Many happy returns!	
chronia pola/(na zisis)!	Χρόνια πολλά/(Να ζήσεις)!
May you reach 100 years! (for birthdays only)	
na ta ekatostisis!	Να τα εκατοστήσεις!

FESTIVALS & HOLIDAYS

TOASTS

To your health; Cheers!	stin iyia su (inf)/sas (pol)!
	Στην υγειά σου/σας!
Bon appetit!	kali oreksi!
	Καλή όρεξη!
Hurray!	zito!
	Ζήτω!

FESTIVALS & HOLIDAYS

CHRISTMAS & NEW YEAR

ΧΡΙΣΤΟΥΓΕΝΝΑ & ΠΡΩΤΟΧΡΟΝΙΑ

Christmas is primarily a family celebration, whereas New Year revolves around large parties and going out. The Christmas tree is a post-war introduction – on most islands and coastal areas, you'll see people decorating boats, and even placing brightly decorated boats on the main square. The main Christmas meal is at lunchtime on Christmas day, and consists traditionally of pork, but nowadays of turkey.

The equivalent of Santa Claus in Greece is not the Western European St. Nicholas, but in fact St. Vasilios, a 4th century administrator from Caesaria in Asia Minor, who allegedly gave all his property to the poor. Today, people dress up in the red garments of Santa, but they call themselves Άγιος Βασίλης ayios vasilis St. Vasilios. His saint's day is on 1 January, which is why traditionally, presents are opened on New Year's day. Many families have now switched to opening presents on Christmas day.

Season's greetings!	
chronia pola!	Χρόνια Πολλά!
Happy New Year!	
kali chronia!	Καλή Χρονιά!
Christmas Eve	
i paramoni ton	η παραμονή των
christuyenon	Χριστουγέννων
Christmas Day	
i imera ton christuyenon	η ημέρα των Χριστουγέννων
present	
to christuyeniatiko dhoro	το Χριστουγεννιάτικο δώρο
Santa	
o aghios vasilis	ο Άγιος Βασίλης
New Year's Eve	
i paramoni tis protochronias	η παραμονή της Πρωτοχρονιάς
New Year's Day	
i protochronia	η Πρωτοχρονιά

EASTER   ΤΟ ΠΑΣΧΑ

Holy week is the most important week of the Orthodox calendar. Good Friday is a day of mourning and most places including restaurants are shut. At around 10pm, a bier of Christ ο Επιτάφιος o epitafios sets out from every church and is carried around the streets of the parish, followed by a procession of people holding candles. On Saturday at midnight, the Resurrection η Ανάσταση i anastasi is celebrated at church with fireworks and is followed by a food feast (Easter soup μαγειρίτσα mayiritsa, red eggs, Easter bread). Easter Sunday is a day for the outdoors with hundreds of people roasting lamb on a spit, feasting, dancing and drinking.

Lent	i sarakosti	η Σαρακοστή
Easter	to pascha	το Πάσχα
Easter Saturday	to meghalo savato	το Μεγάλο Σάββατο
Christ's bier/ the Epitaph	o epitafios	ο Επιτάφιος
Easter candle	i lambadha	η λαμπάδα
the Resurrection	i anastasi	η Ανάσταση

FESTIVALS & HOLIDAYS

THEY MAY SAY ...

On Easter Sunday and for the next few days people greet each other with:

christos anesti!   Christ has risen!

to which you reply:

alithos anesti!   He is truly risen!

A general greeting for most festive occasions is:

chronia pola!   This literally means 'many years'. This is a good expression to remember as it can be used for 'Happy Birthday', 'Merry Christmas', 'Happy New Year' or 'Happy Saint's day'.

WEDDINGS

ΓΑΜΟΙ & ΒΑΦΤΙΣΕΙΣ

Long life! (at weddings)
   na zisete!
Να ζήσετε!

To your wedding! (a wish to
single people at weddings)
   ke sta dhika su!
Και στα δικά σου!

bridegroom	o ghambros	ο γαμπρός
bride	i nifi	η νύφη
best man	o kumbaros	ο κουμπάρος
best woman	i kumbara	η κουμπάρα
bridesmaids	i paranifi	οι παράνυφοι
wedding	o ghamos	ο γάμος
wedding present	to dhoro ghamu	το δώρο γάμου
wedding reception	i deksiosi	η δεξίωση

Ailments that you are most likely to suffer from in Greece are a touch of diarrhoea and stomach upsets, insect bites and sunstroke. Most large pharmacies will be able to help you out with these and other minor complaints. If anything more major happens, you can either contact the local surgery (ΙΑΤΡΕΙΟ iatrio) or go to the nearest hospital (ΝΟΣΟΚΟΜΕΙΟ nosokomio). Apart from the remotest of areas, hospitals are quite well-equipped. You will also find that, as most doctors have completed some training abroad, they are near fluent in English. Being ill and trying to speak Greek might just be too much of a challenge.

Where is the ...?	pu ine ...?	Πού είναι ...;
doctor	o yiatros	ο γιατρός
hospital	to nosokomio	το νοσοκομείο
pharmacy	to farmakio	το φαρμακείο

AT THE DOCTOR   ΣΤΟ ΓΙΑΤΡΟ

I'm sick.
    ime arostos   Είμαι άρρωστος.
My friend is sick.
    o filos mu(m)/(i fili (f) mu)   Ο φίλος μου/(η φίλη μου)
    ine arostos (m)/arosti (f)   είναι άρρωστος/άρρωστη.
I need a doctor.
    chriazome ena yiatro   Χρειάζομαι ένα γιατρό.
I've been vomiting.
    ekana emeto   Έκανα εμετό.
I've had diarrhoea for
(three) days.
    echo dhiaria edho ke (tris)   Έχω διάρροια εδώ και (τρεις)
    meres   μέρες.
I feel shivery/dizzy.
    echo riyi/zaladhes   Έχω ρίγη/ζαλάδες.
I can't sleep.
    echo aipnia   Έχω αϋπνία.

It hurts here.
  me ponai edho   Με πονάει εδώ.
I feel better/worse.
  esthanome kalitera/   Αισθάνομαι καλύτερα/
  chirotera   χειρότερα.
I need a rabies vaccine.
  chriazome andilisiko   Χρειάζομαι αντιλυσσικό.

I've been	me tsimbise ...	Με τσίμπησε ...
stung by a ...		
bee	melisa	μέλισσα
jelly fish	tsuchtra	τσούχτρα
wasp	sfika	σφήκα

I've had the vaccine.
  echo kani emvolio   Έχω κάνει εμβόλιο.
I have my own syringe.
  echo dhiki mu siringa   Έχω δική μου σύριγγα.
I don't want a blood transfusion.
  dhen thelo metangisi   Δεν θέλω μετάγγιση
  ematos   αίματος.
I'd like to have my eyes/
teeth checked.
  thelo na mu eksetasete ta   Θέλω να μου εξετάσετε τα
  matia mu/ta dhondia mu   μάτια μου/τα δόντια μου.
I need a new pair of glasses.
  chriazome ena kenuryio   Χρειάζομαι ένα καινούργιο
  zevghari yialia   ζευγάρι γυαλιά.

SICKNESS & CONDOLENCES

Get well soon!	perastika!
	Περαστικά!
My deepest sympathy.	ta therma mu silipitiria
	Τα θερμά μου συλλυπητήρια.

HEALTH

THE DOCTOR MAY ASK ...

ti ine to provlima?	What's the problem?
Τι είναι το πρόβλημα;	
pu ponate?	Where does it hurt?
Πού πονάτε;	
poso kero to echete?	How long have you
Πόσο καιρό το έχετε;	had it?
kapnizete?	Do you smoke?
Καπνίζετε;	
posa tsighara kapnizete	How many cigarettes
tin imera?	do you smoke a day?
Πόσα τσιγάρα καπνίζετε	
την ημέρα;	
pinete?	Do you drink?
Πίνετε;	
poso pinete?	How much do you drink?
Πόσο πίνετε;	
pernete narkotika?	Do you take drugs
Παίρνετε ναρκωτικά;	(narcotics)?
pernete farmaka?	Do you take any
Παίρνετε φάρμακα;	medication?
echete kapia aleryia?	Do you have any
Έχετε κάποια αλλεργία;	allergies?
iste engios?	Are you pregnant?
Είστε έγκυος;	
isastan pote engios?	Have you ever been
Ήσαστan ποτέ έγκυος;	pregnant?
iparchi istoriko (dhiaviti)	Is there a family
stin ikoyenia sas?	history of (diabetes)?
Υπάρχει ιστορικό (διαβήτη)	
στην οικογένεια σας;	
echete sichna	Are you sexually active?
seksualikes epafes?	
Έχετε συχνά σεξουαλικές	
επαφές;	

AILMENTS

ΑΡΡΩΣΤΕΙΕΣ

I have (a/an)...	echo ...	Έχω ...
allergy	aleryia	αλλεργία
high/low blood pressure	psili/chamili piesi	ψηλή/χαμηλή πίεση
bronchitis	vronchika	βρογχικά
burn	ena engavma	ένα έγκαυμα
(dry) cough	(ksiro) vicha	(ξηρό) βήχα
earache	pono stafti	πόνο στ' αυτί
eczema	ekzema	έκζεμα
fever	pireto	πυρετό
sunburn	engavma iliu	έγκαυμα ηλίου
sunstroke	iliasi	ηλίαση
dehydration	afidhatosi	αφυδάτωση
indigestion	dhispepsia	δυσπεψία
infection	mia molinsi	μια μόλυνση
influenza	ghripi	γρίπη
lump	ena volo	ένα βώλο
migraine	imikrania	ημικρανία
pain	enan pono	έναν πόνο
rash	anafilaksia/ eksanthima	αναφυλαξία/ εξάνθημα
sore throat	ponolemo	πονόλαιμο
sting	ena tsibima	ένα τσίμπημα
sprain	ena strabulighma	ένα στραμπούληγμα
swollen (ankle)	prizmeno (astraghalo)	πρησμένο (αστράγαλο)
stomach-ache	stomachopono	στομαχόπονο
travel/motion sickness	naftia	ναυτία
venereal disease	mia afrodhisiaki noso	μια αφροδισιακή νόσο

WOMEN'S HEALTH Η ΥΓΕΙΑ ΤΗΣ ΓΥΝΑΙΚΑΣ

I'm pregnant.
ime engios — Είμαι έγκυος.

I think I'm pregnant.
nomizo oti ime engios — Νομίζω ότι είμαι έγκυος.

I haven't had my period
for (five) weeks.
dhen echo periodho edho
ke (pende) evdhomadhes — Δεν έχω περίοδο εδώ
και (πέντε) εβδομάδες.

I'm on the pill.
perno to andisiliptiko
chapi — Παίρνω το αντισυλληπτικό
χάπι.

I'd like to see a female doctor.
thathela na dho mia yineka
yiatro — Θα'θελα να δω μια γυναίκα
γιατρό.

I have a vaginal infection.
echo kolpiki molinsi — Έχω κολπική μόλυνση.

Can I have something
for period pain?
mu dhinete kati yia tus
ponus tis periodhu? — Μού δίνετε κάτι για τους
πόνους της περιόδου;

Can I have a pregnancy test?
boro na kano ena test
engimosinis? — Μπορώ να κάνω ένα τεστ
εγκυμοσύνης;

I want an abortion.
thelo na kano ektrosi — Θέλω να κάνω έκτρωση.

I'd like (the/a/an) ...	thelo ...	Θέλω ...
diaphragm	ena dhiafraghma	ένα διάφραγμα
morning after pill	to chapi tis epomenis	το χάπι της 'επόμενης'
IUD	mia spira	μια σπείρα
pill	to andisiliptiko chapi	το αντισυλληπτικό χάπι

cramps	i krambes	οι κράμπες
cystitis	i kistitidha	η κυστίτιδα
menstruation	i periodhos	η περίοδος
miscarriage	i apovoli	η αποβολή
pap smear	to test pap	το τεστ παπ
period pains	i poni tis periodhu	οι πόνοι της περιόδου
thrush	i kolpiki molinsi	η κολπική μόλυνση

BODYTALK

Parts of the body are often used in some colloquial expressions:

vghazo glosa   Βγάζω γλώσσα.
To be impudent. (lit: bring out one's tongue)

dhen mu ghemizi to mati   Δεν μου γεμίζει το μάτι
I'm not impressed. (lit: it doesn't fill my eye)

dhen ton chonevo   Δεν τον χωνεύω.
I can't stand him. (lit: I can't digest him)

meprikses   Μ' έπρηξες.
I've had enough of you; You have pissed me off. (lit: you have made me swollen)

mirizo ta nichia mu   Μυρίζω τα νύχια μου.
There's nothing I can do. (lit: I am sniffing my nails)

mu vyike apo ti miti   Μου βγήκε από τη μύτη.
I regretted it. (lit: It came out of my nose)

muvale ta dhio podhia   Μου' βαλε τα δυο πόδια
    sena paputsi   σ'ενα παπούτσι.
He put me under pressure. (lit: he put both my feet in one shoe)

SPECIAL HEALTH NEEDS

ΕΙΔΙΚΕΣ ΑΠΑΙΤΗΣΕΙΣ ΣΤΗΝ ΥΓΕΙΑ

I'm on a special diet.
kano mia idhiki dieta
Κάνω μια ειδική δίαιτα.

I'm on medication for ...
perno farmaka yia ...
Παίρνω φάρμακα για ...

This is my usual medicine.
afta ine ta sinithizmena
mu farmaka
Αυτά είναι τα συνηθισμένα
μου φάρμακα.

I'm allergic to ...
ime aleryikos/
aleryiki ...
Είμαι αλλεργικός/
αλλεργική ...

antibiotics	sta andiviotika	στα αντιβιοτικά
penicillin	stin penikilini	στην πενικιλλίνη
dairy products	sta ghalaktera pro-ionda	στα γαλακτερά προϊόντα
bees	stis melises	στις μέλισσες
acarids	sta akarea	στα ακάρεα
ventolin	sti ventolini	στη βεντολίνη
wasps	stis sfikes	στις σφήκες

I have ...
echo ...
Έχω ...

diabetes	zacharodhiaviti	ζαχαροδιαβήτη
epilepsy	epilipsia	επιληψία
asthma	asthma	άσθμα
anaemia	anemia	αναιμία
HIV	ton ios HIV	τον ιός HIV

I need ventolin.
chriazome ventolini
Χρειάζομαι βεντολίνη.

I have a hearing aid.
forao akustiko variko-ias
Φοράω ακουστικό βαρυκοΐας.

I have a pacemaker.
echo vimatodhoti
Έχω βηματοδότη.

ALTERNATIVE **TREATMENTS**		**ΕΝΑΛΛΑΚΤΙΚΕΣ** **ΘΕΡΑΠΕΙΕΣ**
acupuncture	o velonizmos	ο βελονισμός
aromatherapy	i aromatotherapia	η αρωματοθεραπεία
homoeopathy	i omiopathitiki	η ομοιπαθητική
massage	to masaz	το μασάζ
meditation	i aftosingendrosi	η αυτοσυγκέντρωση
physiotherapy	i fisiotherapia	η φυσιοθεραπεία
yoga	i yoga	η γιόγκα

PARTS OF THE BODY   ΜΕΡΗ ΤΟΥ ΣΩΜΑΤΟΣ

I can't move my ...
(use accusative)

dhen boro na kuniso ... mu   Δεν μπορώ να κουνήσω ... μου.

My ... hurts.	me ponai ... mu	Με πονάει ... μου.
ankle	o astraghalos	ο αστράγαλος
appendix	i skolikoidhitis	η σκωληκοειδίτις
arm	to cheri	το χέρι
back	i plati	η πλάτη
blood	to ema	το αίμα
chest	to stithos	το στήθος
ear	to afti	το αυτί
eye	to mati	το μάτι
finger	to dhaktilo	το δάκτυλο
foot	to podhi	το πόδι
hand	to cheri	το χέρι
head	to kefali	το κεφάλι
heart	i kardhia	η καρδιά
jaw	to saghoni	το σαγόνι
knee	to ghonato	το γόνατο
leg	to podhi	το πόδι
mouth	to stoma	το στόμα
muscle	o mis	ο μυς
nose	i miti	η μύτη
penis	to peos	το πέος

ribs	ta pa-idhia	τα παΐδια
shoulder	o omos	ο ώμος
skin	to dherma	το δέρμα
spine	i spondhiliki stili	η σπονδυλική στήλη
stomach	to stomachi	το στομάχι
teeth	ta dhondia	τα δόντια
testicles	i orchis	οι όρχεις
throat	o lemos/faringas	ο λαιμός/ φάρυγγας
vagina	o kolpos	ο κόλπος

AT THE CHEMIST   ΣΤΟ ΦΑΡΜΑΚΕΙΟ

In Greece all dispensing chemists have a licence to take blood pressure, administer injections, and carry out simple tests. For minor ailments, it might save you from having to go to a doctor. A lot of drugs that would need a prescription elsewhere, can be given over the counter. Insulin is given free.

I need medication for ...
    chriazome farmaka ya ...   Χρειάζομαι φάρμακα για ...
I have a prescription.
    echo sindayi yiatru   Έχω συνταγή γιατρού.
Where is the nearest
all-night pharmacy?
    pu ine to kondinotero   Πού είναι το κοντινότερο
    nichterino farmakio?   νυχτερινό φαρμακείο;

HEALTH

Do I need a prescription for ...?
    chriazome sintayi yiatru ya ...?   Χρειάζομαι συνταγή γιατρού για ...;
How many times a day?
    poses fores tin imera?   Πόσες φορές την ημέρα;
Take (two) pills ...
    parte (dhio) chapia   Πάρτε (δύο) χάπια ...
(...) times a day.
    (...) fores tin imera   (...) φορές την ημέρα.
before/after meals.
    prin/meta to fayito   πριν/μετά το φαγητό

antibiotics	ta andiviotika	τα αντιβιοτικά
aspirin	i aspirini	η ασπιρίνη
bandage	i ghaza	η γάζα
Band-aid	o lefkoplastis	ο λευκοπλάστης
contraceptive	to profilaktiko	το προφυλακτικό
cough medicine	to farmako ya ton vicha	το φάρμακο για τον βήχα
insect repellent	i alifi ya ta kunupia	η αλειφή για τα κουνούπια
laxative	to katharsio	το καθάρσιο
painkillers	ta analghitika	τα αναλγητικά
solutions for soft/ hard contact lenses	ta ighra ya malakus/ sklirus fakus epafis	τα υγρά για μαλακούς/σκληρούς φακούς επαφής
spray for insect bites	sprei ya ta tsim bimata endomon	σπρέυ για τα τσιμπήματα εντόμων

HEALTH

THE NIKOS, THE HELEN

In Greek, people's names also need a definite article as in ο Νίκος or η Ελένη (lit: the Nikos, the Helen).

AT THE DENTIST   ΣΤΟΝ ΟΔΟΝΤΙΑΤΡΟ

I have a toothache.
    echo ponodhondo   Έχω πονόδοντο.

I have a cavity.
    echo mia tripa sto dhondi   Έχω μια τρύπα στο δόντι.

I've lost a filling.
    mupese ena sfrayizma   Μού' πεσε ένα σφράγισμα.

I've broken a tooth.
    espasa to dhondi mu   Έσπασα το δόντι μου.

My gums hurt.
    me ponane ta ula mu   Με πονάνε τα ούλα μου.

This tooth is bothering me.
    me enochli afto to dhondi   Με ενοχλεί αυτό το δόντι.

I don't want it extracted.
    dhen thelo na mu to vghalete   Δεν θέλω να μου το βγάλετε.

DID YOU KNOW ... Γυμναστική yimnastiki is a general word for exercising, not just gymnastics, from the word γυμνάζομαι yimnazome 'to train both physically and mentally'. In classical times, physical and intellectual exercise were always seen as inseparable. That's why in some archaeological sites, you will find a γυμνάσιο yimnasio 'gymnasium' where young men trained, while nowadays γυμνάσιο means only a secondary school. From the same root is the word γυμνός yimnos 'naked', as Greeks, of course, always exercised naked.

HEALTH

USEFUL WORDS   ΧΡΗΣΙΜΕΣ ΛΕΞΕΙΣ

accident	to atichima	το ατύχημα
addiction	i toksikomania	η τοξικομανία
antiseptic	to andisiptiko	το αντισηπτικό
bandage	i ghaza	η γάζα
blood group	i omadha ematos	η ομάδα αίματος
blood pressure	i piesi	η πίεση
contact lenses	i faki epafis	οι φακοί επαφής
disease	i arostia	η αρρώστεια
injury/wound	to travma	το τραύμα
oxygen	to oksighono	το οξυγόνο
psychotherapy	i psichotherapia	η ψυχοθεραπεία
virus	o ios	ο ιός

ΕΙΔΙΚΕΣ ΑΝΑΓΚΕΣ

SPECIFIC NEEDS

DISABLED TRAVELLERS

ΤΑΞΙΔΙΩΤΕΣ ΜΕ ΕΙΔΙΚΕΣ ΑΝΑΓΚΕΣ

Unfortunately, many of the archaeological sites in Greece are accessed with difficulty by a person in a wheelchair, not so much through lack of infrastructure, but simply because a lot of them were built on rocky, inaccessible hilltops. However, most museums and theaters now have facilities for the disabled such as ramps, lifts and toilets. Public transport will be difficult, but you will find that, as a person with special needs, people around you will be helpful and understanding.

I'm disabled.
   ime anapiros/anapiri   Είμαι ανάπηρος/ανάπηρη.
I need help.
   chriazome voithia   Χρειάζομαι βοήθεια.
Is there wheelchair access?
   iparchi prozvasi yia   Υπάρχει πρόσβαση για
   anapiriki karekla?   αναπηρική καρέκλα;
I'm deaf.
   ime kufos/kufi   Είμαι κουφός/κουφή.
Could you speak louder?
   parakalo, milate pio dhinata? Παρακαλώ, μιλάτε πιο δυνατά;
Do you know sign language?
   kserete tin ghlosa ton   Ξέρετε τη γλώσσα των
   kofalalon?   κωφαλάλων;

disabled person	to atomo me idhikes ananges	το άτομο με ειδικές ανάγκες
wheel chair	i anapiriki karekla	η αναπηρική καρέκλα

SPECIFIC NEEDS

GAY TRAVELLERS
ΟΜΟΦΥΛΟΦΙΛΟΙ ΤΑΞΙΔΙΩΤΕΣ

Homosexuality is generally accepted as a fact of life in Greece. However, exercise your common sense as to when and where you are going to be extrovert about it – for example, it is fine in clubs and bars and when socialising with young people, but it may be considered offensive in front of the village's older community.

Is there a gay bar round here?
    iparchi gei bar edho?   Υπάρχει γκέι μπαρ εδώ;
Where can I buy gay magazines?
    apo pu boro naghoraso   Από πού μπορώ ν'αγοράσω
    periodhika yia gei?   περιοδικά για γκέι;
Where do gay people hang out?
    pu sichnazun i gei?   Πού συχνάζουν οι γκέι;

TRAVELLING WITH THE FAMILY
ΤΑΞΙΔΕΥΟΝΤΑΣ ΜΕ ΤΗΝ ΟΙΚΟΓΕΝΕΙΑ

Greeks have a very relaxed attitude to children. You'll notice that Greek families take their children out to restaurants, even late at night, and let them roam around the tables. You'll also find that people will come up and chat to you about your kids.

I'm travelling with my family.
    taksidhevo me tin ikoyenia   Ταξιδεύω με την οικογένεια
    mu   μου.
Is there a babysitter?
    iparchi beibisiter?   Υπάρχει μπειμπισίτερ;

THEY MAY SAY ...

Common terms for gay men are ομοφυλόφαλος omofilofilos, ομό omo, γκέι gei and for women λεσβία lesvia. Some unfriendly terms you hopefully won't have to deal with are τοιούτος tiutos, πούστης pustis, αδελφή adhelfi (sister), συκιά sikia (figtree). A transvestite is τραβεστί travesti.

Could you put a small bed/a
cot in the room?
    borite na valete ena
    krevataki/mia kunia sto
    dhomatio?   Μπορείτε να βάλετε ένα
    κρεβατάκι/μια κούνια στο
    δωμάτιο;

Where can the children play?
    pu borun na peksun ta
    pedhia?   Πού μπορούν να παίξουν τα
    παιδιά;

Is there a family discount?
    kanete ekptosi yia
    ikoyenies?   Κάνετε έκπτωση για
    οικογένειες;

Could we have a children's
portion?
    mas fernete mia pedhiki
    meridha?   Μας φέρνετε μια παιδική
    μερίδα;

Where is the playground?
    pu ine i pedhiki chara?   Πού είναι η παιδική χαρά;

Where are they showing a
children's film?
    pezhete puthena mia
    pediki tenia?   Παίζεται πουθενά μια
    παιδική ταινία;

LOOKING FOR A JOB   ΨΑΧΝΟΝΤΑΣ ΓΙΑ ΕΡΓΑΣΙΑ

Seasonal work in the form of fruit picking is often available during
harvest season, especially during November/December in the olive
groves, August in the peach orchards, August/September in the vine-
yards and late spring/late autumn in citrus groves.

Another option is teaching English. Jobs are advertised in the
paper under the section ΜΙΚΡΕΣ ΑΓΓΕΛΙΕΣ mikres angelies.

I'm looking for a temporary job.
    psachno yia prosorini
    dhulia   Ψάχνω για προσωρινή
    δουλειά.

Do you need help in the field?
    chriazeste voithia sto
    chorafi?   Χρειάζεστε βοήθεια στο
    χωράφι;

SPECIFIC NEEDS

Can I help with the harvest?
boro na voithiso me tin singomidhi?
Μπορώ να βοηθήσω με την συγκομιδή;

What salary are you offering?
ti misthó prosferete?
Τι μισθό προσφέρετε;

Do you pay by the hour?
plironete me tin ora?
Πληρώνετε με την ώρα;

Do you pay cash?
plironete metrita?
Πληρώνετε μετρητά;

Do I need to pay tax?
prepi na pliroso foro?
Πρέπει να πληρώσω φόρο;

When can I start?
pote boro narchiso?
Πότε μπορώ ν'αρχίσω;

Today.	simera	Σήμερα.
Tomorrow.	avrio	Αύριο.

What kind of work can I find here?
ti idhus dhulia boro na vro edho?
Τι είδους δουλειά μπορώ να βρω εδώ;

Do I need a work permit?
chriazome adhia erghasias?
Χρειάζομαι άδεια εργασίας;

Where can I get a work permit?
apo pu boro na vghalo adhia erghasias?
Από πού μπορώ να βγάλω άδεια εργασίας;

What qualifications do I need?
ti prosonda chriazome?
Τι προσόντα χρειάζομαι;

application	i etisi	η αίτηση
temporary work	i prosorini dhulia	η προσωρινή δουλειά
degree	to ptichio	το πτυχίο
employer	o erghodhotis	ο εργοδότης
employee	o ipalilos	ο υπάλληλος
summer job	i kalokerini dhulia	η καλοκαιρινή δουλειά
position	i thesi	η θέση
resume/CV	to vioghrafiko	το βιογραφικό
experience	i pira	η πείρα
volunteer	o ethelondis	ο εθελοντής

BUSINESS   ΜΠΙΖΝΕΣ

If you are conducting business in Greece, it is most likely to be in English. The following phrases, however, could help you with support and secretarial staff that may not speak English.

Can I make some photocopies?
 boro na vghalo merikes fototipies? — Μπορώ να βγάλω μερικές φωτοτυπίες;

Can I send a fax/email?
 boro na stilo ena faks/email? — Μπορώ να στείλω ένα φαξ/e-mail;

Can I use my mobile in here?
 boro na chrisimopi-iso to kinito mu edho? — Μπορώ να χρησιμοποιήσω το κινητό μου εδώ;

Where is the conference room?
 pu ine i ethusa sinedhriaseon? — Πού είναι η αίθουσα συνεδριάσεων;

Can I use this computer?
 boro na chrisimopi-iso afto ton ipologhisti? — Μπορώ να χρησιμοποιήσω αυτό τον υπολογιστή;

For more information on computers see pages 90–91.

SPECIFIC NEEDS

ON TOUR

We're on tour.		
	vriskomaste se periodhia	Βρισκόμαστε σε περιοδεία.
I'm with this group.		
	ime mafto to grup	Είμαι μ'αυτό το γκρουπ.
We lost our things.		
	chasame ta praghmata mas	Χάσαμε τα πράγματά μας.
We sent our things ...		
	stilame ta praghmata mas ...	Στείλαμε τα πράγματά μας ...
on this flight		
	mafti tin ptisi	μ' αυτή την πτήση
on this train		
	mafto to treno	μ' αυτό το τραίνο
We're playing on the (2) July.		
	pezume stis (dhio) iuliu	Παίζουμε στις (δύο) Ιουλίου.

ΣΕ ΠΕΡΙΟΔΕΙΑ

FILM & TV   ΤΑΙΝΙΕΣ & ΤΗΛΕΟΡΑΣΗ

We're shooting a film here.		
	yirname mia tenia edho	Γυρνάμε μια ταινία εδώ.
Can we shoot a film here?		
	borume na ghirisume mia tenia edho?	Μπορούμε να γυρίσουμε μια ταινία εδώ;

We're shooting a ...	yirname ...	Γυρνάμε ...
documentary	ena dokimanter	ένα ντοκιμαντέρ
film	mia tenia	μια ταινία
TV program	ena tileoptiko proghrama	ένα τηλεοπτικό πρόγραμμα

actor/actress	o/i ithopios	ο/η ηθοποιός
cameraman	o kameraman	ο κάμεραμαν
cast	o thiasos	ο θίασος
director	o skinothetis	ο σκηνοθέτης
producer	o paraghoghos	ο παραγωγός

SPECIFIC NEEDS

RELIGION ΘΡΗΣΚΕΙΑ

As long as you are dressed appropriately, you are welcome to take part in an Orthodox service. You won't be allowed into the church if you are wearing shorts, a strapless top, a bathing suit, or anything that leaves too much bare flesh. Just use common sense.

What's your religion?
   ti thriskevma ise (inf)/   Τι θρήσκευμα είσαι/
   iste (pol)?   είστε;
I am not religious.
   dhen ime thriskos/thriski   Δεν είμαι θρήσκος/θρήσκη.

I'm	ime ...	Είμαι ...
Orthodox	orthodhoxos/ orthodhoxi	ορθόδοξος/ ορθόδοξη
Catholic	katholikos/ katholiki	καθολικός/ καθολική
Protestant	dhiamartiromenos/ dhiamartiromeni	διαμαρτυρόμενος/ διαμαρτυρόμενη
Jewish	evreos/evrea	εβραίος/εβραία
Muslim	moamethanos/ moamethani	μωαμεθανός/ μωαμεθανή

I believe in God.
   pistevo sto theo   Πιστεύω στο Θεό.
I'm an atheist.
   ime atheos/athei   Είμαι άθεος/άθεη.
I'm agnostic.
   ime aghnostikistis   Είμαι αγνωστικιστής.
Can I attend the service?
   boro na parakoluthiso tin   Μπορώ να παρακολουθήσω
   liturgia?   την λειτουργία;
Can I receive communion?
   boro na metalavo?   Μπορώ να μεταλάβω;

christening	i vaptisi	η βάπτιση
Communion	i metalipsi	η Μετάληψη
prayer	i prosefchi	η προσευχή
priest	o papas	ο παπάς
wedding	o ghamos	ο γάμος

SIGNS

ΓΙΑ ΤΑ ΑΤΟΜΑ ΜΕ ΕΙΔΙΚΕΣ ΑΝΑΓΚΕΣ	RESERVED FOR THE DISABLED

TELLING THE TIME ΛΕΩ ΤΗΝ ΩΡΑ

Except for official announcements in airports, stations etc, the Greeks use the 12-hour clock. For numbers see page 229.

What time is it?
   ti ora ine?   Τι ώρα είναι;

It's ... o'clock.
   ine ... i ora   Είναι ... η ώρα.

It's one o'clock.
   ine mia i ora   Είναι μία η ώρα.

It's two o'clock.
   ine dhio i ora   Είναι δύο η ώρα.

It's three o'clock.
   ine tris i ora   Είναι τρεις η ώρα.

It's five past four.
   ine teseris ke pende   Είναι τέσσερις και πέντε.

It's quarter past four.
   ine teseris ke tetarto   Είναι τέσσερις και τέταρτο.

It's half past four.
   ine teserisimisi   Είναι τεσσερισήμιση.

It's quarter to four.
   ine teseris para tetarto   Είναι τέσσερις παρά τέταρτο.

It's exactly five.
   ine pende akrivos   Είναι πέντε ακριβώς.

It's almost six.
   ine schedhon eksi   Είναι σχεδόν έξι.

It's 8am.
   ine ochto to proi   Είναι οχτώ το πρωί.

It's 8pm.
   ine ochto to vradhi   Είναι οχτώ το βράδι.

It's early/late.
   ine noris/argha   Είναι νωρίς/αργά.

TIME & DATES

We're early.
irthame noris — Ήρθαμε νωρίς.

We're late.
aryisame — Αργήσαμε.

in the ...	to ...	το ...
morning	proi	πρωί
afternoon	aroyevma	το απόγευμα
evening	vradhi	το βράδι

at ten — stis dheka — στις δέκα

DAYS — ΗΜΕΡΕΣ

Monday	dheftera	Δευτέρα
Tuesday	triti	Τρίτη
Wednesday	tetarti	Τετάρτη
Thursday	pempti	Πέμπτη
Friday	paraskevi	Παρασκευή
Saturday	savato	Σάββατο
Sunday	kiriaki	Κυριακή

the weekend	to savatokiriako	το Σαββατοκύριακο
on (Monday)	tin (dheftera)	την (Δευτέρα)

MONTHS — ΜΗΝΕΣ

January	ianuarios	Ιανουάριος
February	fevruarios	Φεβρουάριος
March	martios	Μάρτιος
April	aprilios	Απρίλιος
May	maios	Μάιος
June	iunios	Ιούνιος
July	iulios	Ιούλιος
August	avghustos	Αύγουστος
September	septemvrios	Σεπτέμβριος
October	oktovrios	Οκτώβριος
November	noemvrios	Νοέμβριος
December	dhekemvrios	Δεκέμβριος

In (June) ... — ton (iunio) ... — Τον (Ιούνιο) ...

DATES

What's the date today?
    ti imerominia echume
    simera?
It's 13 July.
    ine dhekatris iuliu
It's 1 August.
    ine proti avghustu

1999
    chilia eniakosia eneninda
    enea
2000
    dhio chiliadhes
the millennium
    i chilietiridda

ΗΜΕΡΟΜΗΝΙΕΣ

Τι ημερομηνία έχουμε
σήμερα;

Είναι δεκατρείς Ιουλίου.

Είναι πρώτη Αυγούστου.

χίλια εννιακόσια ενενήντα
εννέα

δύο χιλιάδες

η χιλιετηρίδα

TIME & DATES

DID YOU KNOW ...

The days from Monday to Thursday in Greek are simply called second, third, fourth and fifth respectively. This is because when the seven day week was adopted, the Western European names for the days of the week were considered far too pagan. Παρασκευή paraskevi 'Friday' means 'the day of preparation' and Κυριακή kiriaki 'Sunday' means 'the day of the master' from the word Κύριος kirios.

TIME & DATES

PRESENT   ΤΟ ΠΑΡΟΝ

It's on time.
   ine stin ora tu   Είναι στην ώρα του.

today	simera	σήμερα
this morning	simera to proi	σήμερα το πρωί
this afternoon	simera to apoyevma	σήμερα το απόγευμα
tonight	apopse	απόψε
this week	afti tin evdhomadha	αυτή την εβδομάδα
this month	afto ton mina	αυτό τον μήνα
this year	fetos	φέτος
immediately	amesos	αμέσως
now	tora	τώρα

PAST   ΤΟ ΠΑΡΕΛΘΟΝ

yesterday	chtes (chthes)	χτες (χθες)
the day before yesterday	prochtes (prochthes)	προχτές (προχθές)
yesterday morning	chtes to proi	χτες το πρωί
yesterday evening	chtes to apoyevma	χτες το απόγευμα
last week	tin pro-ighumeni evdhomadha	την προηγούμενη εβδομάδα
last month	ton pro-ighumeno mina	τον προηγούμενο μήνα
last year	persi	πέρσι
half an hour ago	prin apo misi ora	πριν από μισή ώρα

FUTURE

		ΤΟ ΜΕΛΛΟΝ
tomorrow	avrio	αύριο
the day after tomorrow	methavrio	μεθαύριο
tomorrow morning	avrio to proi	αύριο το πρωί
tomorrow night	avrio to vradhi	αύριο το βράδι
next week	tin epomeni evdhomadha	την επόμενη εβδομάδα
next month	ton epomeno mina	τον επόμενο μήνα
next year	tu chronu	του χρόνου
soon	sindoma	σύντομα
in ... minutes/ hours/days	se ... lepta/ ores/meres	σε ... λεπτά/ώρες/ μέρες

DURING THE DAY

		ΚΑΤΑ ΤΗ ΔΙΑΡΚΕΙΑ ΤΗΣ ΗΜΕΡΣ
day	i imera/mera	η ημέρα/μέρα
dawn	i anatoli	η ανατολή
early	noris	νωρίς
the morning	to proi	το πρωί
noon/early afternoon	to mesimeri	το μεσημέρι
late afternoon/ evening	to apoyevma	το απόγευμα
sunset	i dhisi	η δύση
evening	to vradhi	το βράδι
night	i nichta	η νύχτα
midnight	ta mesanichta	τα μεσάνυχτα

USEFUL WORDS   ΧΡΗΣΙΜΕΣ ΛΕΞΕΙ

always	panda	πάντα
annual	etisios/etisia/etisio	ετήσιος/ετήσια/ετήσιο
before	prin	πριν
calendar/diary	to imerologhio	το ημερολόγιο
clock/watch	to roloi	το ρολόι
daily	kathimerina	καθημερινά
forever	ya panda	για πάντα
fortnight	to dhekapenthimero	το δεκαπενθήμερο
from time to time	kapu kapu	κάπου κάπου
later	arghotera	αργότερα
a minute	ena lepto	ένα λεπτό
never	pote	ποτέ
not yet	ochi akomi	όχι ακόμη
often	sichna	συχνά
recently	prosfata	πρόσφατα
a second	to dhefterolepto	το δευτερόλεπτο
seldom	spania	σπάνια
sometime	kapote	κάποτε
sometimes	kamia fora	καμμιά φορά
soon	sindoma	σύντομα
the future	to melon	το μέλλον
the past	to parelthon	το παρελθόν
the present	to paron	το παρόν

TIME & DATES

ΑΡΙΘΜΟΙ & ΠΟΣΑ

NUMBERS & AMOUNTS

CARDINAL NUMBERS   ΑΠΟΛΥΤΟΙ ΑΡΙΘΜΟΙ

0	midhen	μηδέν
1	enas/mia/ena	ένας/μία/ένα
2	dhio	δύο
3	tris/tris/tria	τρεις/τρεις/τρία
4	teseris/teseris/tesera	τέσσερις/τέσσερις/τέσσερα
5	pende	πέντε
6	eksi	έξι
7	efta/epta (written)	εφτά/επτά
8	ochto/okto (written)	οχτώ/οκτώ
9	enia/enea (written)	εννιά/εννέα
10	dheka	δέκα
11	endeka	έντεκα
12	dhodheka	δώδεκα
13	dhekatris/dhekatria	δεκατρείς/δεκατρία
14	dhekateseris/dhekatesera	δεκατέσσερις/δεκατέσσερα
15	dhekapende	δεκαπέντε
16	dhekaeksi	δεκαέξι
17	dhekaefta	δεκαεφτά
18	dhekaochto	δεκαοχτώ
19	dhekaenea	δεκαεννέα
20	ikosi	είκοσι
21	ikosi enas/ikosi	είκοσι ένας/είκοσι
	mia/ikosi ena	μία/είκοσι ένα
22	ikosi dhio	είκοσι δύο
30	trianda	τριάντα
40	saranda	σαράντα
50	peninda	πενήντα
60	eksinda	εξήντα
70	evdhominda	εβδομήντα
80	oghdhonda	ογδόντα
90	eneninda	ενενήντα

229

100	ekato	εκατό
101	ekaton ena	εκατόν ένα
120	ekaton ikosi	εκατόν είκοσι
1000	chili-i/chilies/chilia	χίλιοι/χίλιες/χίλια
2000	dhio chiliadhes	δύο χιλιάδες
3000	tris chiliadhes	τρεις χιλιάδες
one million	ena ekatomirio	ένα εκατομμύριο

In Greek, the decimal point is shown as a comma (3,5 is three and a half), while a full stop separates the thousands (3.000 is three thousand)

ORDINAL NUMBERS   ΤΑΚΤΙΚΟΙ ΑΡΙΘΜΟΙ

first
    protos/proti/proto   πρώτος/πρώτη/πρώτο (1ος/1η/1ο)
second
    dhefteros/dhefteri/   δεύτερος/δεύτερη/
    dhefero   δεύτερο (2ος/2η/2ο)
third
    tritos/triti/trito   τρίτος/τρίτη/τρίτο (3ος/3η/3ο)
fourth
    tetartos/tetarti/tetarto   τέταρτος/τέταρτη/τέταρτο
fifth
    pemptos/pempti/pempto   πέμπτος/πέμπτη/πέμπτο

THE REST ARE ANDROGENOUS

The numbers 1, 3, 4 and 1000 and any number ending in one, three and four have genders, for example three can be τρεις tris (m/f) or τρία (n) tria. Remember that a drachma η δραχμή i dhrachmi is feminine. You therefore say χίλιες δραχμές chilies dhrachmes 1000 drachmas, εκατόν πενήντα τρεις δραχμές ekaton peninda tris dhrachmes 153 drachmas.

sixth
   ektos/ekti/ekto   έκτος/έκτη/έκτο
seventh
   evdhomos/evdhomi/   έβδομος/έβδομη/έβδομο
   evdhomo
eighth
   oghdhoos/oghdhoi/   όγδοος/όγδοη/όγδοο
   oghdho-o
ninth
   enatos/enati/enato   ένατος/ένατη/ένατο
tenth
   dhekatos/dhekati/dhekato δέκατος/δέκατη/δέκατο
twentieth
   ikostos/ikosti/ikosto   εικοστός/εικοστή/εικοστό
hundredth
   ekatostos/ekatosti/ekatosto εκατοστός/εκατοστή/εκατοστό
thousandth
   chiliostos/chiliosti/chiliosto χιλιοστός/χιλιοστή/χιλιοστό
last
   telefteos/teleftea/telefteo τελευταίος/τελευταία/τελευταίο

SURNAME = REGION

Despite generations of emigration, you can sometimes guess which region of Greece people come from depending on the ending of their surname. Names ending in -ακης -akis are from Crete, -ατος -atos from Cephallonia, -ιδης -idhis from Lefkas and -πουλος -pulos from the Peloponnese. Greeks living abroad often shorten their names. Nick Pappas for example, stands for Νικόλαος Παπαδόπουλος nikolaos papadhopulos.

NUMBERS &
AMOUNTS

·EXPRESSING QUANTITIES·

There is no distinction between the words 'a few'/'a little' (lighos), and also between 'much'/'many'/'a lot of' (polis) in Greek. Both these words function as adjectives, and therefore have to agree with the noun that they qualify (see page 29). For example:

We have little time.
   echume ligho kero
There are a few tickets left.
   echun mini ligha isitiria
We have many friends in Greece.
   echume polus filus stin eladha
I've sent a lot of postcards.
   estila poles kartes
I haven't got much money.
   dhen echo pola lefta
(NB. 'money' is always plural in Greek)

The adjective 'some' merikos also behaves in the same way:

I'd like some stamps.
   tha ithela merika ghramatosima
I invited some friends.
   kalesa merikus filus

Note that the word merikos can only be used with countable nouns:

Can I have some oranges?
   boro na echo merika portokalia?

as opposed to:

Can I have some milk?
   boro na echo ligho ghala?

GREEK NUMERALS ΟΙ ΕΛΛΗΝΙΚΟΙ ΑΡΙΘΜΟΙ

The Greek numerals are formed using combinations of letters. They are still used quite widely, especially to denote floor number, room number, class (when travelling), hotel class, and occasionally year. Knowing the first 10 should suffice for everyday purposes.

1	α´
2	β´
3	γ´
4	δ´
5	ε´
6	στ´/ς´
7	ζ´
8	η´
9	θ´
10	ι´

1000 FEMINISTS

The word χιλιάδες chiliadhes – thousands (more than 1000) is always feminine and takes the feminine form of 'one','three' and 'four' for example:

είκοσι μία χιλιάδες
ikosi mia chiliadhes
twenty one thousand.

FRACTIONS ΚΛΑΣΜΑΤΑ

1/4	ena tetarto	ένα τέταρτο
1/3	ena trito	ένα τρίτο
1/2	imisi/to miso	ήμισυ/το μισό
3/4	tria tetarta	τρία τέταρτα

NUMBERS & AMOUNTS

FAMILY ROOTS

You may be asked από πού κατάγεσαι; apo pu katayese? (lit: where do you originate from). Greeks have a strong sense of family roots. Your origin (η καταγωγή i kataghoyi) is not just where you were born, but in which village your family roots are. This is because a lot of Greeks have emigrated to Athens or overseas, but they feel that their family home is still a village or an island.

USEFUL WORDS ΧΡΗΣΙΜΕΣ ΛΕΞΕΙΣ

a little bit	ligho	λίγο
double	dhiplos/dhipli/ dhiplo	διπλός/διπλή/διπλό
a dozen	mia dhodhekadha/ mia duzina	μια δωδεκάδα/μια ντουζίνα
enough	arketa	αρκετά
few/little/a little	lighos/lighi/ligho (sg) lighi/lighes/ligha (pl)	λίγος/λίγη/λίγο λίγοι/λίγες/λίγα
some	meriki/merikes/ merika	μερικοί/μερικές/ μερικά
(about) a hundred	(peripu) mia ekatosti	(περίπου) μια εκατοστή
less	lighotero	λιγότερο
many/much/ a lot of	polis/poli/poli (sg) poli/poles/pola (pl)	πολύς/πολλή/πολύ πολλοί/πολλές/ πολλά
more	perisotero	περισσότερο
once	mia fora/apaks	μια φορά/άπαξ
percent	tis ekato	τοις εκατό
very/a lot/ too much	poli	πολύ

ΕΠΕΙΓΟΝΤΑ **EMERGENCIES**
ΠΕΡΙΣΤΑΤΙΚΑ

Take care/Attention!
   prosochi!   Προσοχή!
Go away!
   fiye!   Φύγε!
Fire!
   fotia!   Φωτιά!
Thief!
   kleftis!   Κλέφτης!
Theft!
   listia!   Ληστεία!
It's an emergency!
   ine amesi anangi!   Είναι άμεση ανάγκη!
There's been an accident.
   eyine atichima   Έγινε ατύχημα.
Call a doctor.
   fonakste ena yiatro   Φωνάξτε ένα γιατρό.
Call the police.
   fonakste tin astinomia   Φωνάξτε την αστυνομία.
Call an ambulance.
   fonakste ena asthenoforo   Φωνάξτε ένα ασθενοφόρο.
Where is the police station?
   pu ine to astinomiko   Πού είναι το αστυνομικό
   tmima?   τμήμα;
Can you help me?
   borite na me voithisete?   Μπορείτε να με βοηθήσετε;

WHEN YOU'RE IN TROUBLE		
HELP!	voithia!	Βοήθεια!
POLICE!	astinomia!	Αστυνομία!

EMERGENCY NUMBER: 100

I've been raped.
    me viasan   Με βίασαν.
I've been robbed.
    me eklepsan   Με έκλεψαν.
They've taken my wallet.
    mu eklepsan to portofoli   Μου έκλεψαν το πορτοφόλι
    mu   μου.
I've lost my passport.
    echasa to dhiavatirio mu   Έχασα το διαβατήριό μου.
I'm ill.
    ime arostos/arosti   Είμαι άρρωστος/άρρωστη.
My friend is ill.
    o filos mu ine arostos (m)   Ο φίλος μου είναι άρρωστος.
    i fili mu ine arosti (f)   Η φίλη μου είναι άρρωστη.
I'm lost.
    echo chathi   Έχω χαθεί.
I've lost my friend.
    echasa ton filo mu/tin fili   Έχασα τον φίλο μου/την φίλη
    mu   μου.

Where are the toilets?
    pu ine i tualetes?   Πού είναι οι τουαλέτες;
I speak English.
    milao anglika   Μιλάω αγγλικά.
Can I use the phone?
    boro na chrisimopi-iso to   Μπορώ να χρησιμοποιήσω το
    tilefono?   τηλέφωνο;
I have medical insurance.
    echo iatriki asfalia   Έχω ιατρική ασφάλεια.
My personal belongings
are insured.
    echo asfalisi ta prosopika   Έχω ασφαλίσει τα προσωπικά
    mu andikimena   μου αντικείμενα.

I've lost my ...	echasa ...	Έχασα ...
My ... was stolen.	mu eklepsan ...	Μου έκλεψαν ...
handbag	tin tsanda mu	την τσάντα μου
luggage	tis aposkeves mu	τις αποσκευές μου
money	ta chrimata mu	τα χρήματά μου
travellers cheques	tis taksidhiotikes epitayes mu	τις ταξιδιωτικές επιταγές μου
credit card	tin pistotiki karta mu	την πιστωτική κάρτα μου
passport	to dhiavatirio mu	το διαβατήριό μου

DEALING WITH THE POLICE

ΑΝΤΙΜΕΤΩΠΙΖΟΝΤΑΣ ΤΗΝ ΑΣΤΥΝΟΜΙΑ

I want to report an offence.
    thelo na katangilo
    ena adhikima

Θέλω να καταγγείλω
ένα αδίκημα.

I apologise.
    sas zito sighnomi

Σας ζητώ συγγνώμη.

I didn't know I was doing
something illegal.
    dhen iksera oti ekana kati
    paranomo

Δεν ήξερα ότι έκανα κάτι
παράνομο.

THEY MAY SAY ...

onoma ke dhiefthinsi,
    parakalo
Όνομα και διεύθυνση,
    παρακαλώ.

Your name and
    address, please.

to dhiavatirio sas, parakalo
Το διαβατήριό σας παρακαλώ.

Your passport,
    please.

mia taftotita, parakalo
Μια ταυτότητα, παρακαλώ.

A form of identity,
    please.

pu ine i adhia erghasias sas?
Πού είναι η άδεια εργασίας σας;

Where is your work
    permit?

sas vazo prostimo
Σας βάζω πρόστιμο.

I'm giving you a
    fine.

iste ipo kratisi
Είστε υπό κράτηση.

You're under arrest.

parakalo na mas
    akoluthisete os to
    astinomiko tmima
Παρακαλώ, να μας ακολουθήσετε
    ως το αστυνομικό τμήμα.

Please follow us to
    the police
    station.

echete to dhikeoma
    na mi milisete
Έχετε το δικαίωμα να μη μιλήσετε.

You have the right
    to remain silent.

I am innocent.
    ime athoos/athoa

Είμαι αθώος/αθώα.

I didn't do it.
    dhen to ekana egho

Δεν το έκανα εγώ.

What am I accused of?
    yia pio adhikima
    katighorume?

Για ποιο αδίκημα
κατηγορούμαι;

Do I have the right to make
a phonecall?
    echo to dhikeoma na kano
    ena tilefonima?

Έχω το δικαίωμα να κάνω
ένα τηλεφώνημα;

I want to inform my
embassy/consulate.
    thelo na idhopi-iso tin
    prezvia/to proksenio mu

Θέλω να ειδοποιήσω την
πρεσβεία/το προξενείο μου.

Can I have a lawyer?
    boro na kaleso ena
    dhikighoro?

Μπορώ να καλέσω ένα
δικηγόρο;

I will make a statement only
in front of a lawyer.
    tha kano dhilosi mono
    brosta se dhikigoro

Θα κάνω δήλωση μόνο
μπροστά σε δικηγόρο.

I will not be searched unless
my lawyer is present.
    tha me psaksete mono an o
    dhikighoros mu ine paron

Θα με ψάξετε μόνο αν ο
δικηγόρος μου είναι παρών.

I want to see a policewoman.
    thelo na dho mia yineka
    astinomiko

Θέλω να δω μια γυναίκα
αστυνομικό.

Does anyone speak English?
    milai kanis anglika?

Μιλάει κανείς Αγγλικά;

EMERGENCIES

SIGNS

ΑΣΤΥΝΟΜΙΑ	**POLICE**
ΑΣΤΥΝΟΜΙΚΟ ΤΜΗΜΑ	**POLICE STATION**

Can I pay an on-the-spot fine?
> boro na pliroso to prostimo epi topu?

Μπορώ να πληρώσω το πρόστιμο επι τοπου;

This is for personal use.
> afto ine ya prosopiki chrisi

Αυτό είναι για προσωπική χρήση.

aiding & abetting	i sinenochi	η συνενοχή
to arrest	silamvano	συλλαμβάνω
cell	to keli	το κελί
cop	o batsos	ο μπάτσος
court	to dhikastirio	το δικαστήριο
disturbing the peace	i dhiataraksi tis dhimosias taksis	η διατάραξη της δημόσιας τάξης
drug possession	i katochi narkotikon	η κατοχή ναρκωτικών
drug use	i chrisi narkotikon	η χρήση ναρκωτικών
judge	i dhikastis	ο δικαστής
lawyer	o/i dhikighoros	ο/η δικηγόρος
murder	o fonos	ο φόνος
police car	to astinomiko	το αστυνομικό
policeman/ policewoman	o/i astinomikos	ο/η αστυνομικός
prison	i filaki	η φυλακή
rape	o viazmos	ο βιασμός
to release	afino eleuthero	αφήνω ελεύθερο
theft	i klopi	η κλοπή

In this dictionary, as in the rest of the book, the masculine form of a word appears first followed by the feminine and neuter (where applicable), separated by a slash. For adjectives, the masculine form has been given in full, followed by the feminine and neuter endings only. For example μεγάλος/-η/-ο meghalos/-i/-o means that the three genders are formed as: μεγάλος/μεγάλη/μεγάλο meghalos/meghali/meghalo. The article has been included in the definite form (the), unless it's inappropriate for the particular expression. Verbs have been listed in the first person present tense. (see Grammar page 30).

A

able (to be); can	boro	μπορώ
above	epano	επάνω
abroad	sto eksoteriko	στο εξωτερικό
accident	to atichima	το ατύχημα
accommodation	i dhiamoni	η διαμονή
across	apenandi	απέναντι
address	i dhiefthinsi	η διεύθυνση
admire	thavmazo	θαυμάζω
admission	i isodhos	η είσοδος
advantage	to pleonektima	το πλεονέκτημα
advice	i simvuli	η συμβουλή
after	meta	μετά
again	ksana	ξανά
against	enandion	εναντίον
age	i ilikia	η ηλικία
aggressive	epithetikos/-i/-o	επιθετικός/-η/-ο
ago	prin apo	πριν από
to agree	simfono	συμφωνώ

Agreed!		
simfoni!	**Σύμφωνοι!**	

ahead	brosta	μπροστά
aid (help)	i voithia	η βοήθεια
AIDS	to eids	το AIDS
air	o aeras	ο αέρας
air-conditioned	klimatizomenos/-i/-o	κλιματιζόμενος/-η/-ο
airport	to aerodhromio	το αεροδρόμιο
alarm clock	to ksipnitiri	το ξυπνητήρι
all (pl)	oli/-es/-a	όλοι/-ες/-α
to allow	epitrepo	επιτρέπω

It's (not) allowed. {dhen} epitrepete	(δεν) επιτρέπεται.	
almost	schedhon	σχεδόν
alone	monos/-i/-o	μόνος/-η/-ο
already	kiolas	κιόλας
also	episis	επίσης
always	panda	πάντα
among	anamesa	ανάμεσα
ancient	archeos/-a/-o	αρχαίος/-α/-ο
and	ke/ki	και/κι
angry	thimomenos/-i/-o	θυμωμένος/-η/-ο
answer	i apandisi	η απάντηση
antiques	i andikes	οι αντίκες
any	kanenas/kamia/kanena	κανένας/καμία/ κανένα
appointment	to randevu	το ραντεβού
architecture	i architektoniki	η αρχιτεκτονική
arm	to cheri	το χέρι
to arrive	ftano	φτάνω
art	i techni	η τέχνη
art gallery	i galeri technis	η γκαλλερί τέχνης
artwork	to ergho technis	το έργο τέχνης
ashtray	to tasaki	το τασάκι
to ask (for something)	zito	ζητώ
to ask (a question)	rotao	ρωτάω
atmosphere	i atmosfera	η ατμόσφαιρα
aunt	i thia	η θεία
autumn	to fthinoporo	το φθινόπωρο
avenue	i leoforos	η λεωφόρος
awful	apesios/-a/-o	απαίσιος/-α/-ο

B

baby	to moro	το μωρό
back (body)	i plati	η πλάτη
backpack (n)	to sakidhio	το σακκίδιο
bad	kakos/kakia/kako	κακός/κακιά/κακό
bag	i tsanda	η τσάντα
baggage	i aposkeves	οι αποσκευές
baggage claim	i paralavi aposkevon	η παραλαβή αποσκευών
bandage	i ghaza	η γάζα
basket	to kalathi	το καλάθι

bath	to banio	το μπάνιο
to be	ime	είμαι
beautiful	omorfos/-i/-o	όμορφος/-η/-ο
because	epidhi/yiati	επειδή, γιατί
bed	to krevati	το κρεββάτι
bedroom	i krevatokamara	η κρεββατοκάμαρα
beside	dhipla	δίπλα
best	o kaliteros/i kaliteri/	ο καλύτερος/η
	to kalitero	καλύτερη/το
		καλύτερο
bet	to stichima	το στοίχημα
between	metaksi	μεταξύ
the Bible	i vivlos	η Βίβλος
bicycle/bike	to podhilato	το ποδήλατο
big	meghalos/-i/-o	μεγάλος/-η/-ο
bill (restaurant)	o loghariazmos	ο λογαριασμός
bird	to puli	το πουλί
birth certificate	to pistopi-itiko yeniseos	το πιστοποιητικό
		γεννήσεως
birthday	ta yenethlia	τα γενέθλια
bite (dog)	to dhangoma	το δάγκωμα
bite (insect)	to tsibima	το τσίμπημα
blanket	i kuverta	η κουβέρτα
to bleed	matono	ματώνω
to bless	evlogho	ευλογώ

Bless you! (sneezing)		
stin ighia su!	Στην υγειά σου!	

blind	tiflos/-i/-o	τυφλός/-η/-ο
blood	to ema	το αίμα
to board (ship, etc)	epivivazome	επιβιβάζομαι
boarding pass	i karta epivivasis	η κάρτα επιβίβασης
boat	to plio/karavi/vaporio	το πλοίο/καράβι/
		βαπόρι
body	to soma	το σώμα

Bon appetit!		
kali oreksi!	Καλή όρεξη!	

Bon voyage!		
kalo taksidhi!	Καλό ταξίδι!	

book	to vivlio	το βιβλίο
to book	klino thesi	κλείνω θέση
(make booking)		

bookshop	to vivliopolio	το βιβλιοπωλείο
border	ta sinora	τα σύνορα
bored	variestimenos/-i/-o	βαριεστημένος/-η/-ο
boring	varetos/-i/-o	βαρετός/-η/-ο
borrow	dhanizome	δανείζομαι
both	ke ta dhio	και τα δύο
bottle	to bukali	το μπουκάλι
bottle opener	to anichtiri	το ανοιχτήρι
box	to kuti	το κουτί
boy	to aghori	το αγόρι
boyfriend	to aghori/o filos	το αγόρι/ο φίλος
brave	yeneos/-a/-o	γενναίος/-α/-ο
breakfast	to proino	το πρωινό
to bribe	dhorodhoko	δωροδοκώ
bridge	i yefira	η γέφυρα
brilliant	katapliktikos/-i/-o	καταπληκτικός/-η/-ο
to bring	ferno	φέρνω
broken	spazmenos/-i/-o	σπασμένος/-η/-ο
brother	o adhelfos	ο αδελφός
bruise	i melania	η μελανιά
bucket	o kuvas	ο κουβάς
building	to ktirio	το κτίριο
bus (city)	to leoforio (astiko)	το λεωφορείο (αστικό)
bus (intercity)	to leoforio (iperastiko)	το λεωφορείο (υπεραστικό)
business (company)	i epichirisi	η επιχείρηση
business (to do)	kano dhulia	κάνω δουλειά
busy	apascholimenos/-i/-o	απασχολημένος/-η/-ο
butterfly	i petaludha	η πεταλούδα
buttons	ta kubia	τα κουμπιά
to buy	aghorazo (aghorasa)	αγοράζω (αγόρασα)

I'd like to buy ...
thathela naghoraso ...
Θα 'θελα ν' αγοράσω ...

C

calendar	to imerologhio	το ημερολόγιο
camera	i fotoghrafiki michani	η φωτογραφική μηχανή
to camp	kataskinono	κατασκηνώνω
campsite	o choros kataskinosis	ο χώρος κατασκήνωσης

C

can (to be able)	boro	μπορώ

I can.		
boro	Μπορώ.	

I can't do it.		
dhen boro	Δεν μπορώ.	

can (tin)	i konserva	η κονσέρβα
can opener	to anichtiri (konservas)	το ανοιχτήρι (κονσέρβας)
cancel	akirono	ακυρώνω
candle	to keri	το κερί
car	to aftokinito	το αυτοκίνητο
car registration	o arithmos kikloforias	ο αριθμός κυκλοφορίας
to care (about)	endhiaferome	ενδιαφέρομαι
to care (for someone)	frondizo	φροντίζω

Careful!		
prosochi!	προσοχή!	

cash register	to tamio	το ταμείο
cat	i ghata	η γάτα
cathedral	o kathedhrikos naos	ο καθεδρικός ναός
caves	i spilies/ta spilea	οι σπηλιές/τα σπήλαια
to celebrate	yiortazo	γιορτάζω
centimetre	to ekatosto	το εκατοστό
ceramic	keramikos/-i/-o	κεραμικός/-η/-ο
certificate	to pistopi-itiko	το πιστοποιητικό
chair	i karekla	η καρέκλα
to change	alazo (alaksa)	αλλάζω (άλλαξα)
change (spare coins)	tapsila	τα ψιλά
change (after a purchase)	taresta	τα ρέστα
changing rooms	ta dhokimastiria	τα δοκιμαστήρια
charming	simbathitikos/-i/-o	συμπαθητικός/-η/-ο
cheap	ftinos/-i/-o	φτηνός/-η/-ο
to check	elencho	ελέγχω
cheese	to tiri	το τυρί
chest (part of body)	to stithos	το στήθος
chewing gum	i tsichla	η τσίχλα
chicken	i kota	η κότα
children	tapedhia	τα παιδιά

D I C T I O N A R Y

to choose	dhialegho	διαλέγω
Christian	christianos/-i	Χριστιανός/-η
Christmas	ta christuyena	τα Χριστούγεννα
church	i eklisia	η εκκλησία
cigarettes	ta tsighara	τα τσιγάρα
cinema	o kinimatoghrafos	ο κινηματογράφος
circus	to tsirko	το τσίρκο
citizenship	i ipiko-otita	η υπηκοότητα
city	i poli	η πόλη
city centre	to kendro tis polis	το κέντρο της πόλης
clean	katharos/-i/-o	καθαρός/-η/-ο
client	o pelatis	ο πελάτης
cliff	o gremos	ο γκρεμός
to climb	skarfalono	σκαρφαλώνω
cloakroom	i gardaroba	η γκαρνταρόμπα
clock	to roloi	το ρολόι
to close	klino	κλείνω
closed	klistos/-i/-o	κλειστός/-η/-ο
clothes	ta rucha	τα ρούχα
cloud	to sinefo	το σύννεφο
cloudy	sinefiazmenos/-i/-o	συννεφιασμένος/-η/-ο
coast	i paralia/akti/akroyialia	η παραλία/ακτή/ ακρογιαλιά
coat	to palto	το παλτό
coins	ta kermata	τα κέρματα
a cold	to krioloyima	το κρυολόγημα
cold (adj)	krios/-a/-o	κρύος/-α/-ο
to have a cold	ime kriomenos/-i	είμαι κρυωμένος/-η
cold water	krio nero	κρύο νερό
colleague	o/i sinadhelfos	ο/η συνάδελφος
college	to koleyio	το κολλέγιο
colour	to chroma	το χρώμα
comb	i chtena	η χτένα
to come	erchome	έρχομαι
comedy	i komodhia	η κωμωδία
communion	i metalipsi	η Μετάληψη
companion	o/i sindrofos	ο/η σύντροφος
company (firm)	i eteria	η εταιρία
compass	i piksidha	η πυξίδα
a concert	i sinavlia	η συναυλία
confession (religious)	i eksomoloyisi	η εξομολόγηση
to confirm (a booking)	epiveveono	επιβεβαιώνω

Congratulations! sincharitiria!	Συγχαρητήρια!	
conservative	sindiritikos/-i/-o	συντηρητικός/-η/-ο
consulate	to proksenio	το προξενείο
contact lenses	i faki epafis	οι φακοί επαφής
contraception	i andisilipsi	η αντισύλληψη
contract	to simvoleo	το συμβόλαιο
convent	to monastiri	το μοναστήρι
to cook	mayirevo (mayirepsa)	μαγειρεύω (μαγείρεψα)
corner	i ghonia	η γωνία
corrupt	dhieftharmenos/-i/-o	διεφθαρμένος/-η/-ο
to cost	kostizo (kostisa)	κοστίζω (κόστισα)
country	i chora	η χώρα
countryside	i eksochi	η εξοχή
cough (n)	o vichas	ο βήχας
to count	metro	μετρώ
court (legal)	to dhikastirio	το δικαστήριο
cow	i agheladha	η αγελάδα
crafts	i chirotechnia	η χειροτεχνία
crazy	trelos/-i/-o	τρελλός/-η/-ο
cross (religious)	o stavros	ο σταυρός
cross (angry)	thimomenos/-i/-o	θυμωμένος/-η/-ο
to cross	perno (perasa)	περνώ (πέρασα)
a cuddle	i angalia	η αγκαλιά
cup	to flitzani	το φλυτζάνι
cupboard	i dulapa	η ντουλάπα
customs (habits)	ta ethima	τα έθιμα
customs	to telonio	το τελωνείο
to cut	kovo (ekopsa)	κόβω (έκοψα)

D

dad	o babas	ο μπαμπάς
daily	imerisios/-a/-o	ημερήσιος/-α/-ο
to dance	chorevo	χορεύω
dance	o choros	ο χορός
dangerous	epikindhinos/-i/-o	επικίνδυνος/-η/-ο
dark	skotinos/-i/-o	σκοτεινός/-η/-ο
date (time)	i imerominia	η ημερομηνία
to date (someone)	vyeno me	βγαίνω με
daughter	i kori	η κόρη

dawn	i avyi/anatoli	η αυγή/ανατολή
day	i imera/mera	η ημέρα/μέρα
dead	nekros/-i/-o	νεκρός/-η/-ο
deaf	kufos/-i/-o	κουφός/-η/-ο
death	o thanatos	ο θάνατος
decide	apofasizo	αποφασίζω
deck (of ship)	to katastroma	το κατάστρωμα
deep	vathis/-ia/-i	βαθύς/-ιά/-ύ
degree	to ptichio	το πτυχίο
delay	i kathisterisi	η καθυστέρηση
delicatessen	ta alandika	τα αλαντικά
dental floss	to odhondiko nima	το οδοντικό νήμα
dentist	o/i odhondiatros	ο/η οδοντίατρος
to deny	arnume (arnithika)	αρνούμαι (αρνήθηκα)
to depart (leave)	anachoro (anachorisa)	αναχωρώ (αναχώρησα)
descendent	o/i apoghonos	ο/η απόγονος
desert	i erimos	η έρημος
destination	o pro-orizmos	ο προορισμός
to destroy	okatastrefo	καταστρέφω
detail	i leptomeria	η λεπτομέρεια
dictionary	to leksiko	το λεξικό
to die	petheno (pethana)	πεθαίνω (πέθανα)
different	dhiaforetikos/-i/-o	διαφορετικός/-η/-ο
difficult	dhiskolos/-i/-o	δύσκολος/-η/-ο
dinner	to dhipno	το δείπνο
direct (flight etc)	apefthias	απ'ευθείας
director	o/i dhiefthindis/ dhiefthindria	ο/η διευθυντής/ διευθύντρια
dirty	vromikos/-i/-o	βρώμικος/-η/-ο
disabled	anapiros/-i/-o	ανάπηρος/-η/-ο
disadvantage	to mionektima	το μειονέκτημα
discount	i ekptosi	η έκπτωση
to discover	anakalipto (anakalipsa)	ανακαλύπτω (ανακάλυψα)
discrimination	i merolipsia	η μεροληψία
disease	i arostia	η αρρώστεια
dizzy	zalizmenos/-i/-o	ζαλισμένος/-η/-ο
to do	kano (ekana)	κάνω (έκανα)

What are you doing?
ti kanis? Τι κάνεις;

doctor	o/i yiatros	ο/η γιατρός
dog	o skilos	ο σκύλος

ENGLISH – GREEK

door	i porta	η πόρτα
dope (drugs)	ta narkotika	τα ναρκωτικά
double	dhiplos/-i/-o	διπλός/-η/-ο
drama	to dhrama	το δράμα
dramatic	dhramatikos/-i/-o	δραματικός/-η/-ο
to dream	onirevome (onireftika)	ονειρεύομαι (ονειρεύτηκα)
dress	to forema	το φόρεμα
a drink	to poto	το ποτό
to drink	pino (ipia)	πίνω (ήπια)
to drive	odhigho	οδηγώ
driver's licence	i adhia odhighisis	η άδεια οδήγησης
drug (medicine)	to farmako	το φάρμακο
drugs (narcotics)	ta narkotika	τα ναρκωτικά
drums	ta timbana	τα τύμπανα
to be drunk	methizmenos/-i/-o	μεθυσμένος/-η/-ο
to dry	steghnono (steghnosa)	στεγνώνω (στέγνωσα)
dummy/pacifier	i pipila	η πιπίλα

E

ear	to afti	το αυτί
early	noris	νωρίς
to earn	kerdhizo	κερδίζω
ears	ta aftia	τα αυτιά
Earth	i yi	η Γη
earth (soil)	to choma	το χώμα
earthquake	o sizmos	ο σεισμός
east (adv)	anatolika	ανατολικά
the east	i anatoli	η Ανατολή
Easter	to pascha	το Πάσχα
easy	efkolos/-i/-o	εύκολος/-η/-ο
to eat	tro-o (efagha)	τρώω (έφαγα)
the economy	i ikonomia	η οικονομία
editor	o/i ekdhotis/ekdhotria	ο/η εκδότης/εκδότρια
education	i ekpedhefsi	η εκπαίδευση
elections	i ekloyes	οι εκλογές
electricity	o ilektrizmos	ο ηλεκτρισμός
embarassment	i dropi	η ντροπή
embassy	i prezvia	η πρεσβεία
emergency	i amesi anangi	η άμεση ανάγκη
empty	adhios/-a/-o	άδειος/-α/-ο
end	to telos	το τέλος

to end	teliono (teliosa)	τελειώνω (τελείωσα)
endangered species	to apilomeno idhos	το απειλούμενο είδος
engagement	o aravonas	ο αρραβώνας
English	ta anglika	τα Αγγλικά
to enjoy (oneself)	dhiaskedhazo	διασκεδάζω
enough	arketos/-i/-o	αρκετός/-η/-ο
to enter	beno (bika)	μπαίνω (μπήκα)
entertaining	dhiaskedhastikos/-i/-o	διασκεδαστικός/-η/-ο
envelope	o fakelos	ο φάκελλος
environment	to perivalon	το περιβάλλον
epileptic	epiliptikos/-i	επιληπτικός/-η
equality	i isotita	η ισότητα
European	evropaikos/-i/-o	Ευρωπαϊκός/-η/-ο
evening	to apoyevma	το απόγευμα
example	to paradhighma	το παράδειγμα

For example …
ya paradhighma/paradhighmatos chari …
Για παράδειγμα/παραδείγματος χάρη …

excellent	thavmasios/-a/-o	θαυμάσιος/-α/-ο
to exhibit	ektheto (eksethesa)	εκθέτω (εξέθεσα)
exhibition	i ekthesi	η έκθεση
exit	i eksodhos	η έξοδος
expensive	akrivos/-i/-o	ακριβός/-η/-ο
eye	to mati	το μάτι

F

factory	to erghostasio	το εργοστάσιο
family	i ikoyenia	η οικογένεια
famous	dhiasimos/-i/-o	διάσημος/-η/-ο
fan (machine)	to vendilater	το βεντιλατέρ
fan (of a team)	o opadhos	ο οπαδός
far	makria	μακριά
farm	to aghroktima	το αγρόκτημα
fast (adv)	ghrighora	γρήγορα
fat	chondros/-i/-o	χοντρός/-η/-ο
father	o pateras	ο πατέρας
fault (someone's)	to lathos	το λάθος
faulty	elatomatikos/-i/-o	ελαττωματικός/-η/-ο
fear	fovos	ο φόβος
feast	to paniyiri	το πανηγύρι

to feel	esthanome	αισθάνομαι
feelings	ta sinesthimata	τα συναισθήματα
fence (gate)	o frachtis	ο φράχτης
festival	i yiorti/to festival	η γιορτή/το φεστιβάλ
fever	o piretos	ο πυρετός
fight	o kavghas	ο καυγάς
to fight	palevo	παλεύω
to fill	yemizo	γεμίζω
to find	vrisko	βρίσκω
a fine	to prostimo	το πρόστιμο
finger	to dhaktilo	το δάκτυλο
fire	i fotia	η φωτιά
firewood	to ksilo ya kafsima	το ξύλο για καύσιμα
first	protos/-i/-o	πρώτος/-η/-ο
first-aid kit	to kuti proton voithion	το κουτί πρώτων βοηθειών
fish	to psari	το ψάρι
flag	i simea	η σημαία
flat (adj)	platis/-ia/-i	πλατύς/-ιά/-ύ
flat (apartment)	to dhiamerizma	το διαμέρισμα
flea	o psilos	ο ψύλλος
flashlight (torch)	o fakos	ο φακός
flight	i ptisi	η πτήση
floor (storey)	o orofos	ο όροφος
flour	to alevri	το αλεύρι
flower	to luludhi/anthos	το λουλούδι/άνθος
to follow	akolutho	ακολουθώ
food	to fayito	το φαγητό
foot	to podhi	το πόδι
foreign	ksenos/-i/-o	ξένος/-η/-ο
forest	to dhasos	το δάσος
forever	ya panda	για πάντα
to forget	ksechno (ksechasa)	ξεχνώ (ξέχασα)

Forget about it; Don't worry!
dhen variese! Δεν βαριέσαι!

to forgive	sinchoro	συγχωρώ
fork	to piruni	το πηρούνι
free (not bound)	eleftheros/-i/-o	ελεύθερος/-η/-ο
free (of charge)	dhorean	δωρεάν
to freeze	paghono (paghosa)	παγώνω (πάγωσα)
fresh	freskos/freskia/fresko	φρέσκος/φρέσκια/φρέσκο

DICTIONARY

friend	o/i filos/fili	ο/η φίλος/φίλη
fruit picking	i singomidhi fruton	η συγκομιδή φρούτων
full	yematos/-i/-o	γεμάτος/-η/-ο
fun	i plaka	η πλάκα
funeral	i kidhia	η κηδεία
future	to melon	το μέλλον

G

game (children's)	to pechnidhi	το παιχνίδι
game (sports)	o aghonas	ο αγώνας
garbage	ta skupidhia	τα σκουπίδια
gardens	o kipos	ο κήπος
gift	to dhoro	το δώρο
girl	to koritsi	το κορίτσι
to give	dhino	δίνω

| Could you give me ...? | |
| mu dhinete ...? | Μου δίνετε ...; |

glass (drinking vessel)	to potiri	το ποτήρι
glass (windows)	to yali	το γυαλί
to go	pigheno (pigha)	πηγαίνω (πήγα)

| Let's go. | |
| pame | Πάμε. |

| goat | i katsika | η κατσίκα |
| God | otheos | ο Θεός |

| Good luck! | |
| kali tichi! | Καλή τύχη! |

government	i kivernisi	η κυβέρνηση
gram	to ghramario	το γραμμάριο
grass	to chorto	το χόρτο
grave	o tafos	ο τάφος
great (big)	meghalos/-i/-o	μεγάλος/-η/-ο

| Great! | |
| fandastika! | Φανταστικά! |

to guess	mandevo	μαντεύω
guide	o odhighos	ο οδηγός
guidebook	o turistikos odhighos	ο τουριστικός οδηγός
guitar	i kithara	η κιθάρα
gym	to yimnastirio	το γυμναστήριο

H

hair	ta malia	τα μαλλιά
hairbrush	i vurtsa	η βούρτσα
half	misos/-i/-o	μισός/-η/-ο
ham	to zambon	το ζαμπόν
hammer	to sfiri	το σφυρί
hammock	i kunia	η κούνια
hand	to cheri	το χέρι
handbag	i tsanda	η τσάντα
handsome	omorfos/-i/-o	όμορφος/-η/-ο
happy	charumenos/-i/-o	χαρούμενος/-η/-ο

Happy birthday!
chronia pola!   Χρόνια Πολλά!

harbour	to limani	το λιμάνι
hard	skliros/-i/-o	σκληρός/-η/-ο
harrassment	i enochlisi	η ενόχληση
hash	to chasisi	το χασίσι
to have	echo (icha)	έχω (είχα)

Do you have ...?
echete ...?   Έχετε ...;

he	aftos	αυτός
head	to kefali	το κεφάλι
headache	o ponokefalos	ο πονοκέφαλος
health	i iyia	η υγεία
to hear	akuo	ακούω
hearing aid	to akustiko (variko-ias)	το ακουστικό (βαρυκοΐας)
heart	i kardhia	η καρδιά
heat	i zesti	η ζέστη
heatwave	o kafsonas	ο καύσωνας
heating	i thermansi	η θέρμανση
heavy	varis/-ia/-i	βαρύς/-ια/-υ
hello	yia su	Γειά σου

Hello! (answering telephone)
embros!   Εμπρός!

Help!
voithia!   Βοήθεια!

| to help | voithao (voithisa) | βοηθάω (βοήθησα) |
| herbs | tavotana | τα βότανα |

here	edho	εδώ
high	psilos/-i/-o	ψηλός/-η/-ο
high school	to yimnasio/likio	το γυμνάσιο/λύκειο
hill	olofos	ο λόφος
to hire	nikiazo	νοικιάζω
to hitchhike	kano oto-stop	κάνω ωτο-στοπ
HIV positive	thetikos ya ton io tu eits-ai-vi (HIV)	θετικός για τον ιο του HiV
holidays	i dhiakopes	οι διακοπές
homeless	asteghos	άστεγος
honeymoon	o minas tu melitos	ο μήνας του μέλιτος
horrible	apesios/-a/-o	απαίσιος/-α/-ο
horse	to alogho	το άλογο
horse riding	i ipasia	η ιππασία
hospital	to nosokomio	το νοσοκομείο
hot	zestos/-i/-o	ζεστός/-η/-ο
to be hot	zestenome	ζεσταίνομαι
hot water	zesto nero	ζεστό νερό
house	to spiti	το σπίτι
how	pos	πώς

How do I get to ...?
pos pane se ...? Πώς πάνε σε ...;

hug	i angalia	η αγκαλιά
to be hungry	pinao	πεινάω
husband	oandhras/sizighos	ο άνδρας/σύζυγος

I

I	egho	εγώ
ice	o paghos	ο πάγος
icecream	to paghoto	το παγωτό
idiot	ilithios/-a/-o	ηλίθιος/-α/-ο
ill	arostos/-i/-o	άρρωστος/-η/-ο
immigration	i metanastefsi	η μετανάστευση
important	simandikos/-i/-o	σημαντικός/-η/-ο

It's (not) important.
(dhen) ine simandiko (Δεν) είναι σημαντικό.

to be in a hurry	viazome (viastika)	βιάζομαι (βιάστηκα)
in front of	brosta se	μπροστά σε
incomprehensible	adhiano-ito/-s/-i/-o	αδιανόητο/-ς/-ι/-ο
indicator	o dhiktis	ο δείκτης

indigestion	i dhispepsia	η δυσπεψία
industry	i vi-omichania	η βιομηχανία
inequality	i anisotita	η ανισότητα
to inject	kano enesi	κάνω ένεση
injection	i enesi	η ένεση
injury	o travmatizmos	ο τραυματισμός
insect repellent	to endomoapothitiko	το εντομοαπωθητικό
inside	mesa	μέσα
instructor	o ekpedheftis	ο εκπαιδευτής
intense	endonos/-i/-o	έντονος/-η/-ο
interesting	endhiaferon/-usa/-on	ενδιαφέρων/-ουσα/-ον
international	pangosmios/-a/-o	παγκόσμιος/-α/-ο
island	to nisi	το νησί
itch	i faghura	η φαγούρα
itinerary	i poria	η πορεία

J

jail	i filaki	η φυλακή
jar	i yiala	η γυάλα
jealous	ziliaris/-a	ζηλιάρης/-α
jeans	to blutzin	το μπλουτζήν
jeep	to tzip	το τζιπ
Jewish	evreos/-a	Εβραίος/-α
job	i dhulia/erghasia	η δουλειά/εργασία
joke	to anekdhoto	το ανέκδοτο
to joke	kano plaka	κάνω πλάκα
journalist	o/i dhimosioghrafos	ο/η δημοσιογράφος
journey	to taksidhi	το ταξίδι
judge	o/i dhikastis	ο/η δικαστής
juice	o chimos	ο χυμός
to jump	pidhao (pidhisa)	πηδάω (πήδησα)
justice	i dhikeosini	η δικαιοσύνη

K

key	to klidhi	το κλειδί
to kill	skotono	σκοτώνω
kind (adj)	kalos/kali/kalo	καλός/καλή/καλό
kind (type)	to idhos	το είδος
kindergarten	to nipiaghoyio	το νηπιαγωγείο
king	o vasilias	ο βασιλιάς
kiss	to fili	το φιλί

to kiss	filo	φιλώ
kitchen	i kuzina	η κουζίνα
kitten	to ghataki	το γατάκι
knapsack	to sakidhio	το σακκίδιο
knee	to ghonato	το γόνατο
knife	to macheri	το μαχαίρι
to know	ksero	ξέρω

L

lake	i limni	η λίμνη
land	i yi	η γη
language	i ghlossa	η γλώσσα
large	meghalos/-i/-o	μεγάλος/-η/-ο
last (final)	telefteos/-a/-o	τελευταίος/-α/-ο
last (previous)	pro-ighumenos/-i/-o	προηγούμενος/-η/-ο
late	argha	αργά
to laugh	yelo	γελώ
launderette	to katharistirio	το καθαριστήριο
law	o nomos	ο νόμος
lawyer	o/i dhikighoros	ο/η δικηγόρος
lazy	tembelis/-a	τεμπέλης/-α
leader	o/i odhighos/archiyos	ο/η οδηγός/αρχηγός
to learn	matheno	μαθαίνω (έμαθα)
left (not right)	dheksia	δεξιά
left-wing	aristeros/-i/-o	αριστερός/-η/-ο
leg	to podhi	το πόδι
less	lighoteros/-i/-o	λιγότερος/-η/-ο
letter	to ghrama	το γράμμα
liar	pseftis/pseftra	ψεύτης/ψεύτρα
library	i vivliothiki	η βιβλιοθήκη
to lie	leo psemata	λέω ψέμματα
to lie down	ksaplono	ξαπλώνω
life	i zoi	η ζωή
light (sun/lamp)	to fos	το φως
light (adj)	elafris/-ia/-i	ελαφρύς/-ια/-υ
lighter (n)	o anaptiras	ο αναπτήρας
to like	aresi	αρέσει
lips	ta chilia	τα χείλια
to listen	akuo	ακούω
little (small)	mikros/-i/-o	μικρός/-η/-ο
a little (amount)	ligho	λίγο
to live (to exist)	zo	ζω

to live (somewhere)	meno	μένω
local	topikos/-i/-o	τοπικός/-η/-ο
lock	i klidharia	η κλειδαριά
to lock	klidhono	κλειδώνω
long	makris/-ia/-i	μακρύς/-ια/-υ
to look	vlepo (idha)	βλέπω (είδα)
to look after	frondizo/prosecho	φροντίζω/προσέχω
to look for	psachno	ψάχνω
to lose	chano	χάνω
loser	itimenos/-i/-o	ηττημένος/-η/-ο
loss	i ita	η ήττα
a lot	poli	πολύ
loud	dhinatos/-i/-o	δυνατός/-η/-ο
to love	aghapo (aghapisa)	αγαπώ (αγάπησα)
lover	eromenos/-i	ερωμένος/-η
low	chamilos/-i/-o	χαμηλός/-η/-ο
loyal	pistos/-i/-o	πιστός/-η/-ο
luck	i tichi	η τύχη
lucky	ticheros/-i/-o	τυχερός/-η/-ο
luggage	i aposkeves	οι αποσκευές
lunch	to mesimeriano	το μεσημεριανό
luxury	i politelia	η πολυτέλεια
luxurious	politelis/-is/-es	πολυτελής/-ις/-ες

M

magazine	to periodhiko	το περιοδικό
magician	o maghos	ο μάγος
mail	i aliloghrafia	η αλληλογραφία
mailbox	to tachidhromiko kuti	το ταχυδρομικό κουτί
main road	o kendrikos dhromos	ο κεντρικός δρόμος
main square	i kendriki platia	η κεντρική πλατεία
majority	i pliopsifia	η πλειοψηφία
to make	ftiachno (eftiaksa)	φτιάχνω (έφτιαξα)
make-up	to makiyiaz	το μακιγιάζ
man (male person)	o andhras	ο άνδρας
Man (a human being)	o anthropos	ο άνθρωπος
many	poli/-es/-a	πολλοί/-ες/-α
map	o chartis	ο χάρτης
market	i aghora	η αγορά
marriage	o ghamos	ο γάμος
to marry	pandrevome	παντρεύομαι
marvellous	thavmasios/-a/-o	θαυμάσιος/-α/-ο

M

mat	to stroma	το στρώμα
match (sports)	oaghonas/ to mats	ο αγώνας/το μάτς
matches	ta spirta	τα σπίρτα
mattress	to stroma	το στρώμα
maybe	isos	ίσως
mayor	o dhimarchos	ο δήμαρχος
mechanic	o michanikos	ο μηχανικός
medicine	i iatriki	η ιατρική
to meet	sinando (sinandisa)	συναντώ (συνάντησα)
menstruation	i periodhos	η περίοδος
message	to minima	το μήνυμα
meteor	ometeoritis	ο μετεωρίτης
migraine	i imikrania	η ημικρανία
milk	to ghala	το γάλα
millimetre	to chiliosto	το χιλιοστό
mind (n)	o nus	ο νους
to mind	pirazi	πειράζει

I don't mind.
dhen me pirazi   Δεν με πειράζει.

mineral water	to metaliko nero	το μεταλλικό νερό
a minute	ena lepto	ένα λεπτό

Just a minute.
miso lepto   Μισό λεπτό.

mirror	o kathreftis	ο καθρέφτης
to miss (feel absence)	lipo (elipsa)	λείπω (έλειψα)

I miss you.
mu lipis   Μου λείπεις.

mistake	to lathos	το λάθος
to mix	anakatevo/anamighnio	ανακατεύω/αναμιγνύω
mobile phone	to kinito (tilefono)	το κινητό (τηλέφωνο)
monastery	to monastiri/i moni	το μοναστήρι/η μονή
money	ta chrimata/lefta	τα χρήματα/λεφτά
monk	o omonachos/kalogheros	ο μοναχός/καλόγερος
month	o minas	ο μήνας
monument	to mnimio	το μνημείο
moon	to fengari/i selini	το φεγγάρι/η σελήνη
more	perisoteros/-i/-o	περισσότερος/-η/-ο
morning	to proi	το πρωί
mosque	to tzami	το τζαμί
mother	i mitera	η μητέρα

D I C T I O N A R Y

motorcycle	i motosikleta	η μοτοσυκλέτα
motorway (tollway)	i ethniki odhos	η εθνική οδός
mountain	to oros/vuno	το όρος/βουνό
mountaineering	i orivasia	η ορειβασία
mouse (animal/computer)	to pondiki	το ποντίκι
mouth	to stoma	το στόμα
movie	i tenia	η ταινία
mud	i laspi	η λάσπη
Mum	i mama	η μαμά
muscle	o mis	ο μυς
Muslim	moamethanos/-i	Μωαμεθανός/-ή

N

name	to onoma	το όνομα
nappy	i pana	η πάνα
nationality	i ipiko-otita	η υπηκοότητα
nature	i fisi	η φύση
nausea	i naftia	η ναυτία
near	konda	κοντά
necessary	aparetitos/-i/-o	απαραίτητος/-η/-ο
to need	chriazome	χρειάζομαι
needle	i velona	η βελόνα
neither ... nor	ute ... ute	ούτε ... ούτε
net (fishing)	to dhichti	το δίχτυ
never	pote	ποτέ
new	kenuryios/-a/-o	καινούργιος/-α/-ο
news	ta nea	τα νέα
newspaper	i efimeridha	η εφημερίδα
next	epomenos/-i/-o	επόμενος/-η/-ο
next to	dhipla se	δίπλα σε
nice	kalos/-i/-o	καλός/-η/-ο
night	i nichta	η νύχτα
no	ochi	όχι
noise	o thorivos	ο θόρυβος
none	katholu/tipota	καθόλου/τίποτα
noon	to mesimeri	το μεσημέρι
north (adv)	voria	βόρεια
the north	o voras	ο βορράς
nose	i miti	η μύτη
nothing	tipota	τίποτα
not	dhen	δεν

novel (book)	to mithistorima	το μυθιστόρημα
now	tora	τώρα
nun	i kaloghria	η καλόγρια
nurse	o/i nosokomos/ nosokoma	ο/η νοσοκόμος/ νοσοκόμα

O

obvious	faneros/-i/-o	φανερός/-η/-ο
ocean	o okeanos	ο ωκεανός
offence	to adhikima	το αδίκημα
office	to ghrafio	το γραφείο
often	sichna	συχνά
oil (cooking)	to ladhi	το λάδι
oil (crude)	to petreleo	το πετρέλαιο
OK	endaksi	εντάξει
old (people)	yeros/ghria	γέρος/γριά
old (things)	palios/-a/-o	παλιός/-α/-ο
olive oil	to eleoladho	το ελαιόλαδο
olives	i elies	οι ελιές
once	mia fora	μια φορά
only	mono	μόνο
open	anichtos/-i/-o	ανοιχτός/-η/-ο
to open	anigho	ανοίγω
opening	to anighma	το άνοιγμα
opera	i opera	η όπερα
opinion	i ghnomi	η γνώμη
opponent	o andipalos	ο αντίπαλος
opposite (adj)	andithetos/-i/-o	αντίθετος/-η/-ο
or	i	ή
order	i dhiatayi/parangelia	η διαταγή/παραγγελία
to order (command)	dhiatazo	διατάζω
to order (food)	paragelno	παραγγέλνω
to organise	orghanono	οργανώνω
original (n)	to prototipo	το πρωτότυπο
other	alos/-i/-o	άλλος/-η/-ο
outside	ekso	έξω
over (above)	epano	επάνω
to owe	chrostao	χρωστάω
owner	idhioktitis/idhioktitria	ιδιοκτήτης/ιδιοκτήτρια
oxygen	to oksighono	το οξυγόνο

P

pacifier (dummy)	i pipila	η πιπίλα
padlock	to luketo	το λουκέτο
page	i selidha	η σελίδα
a pain	o ponos	ο πόνος
painful	odhiniros/-i/-o	οδυνηρός/-η/-ο
painkillers	ta analytika	τα αναληπτικά
a pair (a couple)	ena zevghari	ένα ζευγάρι
palace	ta anaktora	τα ανάκτορα
pan	i katsarola	η κατσαρόλα
paper	to charti	το χαρτί
paraplegic	paralitos/-i	παράλυτος/-η
parcel	to dhema	το δέμα
parents	i ghonis	οι γονείς
a park	to parko	το πάρκο
to part	chorizo	χωρίζω
party (fiesta!)	to parti	το πάρτυ
party (politics)	to koma	το κόμμα
pass	pernao	περνάω
passenger	o/i epivatis	ο/η επιβάτης
passive	pathitikos/-i/-o	παθητικός/-η/-ο
passport	to dhiavatirio	το διαβατήριο
past (n)	to parelthon	το παρελθόν
path	to monopati	το μονοπάτι
patient (adj)	ipomonetikos/-i/-o	υπομονετικός/-η/-ο
to pay	plirono	πληρώνω
peace	i irini	η ειρήνη
pedestrian	pezos/pezi	πεζός/πεζή
pen (ballpoint)	to stilo	το στυλό
pencil	to molivi	το μολύβι
penis	to peos	το πέος
penknife	o suyias	ο σουγιάς
pensioner	o/i sindaksiuchos	ο/η συνταξιούχος
people	o kozmos (sg)/ i anthropi (pl)	ο κόσμος/οι άνθρωποι
pepper	to piperi	το πιπέρι
percent	tis ekato	τοις εκατό
performance	i parastasi	η παράσταση
permanent	monimos/-i/-o	μόνιμος/-η/-ο
permission	i adhia	η άδεια
person	to atomo	το άτομο
personality	i charaktiras	ο χαρακτήρας

to perspire	idhrono	ιδρώνω
petrol (fuel)	i venzini	η βενζίνη
phonecard	i tilekarta	η τηλεκάρτα
pie	i pita	η πίτα
piece	to komati	το κομμάτι
pig	to ghuruni	το γουρούνι
pill	to chapi	το χάπι
the Pill	to andisiliptiko chapi	το αντισυλληπτικό χάπι
pillow	to maksilari	το μαξιλάρι
pine	to pefko	το πεύκο
pipe	i pipa	η πίπα
place	to meros/o topos	το μέρος/ο τόπος
plain (simple)	aplos/-i/-o	απλός/-η/-ο
plain (flat area)	i pedhiadha	η πεδιάδα
planet	o planitis	ο πλανήτης
plant	to fito	το φυτό
plate	to piato	το πιάτο
plateau	to oropedhio	το οροπέδιο
play (theatre)	to theatriko ergho	το θεατρικό έργο
to play	pezo	παίζω
player (sports)	o/i pektis/pektria	ο/η παίκτης/παίκτρια
playing cards	i trapula	η τράπουλα
plug (electricity)	i priza	η πρίζα
poetry	i pi-isi	η ποίηση
to point	dichno	δείχνω
police	i astinomia	η αστυνομία
pollen	i yiri	η γύρη
pollution	i molinsi	η μόλυνση
pool (swimming)	i pisina	η πισίνα
poor	ftochos/-i/-o	φτωχός/-η/-ο
popular	dhimofilis/-is/-es	δημοφιλής/-ης/-ες
port	to limani	το λιμάνι
possible	dhinatos/-i/-o	δυνατός/-η/-ο

| It's (not) possible. | | |
| (dhen) ine dhinato | (Δεν) είναι δυνατό. | |

poster	i afisa	η αφίσσα
poverty	i ftochia	η φτώχεια
power	i dhinami	η δύναμη
prayer	i prosefchi	η προσευχή
to prefer	protimo	προτιμώ
pregnant	engios	έγκυος

to prepare	etimazo	ετοιμάζω
present (gift)	to dhoro	το δώρο
present (time)	to paron	το παρόν
president	o/i proedhros	ο/η πρόεδρος
pretty	omorfos/-i/-o	όμορφος/-η/-ο
price	i timi	η τιμή
pride	i iperifania	η υπερηφάνεια
priest	o papas	ο παπάς
prime minister	o/i prothipurghos	ο/η πρωθυπουργός
prison	i filaki	η φυλακή
prisoner	filakizmenos/-i	φυλακισμένος/-η
private	idhiotikos/-i/-o	ιδιωτικός/-η/-ο
producer	o/i paraghoghos	ο/η παραγωγός
profession	to epangelma	το επάγγελμα
profit	to kerdhos	το κέρδος
projector	o provoleas	ο προβολέας
to promise	iposchome	υπόσχομαι
proposal	i protasi	η πρόταση
to protect	prostatevo	προστατεύω
protected forest	to prostatevomeno dhasos	το προστατευόμενο δάσος
to pull	travao	τραβάω
puncture	tripa sto lasticho	τρύπα στο λάστιχο
to punish	timoro	τιμωρώ
pure	aghnos/-i/-o	αγνός/-η/-ο
to push	sprochno	σπρώχνω
to put	vazo	βάζω

Q

qualifications	ta prosonda	τα προσόντα
quality	i piotita	η ποιότητα
quarantine	i karantina	η καραντίνα
quarrel	o kavghas	ο καυγάς
queen	i vasilisa	η βασίλισσα
question	i erotisi	η ερώτηση
queue	i ura	η ουρά
quick	ghrighoros/-i/-o	γρήγορος/-η/-ο
quiet	isichos/-i/-o	ήσυχος/-η/-ο
to quit	parato	παρατώ

R

| race (sport) | o aghonas | ο αγώνας |
| racism | o ratsizmos | ο ρατσισμός |

radiator	to kalorifer	το καλοριφέρ
rain	i vrochi	η βροχή
rape	o viazmos	ο βιασμός
rare	spanios/-a/-o	σπάνιος/-α/-ο
a rash	to eksanthima	το εξάνθημα
rat	o arureos	ο αρουραίος
raw	omos/-i/-o	ωμός/-η/-ο
to read	dhiavazo	διαβάζω
ready	etimos/-i/-o	έτοιμος/-η/-ο
reason (cause)	o loghos/i etia	ο λόγος/η αιτία
receipt	i apodhiksi	η απόδειξη
to receive	dhechome	δέχομαι
recent	prosfatos/-i/-o	πρόσφατος/-η/-ο
recently	prosfata	πρόσφατα
to recognise	anaghnorizo	αναγνωρίζω
to recommend	sistino	συστήνω
recycling	i anakiklosi	η ανακύκλωση
referee	o dhietitis	ο διαιτητής
reference	i sistatiki epistoli	η συστατική επιστολή
reflection (mirror)	i andanaklasi	η αντανάκλαση
reflection (thinking)	i skepsi	η σκέψη
refugee	o prosfighas	ο πρόσφυγας
refund	i epistrofi chrimaton	η επιστροφή χρημάτων
to refuse	arnume	αρνούμαι
to regret	metaniono	μετανιώνω
relationship	i schesi	η σχέση
to relax	chalarono	χαλαρώνω
religion	i thriskia	η θρησκεία
to remember	thimame	θυμάμαι
remote	apomeros	απόμερος
rent	to enikio	το ενοίκιο
to rent	nikiazo	νοικιάζω
to repeat	epanalamvano	επαναλαμβάνω
republic	i dhimokratia	η δημοκρατία
to reserve	klino thesi	κλείνω θέση
resignation	i paretisi	η παραίτηση
respect (n)	o sevazmos	ο σεβασμός
rest (relaxation)	i ksekurasi	η ξεκούραση
rest (what's left)	to ipolipo	το υπόλοιπο
restaurant	to estiatorio	το εστιατόριο
resume (CV)	to vioghrafiko	το βιογραφικό
retired	sindaksiuchos	συνταξιούχος
to return	epistrefo	επιστρέφω

ENGLISH – GREEK

rhythm	o rithmos	ο ρυθμός
rich	plusios/-a/-o	πλούσιος/-α/-ο
to ride (a horse)	kavalikevo	καβαλικεύω
right (correct)	sostos/-i/-o	σωστός/-η/-ο
right (not left)	dheksios/-a/-o	δεξιός/-α/-ο
right-wing	dheksios/-a/-o	δεξιός/-α/-ο
rip-off	i apati	η απάτη
risk	o kindhinos	ο κίνδυνος
river	o potamos	ο ποταμός
road	o dhromos	ο δρόμος
to rob	klevo	κλέβω
rock	o vrachos	ο βράχος
romance	to flert	το φλερτ
room	to dhomatio	το δωμάτιο
rope	to schini	το σχοινί
round	strongilos/-i/-o	στρογγυλός/-η/-ο
route	i dhiadhromi	η διαδρομή
rubbish (garbage)	ta skupidhia	τα σκουπίδια
ruins	ta eripia	τα ερείπια
rules	i kanonizmi	οι κανονισμοί
to run	trecho	τρέχω

S

sad	lipimenos/-i/-o	λυπημένος/-η/-ο
safe (adj)	akindhina	ακίνδυνα
saint	ayios/ayia	άγιος/αγία
salary	o misthos	ο μισθός
salt	to alati	το αλάτι
same	idhios/-a/-o	ίδιος/-α/-ο
sand	i amos	η άμμος
sanitary napkins	i servietes	οι σερβιέτες
to save	sozo	σώζω
to say	leo	λέω
science	i epistimi	η επιστήμη
scissors	to psalidhi	το ψαλίδι
screen	i othoni	η οθόνη
sculpture	i ghliptiki	η γλυπτική
sea	i thalasa	η θάλασσα
seasick	echo naftia	έχω ναυτία
seaside	i paralia	η παραλία
seat	i thesi	η θέση
seatbelt	i zoni asfalias	η ζώνη ασφαλείας

second (n)	to dhefterolepto	το δευτερόλεπτο
second	dhefteros/-i/-o	δεύτερος/-η/-ο
to see	vlepo (idha)	βλέπω (είδα)

| We'll see! | | |
| tha dhume! | **Θα δούμε!** | |

| I see. (understand) | | |
| katalava | **Κατάλαβα.** | |

selfish	eghoistis/eghoistria	εγωιστής/εγωίστρια
to sell	pulo	πουλώ
to send	stelno	στέλνω
sensible	loghikos/-i/-o	λογικός/-η/-ο
sentence (words)	i protasi	η πρόταση
sentence (prison)	i pini	η ποινή
to separate	ksehorizo	ξεχωρίζω
serious	sovaros/-i/-o	σοβαρός/-η/-ο
service (assistance)	i eksipiretisix	η εξυπηρέτηση
service (religious)	i lituryia	η λειτουργία
several	arketi/-es/-a	αρκετοί/-ες/-α
shade/shadow	i skia	η σκιά
shape	to schima	το σχήμα
to share (with)	mirazome	μοιράζομαι
to shave	ksirizome	ξυρίζομαι
she	afti	αυτή
sheep	to provato	το πρόβατο
sheet (bed)	to sendoni	το σεντόνι
sheet (of paper)	i selidha	η σελίδα
shell	to ostrako	το όστρακο
shop (inf)	to katastima/maghazi	το κατάστημα/μαγαζί
short	kondos/-i/-o	κοντός/-η/-ο
shortage	i elipsi	η έλλειψη
to shout	fonazo	φωνάζω
a show	to so-u	το σόου
shower	to duz	το ντουζ
to shut	klino	κλείνω
shy	dropalos/-i/-o	ντροπαλός/-η/-ο
sick	arostos/-i/-o	άρρωστος/-η/-ο
side	to plai	το πλάι
a sign (road)	i pinakidha	η πινακίδα
to sign	ipoghrafo	υπογράφω
signature	i ipoghrafi	η υπογραφή
silk	to metaksi	το μετάξι

silver (adj)	asimenios/-a/-o	ασημένιος/-α/-ο
similar	paromios/-a/-o	παρόμοιος/-α/-ο
simple	aplos/-i/-o	απλός/-η/-ο
sin	i amartia	η αμαρτία
since (May)	apo (ton maio)	από (τον Μάιο)
to sing	traghudho	τραγουδώ
sister	i adhelfi	η αδελφή
to sit	kathome	κάθομαι
size	to meyethos	το μέγεθος
skin	to dherma	το δέρμα
sky	o uranos	ο ουρανός
to sleep	kimame	κοιμάμαι
sleeping bag	o ipnosakos	ο υπνόσακκος
sleepy	nistaghmenos/-i/-o	νυσταγμένος/-η/-ο
slow (adj)	arghos/-i/-o	αργός/-η/-ο
small	mikros/-i/-o	μικρός/-η/-ο
smell (n)	i mirodhia/osmi	η μυρωδιά/οσμή
to smell	mirizo	μυρίζω
to smile	chamoyelao	χαμογελάω
soap	to sapuni	το σαπούνι
solid	stereos/-a/-o	στερεός/-α/-ο
some	meriki/-es/-a	μερικοί/-ες/-α
somebody/someone	kapios/-a/-o	κάποιος/-α/-ο
something	kati	κάτι
sometimes	pote pote	πότε πότε
son	o yios	ο γιος
song	to traghudhi	το τραγούδι
soon	sindoma	σύντομα

I'm sorry.		
sighnomi	Συγγνώμη.	

sound	o ichos	ο ήχος
south (adv)	notia	νότια
the south	o notos	ο Νότος
space (room)	o choros	ο χώρος
space (universe)	to dhiastima	το διάστημα
to speak	milao	μιλάω
special	idhikos/-i/-o	ειδικός/-η/-ο
speed	i tachitita	η ταχύτητα
spoon/teaspoon	to kutali	το κουτάλι
spicy (hot)	pikandikos/-i/-o	πικάντικος/-η/-ο
spring (season)	i aniksi	η άνοιξη
square (shape)	to tetraghono	το τετράγωνο

square (in town)	i platia	η πλατεία
stadium	to stadhio	το στάδιο
stage (theatre)	i skini	η σκηνή
stars	ta astra	τα άστρα
station	o stathmos	ο σταθμός
statue	to aghalma	το άγαλμα
to stay	meno	μένω
to steal	klevo	κλέβω
steep	apotomos/-i/-o	απότομος/-η/-ο
step	to skali	το σκαλί
stone	i petra	η πέτρα
to stop	stamato	σταματώ
storm	i kateyidha	η καταιγίδα
story	i istoria	η ιστορία
straight (adv)	isia	ίσια
strange	perierghos/-i/-o	περίεργος/-η/-ο
stream	to riaki	το ρυάκι
street	i odhos	η οδός
strength	i dhinami	η δύναμη
a strike	i aperyia	η απεργία
stroll	o peripatos	ο περίπατος
strong	dhinatos/-i/-o	δυνατός/-η/-ο
stubborn	pismataris/pismatara	πεισματάρης/ πεισματάρα
stupid	chazos/-i/-o	χαζός/-η/-ο
subtitles	i ipotitli	οι υπότιτλοι
to suffer	ipofero	υποφέρω
suitcase	i valitsa	η βαλίτσα
summer	to kalokeri	το καλοκαίρι
sun	o ilios	ο ήλιος
sunblock	olikis andiliako prostasias	ολικής αντηλιακο προστασίας
sunburn	to engavma iliu	το έγκαυμα ηλίου
sunglasses	ta yialia iliu	τα γυαλιά ηλίου
sunny	i liakadha	η λιακάδα
sunrise	i anatoli	η ανατολή
sunset	i dhisi	η δύση

Sure.		
sighura	Σίγουρα.	

surname	to epitheto	το επίθετο
surprise (n)	i ekpliksi	η έκπληξη
to survive	epizo	επιζώ

sweet	ghlikos/-ia/-o	γλυκός/-ια/-ο
to swim	kolimbao	κολυμπάω
swimsuit	to mayio	το μαγιό
sympathetic	simbonetikos/-i/-o	συμπονετικός/-η/-ο
syringe	i siringa	η σύριγγα

T

table	to trapezi	το τραπέζι
tail	i ura	η ουρά
to take	perno	παίρνω
to talk	milao	μιλάω
tall	psilos/-i/-o	ψηλός/-η/-ο
tampons	ta tampon	τα ταμπόν
tasty	yefstikos/-i/-o	γευστικός/-η/-ο
tax	o foros	ο φόρος
taxi stand	o stathmos taksi	ο σταθμός ταξί
teacher	o/i dhaskalos/dhaskala	ο/η δάσκαλος/ δασκάλα
to teach	dhidhasko	διδάσκω
team	i omadha	η ομάδα
to tear	skizo	σκίζω
telegram	to tileghrafima	το τηλεγράφημα
to tell	leo	λέω
temperature (fever)	o piretos	ο πυρετός
temperature (weather)	i thermokrasia	η θερμοκρασία
temple	o naos	ο ναός
tennis	to tenis	το τένις
tennis court	to yipedho tu tenis	το γήπεδο του τένις
tent	i skini	η σκηνή
tenth	dhekatos/-i/-o	δέκατος/-η/-ο
terrible	foveros/-i/-o	φοβερός/-η/-ο
test	to test/i eksetasi	το τεστ/η εξέταση
to thank	efcharisto	ευχαριστώ

| Thank you. | | |
| efcharisto | | Ευχαριστώ. |

they	afti/aftes/afta	αυτοί/αυτές/αυτά
thick	pachis/-ia/-i	παχύς/-ια/-υ
thief	o kleftis	ο κλέφτης
thin	leptos/-i/-o	λεπτός/-η/-ο
to think	skeftome	σκέφτομαι
third	tritos/-i/-o	τρίτος/-η/-ο

to be thirsty	dipsao	διψάω
this	aftos/afti/afto	αυτός/αυτή/αυτό
tide	i paliria	η παλίρροια
tight	sfichtos/-i/-o	σφιχτός/-η/-ο
time (general)	o keros/o chronos	ο καιρός/ο χρόνος
tin (can)	i konserva	η κονσέρβα
tin opener	to anichtiri konservas	το ανοιχτήρι κονσέρβας
tired	kurazmenos/-i/-o	κουρασμένος/-η/-ο
today	simera	σήμερα
together	mazi	μαζί
toilet paper	to charti iyias	το χαρτί υγείας
toilets	i tualetes	οι τουαλέττες
tomorrow	avrio	αύριο
tonight	apopse	απόψε
too (as well)	ep* isis	επίσης
tooth	to dhondi	το δόντι
toothache	o ponodhondos	ο πονόδοντος
torch (flashlight)	o fakos	ο φακός
to touch	akumbo	ακουμπώ
tour	i peri-iyisi	η περιήγηση
tourist	o/i turistas/turistria	ο/η τουρίστας/ τουρίστρια
towards	pros	προς
towel	i petseta	η πετσέτα
tower	o pirghos	ο πύργος
track (path)	to monopati	το μονοπάτι
trade union	to sindhikato	το συνδικάτο
translate	metafrazo	μεταφράζω
to travel	taksidhevo	ταξιδεύω
tree	to dhendro	το δέντρο
trip	to taksidhi	το ταξίδι
truck	to fortigho	το φορτηγό
to trust	embistevome	εμπιστεύομαι
truth	i alithia	η αλήθεια
to try	prospatho	προσπαθώ
tune	o rithmos	ο ρυθμός
twice	dhio fores	δύο φορές
twins	ta dhidhima	τα δίδυμα
typical	tipikos/-i/-o	τυπικός/-η/-ο

U

| umbrella | i ombrella | η ομπρέλλα |
| to understand | katalaveno | καταλαβαίνω |

ENGLISH – GREEK

V

unemployed	anerghos/-i	άνεργος/-η
unemployment	i aneryia	η ανεργία
universe	to simban	το σύμπαν
university	to panepistimio	το πανεπιστήμιο
unsafe	mi asfales	μη ασφαλές
until	mechri	μέχρι
unusual	asinithistos/-i/-o	ασυνήθιστος/-η/-ο
up	pano	πάνω
urgent	epighon	επείγον
useful	chrisimos/-i/-o	χρήσιμος/-η/-ο

V

vacant	adhios/-a/-o	άδειος/-α/-ο
vaccination	to emvolio	το εμβόλιο
valley	i kiladha	η κοιλάδα
valuable	politimos/-i/-o	πολύτιμος/-η/-ο
value (price)	i aksia	η αξία
van	to fortighaki	το φορτηγάκι
vegetable	to lachaniko	το λαχανικό
vegetation	i vlastisi	η βλάστηση
vein	i fleva	η φλέβα
very	poli	πολύ
view	i thea	η θέα
village	to chorio	το χωριό
vine	to ambeli/klima	το αμπέλι/κλήμα
vineyard	o ambelonas	ο αμπελώνας
virus	o ios	ο ιός
visa	i viza	η βίζα
to visit	episkeftome	επισκέφτομαι
voice	i foni	η φωνή
volume (sound)	i endasi	η ένταση
to vote	psifizo	ψηφίζω

W

| Wait! | perimene! | Περίμενε! |

to walk	perpato	περπατώ
wall	o tichos	ο τοίχος
to want	thelo	θέλω
war	o polemos	ο πόλεμος
warm	zestos/-i/-o	ζεστός/-η/-ο

DICTIONARY

to warn	proidhopio	προειδοποιώ
to wash (something)	pleno (eplina)	πλένω
to wash (oneself)	plenome (plithika)	πλένομαι
watch	to roloi	το ρολόι
to watch	parakolutho	παρακολουθώ
water	to nero	το νερό
waterfall	o katarachtis	ο καταρράχτης
wave	to kima	το κύμα
way (direction)	o dhromos	ο δρόμος

Which way?		
pros ta pu?		προς τα πού;

we	emis	εμείς
weak	adhinamos/-i/-o	αδύναμος/-η/-ο
wealthy	plusios/-a/-o	πλούσιος/-α/-ο
to wear	forao	φοράω
weather	o keros	ο καιρός
wedding	o ghamos	ο γάμος
week	i evdhomadha	η εβδομάδα
weight	to varos	το βάρος
welcome	kalos ilthate	καλώς ήλθατε
welfare	i pronia	η πρόνοια
west (adv)	dhitika	δυτικά
the west	i dhisi	η Δύση
wet	vremenos/-i/-o	βρεμένος/-η/-ο
what	ti	τι
wheel	i rodha	η ρόδα
wheelchair	i anapiriki karekla	η αναπηρική καρέκλα
when	pote	πότε
where	pu	πού
white	aspros/-i/-o	άσπρος/-η/-ο
who/which (sg)	pios/pia/pio	ποιος/ποια/ποιο
(pl)	pii/pies/pia	ποιοι/ποιες/ποια
whole	olokliros/-i/-o	ολόκληρος/-η/-ο
why	yiati	γιατί
wide	fardhis/-ia/-i	φαρδύς/-ια/-υ
wife	i yineka/sizighos	η γυναίκα/σύζυγος
to win	kerdhizo	κερδίζω
wind	o aeras	ο αέρας
window	to parathiro	το παράθυρο
wings	ta ftera	τα φτερά
winner	o nikitis	ο νικητής
winter	o chimonas	ο χειμώνας

wise	sofos/-i/-o	σοφός/-η/-ο
to wish	efchome	εύχομαι
with	me	με
without	choris	χωρίς
woman	i yineka	η γυναίκα
wonderful	thavmasios/-a/-o	θαυμάσιος/-α/-ο
wood	to ksilo	το ξύλο
wool	to mali	το μαλλί
word	i leksi	η λέξη
work	i dhulia/erghasia	η δουλειά/εργασία
world	o kozmos	ο κόσμος
wound	i pliyi	η πληγή
to write	ghrafo	γράφω

I'm wrong (it's my fault).
lathos mu   Λάθος μου.

Y

year	o chronos	ο χρόνος
this year	fetos	φέτος
yellow	kitrinos/-i/-o	κίτρινος/-η/-ο
yesterday	chtes	χτες
yesterday morning	chtes to proi	χτες το πρωί
yet	akomi	ακόμη
you (pol)	esis	εσείς
you (inf)	esi	εσύ
young	neos/-a/-o	νέος/-α/-ο
youth (collective)	i neolea	η νεολαία

Z

| zodiac | to zodhio | το ζώδιο |
| zoo | o zo-oloyikos kipos | ο ζωολογικός κήπος |

The Greek alphabet is as follows: Α Β Γ Δ Ε Ζ Η Θ Ι Κ Λ Μ Ν Ξ Ο Π Ρ Σ Τ Υ

A

αγαπώ	aghapo	to love
τα Αγγλικά	ta anglika	English
η αγελάδα	i agheladha	cow
άγιος/αγία	ayios/ayia	saint
η αγκαλιά	i angalia	cuddle/hug
αγνός/-η/-ο	aghnos/-i/-o	pure
η αγορά	i aghora	market
αγοράζω	aghorazo	to buy
το αγόρι	to aghori	boy/boyfriend
άγριος/-α/-ο	aghrios/-a/-o	wild/savage
το αγρόκτημα	to aghroktima	farm
ο αγρότης	o aghrotis	farmer
ο αγώνας	o aghonas	sports game/match/race
οι αγώνες	i aghones	championships
το αγωνιστικό ποδήλατο	to aghonistiko podhilato	racing bike
η άδεια	i adhia	permission/permit
άδειος/-α/-ο	adhios/-a/-o	empty/vacant
η αδελφή	i adhelfi	sister
ο αδελφός	o adhelfos	brother
αδιανόητο	adhiano-ito	incomprehensible
αδύναμος/-η/-ο	adhinamos/-i/-o	weak
αδύνατος/-η/-ο	adhinatos/-i/-o	thin/impossible
ο αέρας	o aeras	air/wind
το AIDS	to eids	AIDS
η αίθουσα αναμονής	i ethusa anamonis	waiting room
το αίμα	to ema	blood
αισθάνομαι	esthanome	to feel
ακίνδυνος/-η/-ο	akindhinos/-i/-o	safe (adj)
ακυρώνω	akirono	to cancel
ακόμη	akomi	yet
ακουμπώ (ακούμπησα)	akumbo (akumbisa)	to touch
ακούω (άκουσα)	akuo (akusa)	to hear/listen
ακριβός/-η/-ο	akrivos/-i/-o	expensive
η ακρογιαλιά	i akroyialia	beach/coast
το αλάτι	to alati	salt
το αλεύρι	to alevri	flour
η αλήθεια	i alithia	truth

Αλήθεια. alithia	It's true.	
αλλάζω	alazo	to change
αλλά	ala	but
η αλληλογραφία	i alilografia	mail/correspondence
άλλος/-η/-ο	alos/-i/-o	other
η αμαρτία	i amartia	sin
η άμεση ανάγκη	i amesi anangi	emergency
αμέσως	amesos	right now
η άμμος	i amos	sand
το αμπέλι	to ambeli	vine
ο αμπελώνας	o ambelonas	vineyard
αν/εάν	an/ean	if
αναγνωρίζω	anaghnorizo	to recognise
ανακαλύπτω	anakalipto	to discover
ανακατεύω	anakatevo	to mix
τα ανάκτορα	ta anaktora	palace
η ανακύκλωση	i anakiklosi	recycling
αναπαυτικός/-η/-ο	anapaftikos/-i/-o	comfortable
η αναπηρική καρέκλα	i anapiriki karekla	wheelchair
ανάπηρος/-η/-ο	anapiros/-i/-o	disabled
αναπνέω	anapneo	to breathe
ο αναπτήρας	o anaptiras	lighter (n)
η Ανατολή	i anatoli	the east/sunrise/dawn
ανατολικά	anatolika	east (adv)
η αναχώρηση	i anachorisi	departure
ο άνδρας	o andhras	man/husband
το ανέκδοτο	to anekdhoto	joke
το άνθος	to anthos	flower
οι άνθρωποι	i anthropi	people
ανοίγω (άνοιξα)	anigho (aniksa)	to open
η άνοιξη	i aniksi	spring (season)
ανοιχτά	anichta	open (shops)
το ανοιχτήρι	to anichtiri	bottle opener
το ανοιχτήρι κονσέρβας	to anichtiri konservas	tin opener
ανταλλάζω	andalaso	to exchange

Άντε χάσου! ande chasu!	Get lost!	
αντίθετος/-η/-ο	andithetos/-i/-o	opposite (adj)
αντιλαμβάνομαι	andilamvanome	to realise

Greek	Transliteration	English
η αντλία	i andlia	pump (hydraulic)
αντιπυρηνικός/-η/-ο	andipirinikos/-i/-o	antinuclear
η αντισύλληψη	i andisilipsi	contraception
το αντισυλληπτικό χάπι	to andisiliptiko chapi	the Pill
η αξία	i aksia	value (price)
απαίσιος/-α/-ο	apesios/-a/-o	awful/horrible
η απάντηση	i apandisi	answer
απαντώ (απάντησα)	apando (apandisa)	to answer
απαραίτητος/-η/-ο	aparetitos/-i/-o	necessary
απασχολημένος/-η/-ο	apascholimenos/-i/-o	busy
η απάτη	i apati	rip-off
το απειλόμενο είδος	to apilomeno idhos	endangered species
απέναντι	apenandi	across/opposite
η απεργία	i aperyia	a strike
απλός/-η/-ο	aplos/-i/-o	plain/simple
από	apo	from/of
απ'ευθείας	apefthias	direct
από (τον Μάιο)	apo (ton maio)	since (May)
από κάτω	apo kato	below
από πίσω	apo piso	behind
το απόγευμα	to apoyevma	afternoon/evening
ο/η απόγονος	o/i apoghonos	descendent
η απόδειξη	i apodhiksi	receipt
απόμερος/-η/-ο	apomeros/-i/-o	remote
οι αποσκευές	i aposkeves	baggage/luggage
απότομος/-η/-ο	apotomos/-i/-o	steep
αποφασίζω (αποφάσισα)	apofasizo (apofasisa)	to decide
απόψε	apopse	tonight
αργά	argha	late (adv)/slowly
αργός/-η/-ο	arghos/-i/-o	slow (adj)
αρέσει	aresi	to like
ο αριθμός	o arithmos	number
αριστερός/-η/-ο	aristeros/-i/-o	left

Αρκετά!		
arketa!	Enough!	

Greek	Transliteration	English
αρκετοί/-ες/-α	arketi/-es/-a	several
αρνούμαι (αρνήθηκα)	arnume (arnithika)	to deny/refuse
ο αρουραίος	o arureos	rat
η αρρώστεια	i arostia	sickness
άρρωστος/-η/-ο	arostos/-i/-o	ill/sick
το αρτοποιείο	to artopi-io	bakery
αρχαίος/-α/-ο	archeos/-a/-o	ancient

Greek	Transliteration	English
ο/η αρχιτέκτονας	o/i architektonas	architect
αρχίζω (άρχισα)	archizo (archisa)	to begin/to start
το ασανσέρ	to asanser	lift/elevator
ασημένιος/-α/-ο	asimenios/-a/-o	silver (adj)
άστεγος/-η/-ο	asteghos/-i/-o	homeless
τα άστρα	ta astra	stars
η αστυνομία	i astinomia	police
ασυνήθιστος/-η/-ο	asinithistos/-i/-o	unusual
η ασφάλεια	i asfalia	insurance
ασφαλής/-ης/-ες	asfalis/-is/-es	safe (n)
ο ατμός	o atmos	steam
το άτομο	to atomo	person/individual
το ατύχημα	to atichima	accident
αύριο	avrio	tomorrow
αύριο το απόγευμα	avrio to apoyevma	tomorrow afternoon/ evening
αύριο το πρωί	avrio to proi	tomorrow morning
η αυγή	i avyi	dawn
αφήνω (άφησα)	afino (afisa)	to leave
αυτή την εβδομάδα	afti tin evdhomadha	this week
το αυτί	to afti	ear
αυτόν τον μήνα	afton ton mina	this month
το αυτοκίνητο	to aftokinito	car
ο αυτόματος	o aftomatos	automatic teller (ATM)

B

Greek	Transliteration	English
το βαγκονλί	to vagonli	sleeping car
βάζω (έβαλα)	vazo (evala)	to put
βαθύς/-ιά/-ύ	vathis/-ia/-i	deep
το βαμβάκι	to vamvaki	cotton
το βαπόρι	to vapori	ship/boat
βαρετός/-η/-ο	varetos/-i/-o	boring
βαριεστημένος/-η/-ο	variestimenos/-i/-o	bored
βαρύς/-ιά/-υ	varis/-ia/-i	heavy
ο βασιλιάς	o vasilias	king
η βασίλισσα	i vasilisa	queen
η βάφτιση	i vaftisi	baptism
βγαίνω (βγήκα)	vyeno (vyika)	to go out/exit
βγαίνω με	vyeno me	to go out with/date (someone)
η βελόνα	i velona	needle (sewing)

το βεντιλατέρ	to vendilater	fan (machine)
ο βήχας	o vichas	cough (n)
ο βιασμός	o viazmos	rape
το βιβλίο	to vivlio	book
η βιβλιοθήκη	i vivliothiki	library
το βιβλιοπωλείο	to vivliopolio	bookshop
η Βίβλος	i vivlos	the Bible
η βίζα	i viza	visa
το βιογραφικό	to vioghrafiko	resume/curriculum vitae
βλέπω (είδα)	vlepo (idha)	to see/look

Θα δούμε. tha dhume		We'll see.

βοηθάω (βοήθησα)	voithao (voithisa)	to help
η βοήθεια	i voithia	aid (help)
βόρεια	voria	north (adv)
ο βορράς	o voras	the north
τα βότανα	ta votana	herbs
το βουνό	to vuno	mountain
η βούρτσα	i vurtsa	hairbrush
το βράδυ	to vradhi	evening
ο βράχος	o vrachos	rock
βρεμένος/-η/-ο	vremenos/-i/-o	wet
βρίσκω (βρήκα)	vrisko (vrika)	to find
η βροχή	i vrochi	rain

Βρέχει. vrechi		It's raining.

Γ

βρώμικος/-η/-ο	vromikos/-i/-o	dirty
η γάζα	i ghaza	bandage
το γάλα	to ghala	milk
ο γάμος	o ghamos	wedding/marriage
η γάτα	i ghata	cat
το γατάκι	to ghataki	kitten
γελώ (γέλασα)	yelo (yelasa)	to laugh
γεμάτος/-η/-ο	yematos/-i/-o	full
γενναίος/-α/-ο	yeneos/-a/-o	brave
τα γενέθλια	ta yenethlia	birthday
γέρος/γριά	yeros/ghria	old (for people)
γευστικός/-η/-ο	yefstikos/-i/-o	tasty

Δ

Greek	Transliteration	English
η γέφυρα	i yefira	bridge
η Γη	i yi	Earth
για	ya	for
για πάντα	ya panda	forever
για πλάκα	ya plaka	for fun
η γιαγιά	i yiayia	grandmother
γιατί	yiati	why/because
ο/η γιατρός	o/i yiatros	doctor
γιορτάζω (γιόρτασα)	yiortazo (yiortasa)	to celebrate
η γιορτή	i yiorti	festival; saint's day
ο γιος	o yios	son
η γκαλερί τέχνης	i galeri technis	art gallery
η γκαρνταρόμπα	i gardaroba	cloakroom
γκαρσόν	garson	waiter
η γκραβούρα	gravura	a print (artwork)
ο γκρεμός	o gremos	cliff
γλυκός/-ια/-ο	ghlikos/-ia/-o	sweet
η γλυπτική	i ghliptiki	sculpture
η γλώσσα	i ghlossa	language
η γνώμη	i ghnomi	opinion
οι γονείς	i ghonis	parents
το γράμμα	to ghrama	letter (alphabet/mail)
το γραμμάριο	to ghramario	gram
τα γραμματόσημα	ta ghramatosima	stamps
η γραμμή	i ghrami	line
το γραφείο πληροφοριών	to ghrafio pliroforion	tourist information office
γράφω	ghrafo	to write
γρήγορα	ghrighora	fast (adv)
γρήγορος/-η/-ο	ghrighoros/-i/-o	quick
η γυάλα	i yiala	jar
το γυαλί	to yiali	glass (windows)
τα γυαλιά ηλίου	ta yialia iliu	sunglasses
η γυναίκα	i yineka	woman/wife
η γωνία	i ghonia	corner

Δ

Greek	Transliteration	English
το δάγκωμα	to dhangoma	bite (dog)
το δάκτυλο	to dhaktilo	finger
δανείζομαι (δανείστηκα)	dhanizome (dhanistika)	to borrow
δανείζω (δάνεισα)	dhanizo (dhanisa)	to lend
ο/η δάσκαλος/δασκάλα	o/i dhaskalos/dhaskala	teacher

Greek	Transliteration	English
το δάσος	to dhasos	forest
ο δείκτης	o dhiktis	indicator
το δείπνο	to dhipno	dinner
το δέμα	to dhema	package/parcel
δεν	dhen	not

Δεν βαριέσαι!		
dhen variese!	Forget about it!; Don't worry!	

Greek	Transliteration	English
το δέντρο	to dhendro	tree
δεξιά	dheksia	right (adv)
το δέρμα	to dherma	leather/skin
το δευτερόλεπτο	to dhefterolepto	second (n)
δεχομαι (δέχτηκα)	dhechome (dhechtika)	to accept/receive
ο δήμαρχος	o dhimarchos	mayor
η δημόσια τουαλέττα	i dhimosia tualeta	public toilet
ο/η δημοσιογράφος	o/i dhimosioghrafos	journalist
δημοφιλής/-ης/-ες	dhimofilis/-is/-es	popular
διαβάζω (διάβασα)	dhiavazo (dhiavasa)	to read
το διαβατήριο	to dhiavatirio	passport
διαβητικός/-η/-ο	dhiavitikos/-i/-o	diabetic
η διαδρομή	i dhiadhromi	route
ο διαιτητής	o dietitis	referee
οι διακοπές	i dhiakopes	holidays
το διάλειμμα	to dhialima	intermission
το διαμέρισμα	to dhiamerizma	flat (appartment)
η διαμονή	i dhiamoni	accommodation
η διάρροια	i dhiaria	diarrhoea
διάσιμος/-η/-ο	dhiasimos/-i/-o	famous
διασκεδαστικός/-η/-ο	dhiaskedhastikos /-i/-o	entertaining
διασκεδάζω (διασκέδασα)	dhiaskedhazo (dhiaskedhasa)	to enjoy oneself
το διάστημα	to dhiastima	space (universe)
η διαταγή	i dhiatayi	order/command
διαφορετικός/-η/-ο	dhiaforetikos/-i/-o	different
διδάσκω (δίδαξα)	dhidhasko (dhidhaksa)	to teach
τα δίδυμα	ta dhidhima	twins
η διεύθυνση	i dhiefthinsi	address
το δικαστήριο	to dhikastirio	court (legal)
ο/η δικαστής	o/i dhikastis	judge
η δικαιοσύνη	i dhikeosini	justice
ο/η δικηγόρος	o/i dhikighoros	lawyer
δίνω (έδωσα)	dhino (edhosa)	to give
δίπλα	dhipla	beside

δίπλα σε	dhipla se	next to
διπλός/-η/-ο	dhiplos/-i/-o	double
το διπλό δωμάτιο	to dhiplo dhomatio	a double room
το διπλό κρεββάτι	to dhiplo krevati	a double bed
διψάω (δίψασα)	dipsao (dipsasa)	to be thirsty
το δόντι	to dhondi	tooth
η δουλειά	i dhulia	work
η δουλειά γραφείου	i dhulia ghrafiu	office work
δουλεύω (δούλεψα)	dhulevo (dhulepsa)	to work
το δράμα	to dhrama	drama
ο δρόμος	o dhromos	road/way (direction)
η δύναμη	i dhinami	power/strength
δυνατός/-η/-ο	dhinatos/-i/-o	loud/strong
δυνατός/-η/-ο	dhinatos/-i/-o	possible

| (Δεν) είναι δυνατό. | (dhen) ine dhinato | It's (not) possible. |

η δύση	i dhisi	west/sunset
δύσκολος/-η/-ο	dhiskolos/-i/-o	difficult
η δυσπεψία	i dhispepsia	indigestion
δυτικά	dhitika	west (adv)
το δωμάτιο	to dhomatio	room
δωρεάν	dhorean	free (of charge)
το δώρο	to dhoro	gift/present
η δωροδοκία	i dhorodhokia	bribery

E

η (ε)βδομάδα	i evdhomadha	week
Εβραίος/-α	evreos/-a	Jewish
το εγγόνι	to engoni	grandchild
το έγκαυμα ηλίου	to engavma iliu	sunburn
έγκυος	engios	pregnant
η εγχείρηση	i enchirisi	operation (medical)
εγώ	egho	I
εγωιστής/εγωίστρια	eghoistis/eghoistria	selfish
εδώ	edho	here
εδώ και	edho ke	ago/since
τα έθιμα	ta ethima	customs (habits)
η εθνική οδός	i ethniki odhos	motorway (tollway)
ο εθνικός δρυμός	o ethnikos dhrimos	national park
ειδικός/-η/-ο	idhikos/-i/-o	special/particular
το είδος	to idhos	kind (type)

Greek	Transliteration	English
η ειρήνη	i irini	peace
το εισιτήριο	to isitirio	ticket
η είσοδος	i isodhos	admission
εκατό	ekato	a hundred
το εκατοστό	to ekatosto	centimetre
η εκδάσωση	i ekdhasosi	deforestation
το εκδοτήριο εισιτηρίων	to ekdhotirio isitirion	ticket office
η έκθεση	i ekthesi	exhibition
η εκκλησία	i eklisia	church
οι εκλογές	i ekloyes	elections
η εκπαίδευση	i ekpedhefsi	education
ο εκπαιδευτής	o ekpedheftis	instructor
η έκπληξη	i ekpliksi	surprise (n)
η έκπτωση	i ekptosi	discount/on sale
η έκτρωση	i ektrosi	abortion
το ελαιόλαδο	to eleoladho	olive oil
ελαττωματικός/-η/-ο	elatomatikos/-i/-o	faulty
ελαφρύς/-ια/-υ	elafris/-ia/-i	light (adj)
ελέγχω	elencho	to check
ελεύθερος/-η/-ο	eleftheros/-i/-o	free/single (person)
οι ελιές	i elies	olives
η έλλειψη	i elipsi	shortage
το εμβόλιο	to emvolio	vaccination
εμείς	emis	we
έμμεσος/-η/-ο	emesos/-i/-o	non-direct
η εμπιστοσύνη	i embistosini	trust
ο έμπορας ναρκωτικών	o emboras narkotikon	drug dealer
το εμφιαλωμένο νερό	to emfialomeno nero	mineral/bottled water
εναντίον	enandion	against
ενδιαφέρων/-ουσα/-ον	endhiaferon/-usa/-on	interesting
η ένεση	i enesi	injection
το ενοίκιο	to enikio	rent
εντάξει	endaksi	OK
η ένταση	i endasi	volume (sound)
έντονος/-η/-ο	endonos/-i/-o	intense
η ενόχληση	i enochlisi	harrassment
το εξάνθημα	to eksanthima	a rash
η έξοδος	i eksodhos	exit
ο εξοπλισμός	o eksoplizmos	equipment
η εξοχή	i eksochi	countryside
έξω	ekso	outside
στο εξωτερικό	sto eksoteriko	abroad

Greek	Transliteration	English
το επάγγελμα	to epangelma	profession
επάνω	epano	above/over
επειδή	epidhi	because
επείγον	epighon	urgent
ο/η επιβάτης	o/i epivatis	passenger
επιβεβαιώνω	epiveveono	to confirm (a booking)
επιβιβάζομαι	epivivazome	to board (ship etc)
επιζώ	epizo	to survive
επιθετικός/-η/-ο	epithetikos/-i/-o	aggressive
το επίθετο	to epitheto	surname
επικίνδυνος/-η/-ο	epikindhinos/-i/-o	dangerous
επίσης	episis	also/too
επισκέφτομαι	episkeftome	to visit
επιστρέφω	epistrefo	to return
η επιστροφή χρημάτων	i epistrofi chrimaton	refund
επιτρέπω	epitrepo	to allow

(Δεν) Επιτρέπεται. (dhen) epitrepete		It's (not) allowed.

Greek	Transliteration	English
η επιτυχία	i epitichia	success
η επιχείρηση	i epichirisi	business (company)
επόμενος/-η/-ο	epomenos/-i/-o	next
την επόμενη εβδομάδα	tin epomeni evdhomadha	next week
τον επόμενο μήνα	ton epomeno mina	next month
εργάζομαι (εργάστηκα)	erghazome (erghastika)	to work
η εργασία	i erghasia	work
τα ερείπια	ta eripia	ruins
η έρημος	i erimos	desert
έρχομαι (ήρθα)	erchome (irtha)	to come
ερωμένος/-η	eromenos/-i	lover
η ερώτηση	i erotisi	question
εσύ/εσείς	esi (inf)/esis (pol)	you
ετοιμάζω (ετοίμασα)	etimazo (etimasa)	to prepare
έτοιμος/-η/-ο	etimos/-i/-o	ready
η ευκαιρία	i efkeria	chance
εύκολος/-η/-ο	efkolos/-i/-o	easy
ευχαριστώ	efcharisto	to thank
εύχομαι	efchome	to wish
η εφημερίδα	i efimeridha	newspaper
έχω	echo	to have
έχω ναυτία	echo naftia	to be seasick

Z

Greek	Transliteration	English
ζαλισμένος/-η/-ο	zalizmenos/-i/-o	dizzy
τα ζάρια	ta zaria	dice
η ζάχαρη	i zachari	sugar
η ζέστη	i zesti	heat
ζεστός/-η/-ο	zestos/-i/-o	hot/warm
ζεστό νερό	zesto nero	hot water
ένα ζευγάρι	enazevghari	a pair/couple
ζηλιάρης/-α	ziliaris/-a	jealous
ο ζητιάνος	o zitianos	beggar
ζητώ (ζήτησα)	zito (zitisa)	to ask for
ζυγίζω (ζύγισα)	ziyizo (ziyisa)	to weigh
ζω (έζησα)	zo (ezisa)	to live (exist)
ζωγραφίζω	zoghrafizo	to paint (art)
η ζωγραφική	i zoghrafiki	painting (art)
το ζώδιο	to zodhio	zodiac
το ζώο	to zo-o	animal
η ζωή	i zoi	life
η ζώνη ασφαλείας	i zoni asfalias	seatbelt

H

ή	i	or
ο ηλεκτρισμός	o ilektrizmos	electricity
ηλίθιος/-α/-ο	ilithios/-a/-o	idiotic
η ηλικία	i ilikia	age
ο ήλιος	o ilios	sun
η (η)μέρα	i (i)mera-a/-o	day
ημερήσιος/-α/-ο	imerisios/-a/-o	daily
η ημερομηνία	i imerominia	date (time)
η ημερομηνία γεννήσεως	i imerominia yeniseos	date of birth
ο ήρωας	o iroas	hero
ήσυχος/-η/-ο	isichos/-i/-o	quiet
η ήττα	i ita	loss
ο ήχος	o ichos	sound

Θ

η θάλασσα	i thalasa	sea
ο θάνατος	o thanatos	death
θαυμάζω	thavmazo	to admire
θαυμάσιος/-α/-ο	thavmasios/-a/-o	wonderful/excellent
η θέα	i thea	view

θέλω (ήθελα)	thelo (ithela)	to want
το θέμα	to thema	topic/issue/subject
ο Θεός	o theos	God
η θέρμανση	i thermansi	heating
η θέση	i thesi	seat
ο θόρυβος	o thorivos	noise
θορυβώδης/-ης/-ες	thorivodhis/-is/-es	noisy
η θρησκεία	i thriskia	religion
θρήσκος/-η	thriskos/-i	religious
θυμάμαι	thimame	to remember
θυμωμένος/-η/-ο	thimomenos/-i/-o	angry/cross

I

ιδιοκτήτης/ιδιοκτήτρια	idhioktitis/idhioktitria	owner
ίδιος/-α/-ο	idhios/-a/-o	same
ιδιωτικός/-η/-ο	idhiotikos/-i/-o	private
ο ιός	o ios	virus
η ισότητα	i isotita	equality
η ιστορία	i istoria	story/history
ίσως	isos	maybe

K

καβαλικεύω	kavalikevo	to ride (a horse)
το καθάρισμα	to katharizma	cleaning
καθαρός/-η/-ο	katharos/-i/-o	clean
κάθε μέρα	kathe mera	every day
ο καθεδρικός ναός	o kathedhrikos naos	cathedral
καθόλου	katholu	none
κάθομαι	kathome	to sit
ο καθρέφτης	o kathreftis	mirror
η καθυστέρηση	i kathisterisi	delay
και/κι	ke/ki	and
και τα δύο	ke ta dhio	both
καινούργιος/-α/-ο	kenuryios/-a/-o	new
ο καιρός	o keros	time (general)/ weather
κακός/κακιά/κακό	kakos/kakia/kako	bad
καλά	kala	well
το καλάθι	to kalathi	basket

Καλή όρεξη!
kali oreksi!   Bon appetit!

Καλή τύχη! kali tichi!		Good luck!
ο/η καλλιτέχνης	o/i kalitechnis	artist
καλός/-η/-ο	kalos/-i/-o	good/nice/kind

Καλό ταξίδι! kalo taksidhi!		Bon voyage!
ο καλόγερος	o kaloyeros	monk
η καλόγρια	i kaloghria	nun
το καλοκαίρι	to kalokeri	summer
το καλοριφέρ	to kalorifer	radiator
καλύτερα	kalitera	better (adv)
καλύτερος/-η/-ο	kaliteros/-i/-o	better (adj)
καλώς ήλθατε	kalos ilthate	welcome
κανένας/καμμία/κανένα	kanenas/kamia/kanena	anyone/noone
οι κανονισμοί	i kanonizmi	rules/regulations
κάνω	kano	to do

Τι κάνεις; ti kanis?		What are you doing?/How are you?
κάνω απεργία	kano aperyia	to be on strike
κάνω ένεση	kano enesi	to inject
κάνω πεζοπορία	kano pezoporia	to hike
κάνω πλάκα	kano plaka	to joke
κάνω ωτοστοπ	kano otostop	to hitchhike
καπνίζω	kapnizo	to smoke
κάποιος/-α/-ο	kapios/-a/-o	somebody/someone
το καράβι	to karavi	ship/boat
η καραντίνα	i karantina	quarantine
η καρδιά	i kardhia	heart
η καρέκλα	i karekla	chair
η κάρτα επιβίβασης	i karta epivivasis	boarding pass
το κασκώλ	to kaskol	scarf
η καταιγίδα	i kateyidha	storm
καταλαβαίνω	katalaveno	to understand
καταπληκτικός/-η/-ο	katapliktikos/-i/-o	brilliant
ο καταρράχτης	o katarachtis	waterfall
κατασκηνώνω	kataskinono	to camp
το κατάστημα	to katastima	shop
καταστρέφω	o katastrefo	to destroy
το κατάστρωμα	to katastroma	deck (of ship)
το καταφύγιο	to katafiyio	mountain hut/refuge

Greek	Transliteration	English
κάτι	kati	something
η κατσαρόλα	i katsarola	pan
ο καυγάς	o kavghas	fight/quarrel
ο καύσωνας	o kafsonas	heatwave
κεντρικός/-η/-ο	kendrikos/-i/-o	central
η κεντρική πλατεία	i kendriki platia	main square
ο κεντρικός δρόμος	o kendrikos dhromos	main road
το κέντρο της πόλης	to kendro tis polis	city centre
κεραμικός/-η/-ο	keramikos/-i/-o	ceramic
κερδίζω	kerdhizo	to win/earn
το κέρδος	to kerdhos	profit
τα κέρματα	ta kermata	coins
το κεφάλι	to kefali	head
η κηδεία	i kidhia	funeral
ο κήπος	o kipos	gardens
ο κίνδυνος	o kindhinos	risk/danger
τα κινούμενα σχέδια	ta kinumena schedhia	cartoons
κιόλας	kiolas	already
κλέβω (έκλεψα)	klevo (eklepsa)	to steal/rob
η κλειδαριά	i klidharia	lock
το κλειδί	to klidhi	key
κλείνω (έκλεισα)	klino (eklisa)	to close/shut
κλείνω θέση	klino thesi	to book (make a booking)
κλειστά	klista	closed (shop)
κλειστός/-η/-ο	klistos/-i/-o	closed (adj)
ο κλέφτης	o kleftis	thief
το κλήμα	to klima	vine
κλιματιζόμενος/-η/-ο	klimatizomenos/-i/-o	air-conditioned
η κλωτσιά	i klotsia	kick
κόβω	kovo	to cut
η κοιλάδα	ii kiladha	valley
κοιμάμαι	kimame	to sleep
η κοινωνική ασφάλεια	i kinoniki asfalia	social security
το κόκκαλο	to kokalo	bone
κόκκινος/-η/-ο	kokinos	red
το κολιέ	to kolie	necklace
το κολλέγιο	to koleyio	college
κολυμπάω (κολύμπησα)	kolimbao (kolimbisa)	to swim
το κολύμπι	to kolibi	swimming
το κόμμα	to koma	party (politics)
το κομμάτι	to komati	piece
η κονσέρβα	i konserva	tin/can

288

GREEK – ENGLISH

Greek	Transliteration	English
κοντά	konda	near/close by
η κόρη	i kori	daughter
το κορίτσι	to koritsi	girl/girlfriend
κοστίζω (κόστισα)	kostizo (kostisa)	to cost
η κότα	i kota	chicken (animal)
το κοτόπουλο	to kotopulo	chicken (food)
το κρασί	to krasi	wine
το κρεββάτι	to krevati	bed
κρύος/-α/-ο	krios/-a/-o	cold (adj)
κρύο νερό	krio nero	cold water
το κρυολόγημα	to krioloyima	a cold
ο κουβάς	o kuvas	bucket
η κουβέρτα	i kuverta	blanket
η κουζίνα	i kuzina	kitchen/cooking stove
τα κουμπιά	ta kubia	buttons
το κουνέλι	to kuneli	rabbit
η κούνια	i kunia	hammock/swing
κουρασμένος/-η/-ο	kurazmenos/-i/-o	tired
το κουτί	to kuti	box/carton
το κτίριο	to ktirio	building
τα κυάλια	ta kialia	binoculars
η κυβέρνηση	i kivernisi	government
η κυκλοφορία	i kikloforia	traffic/circulation
το κύμα	to kima	wave
η κωμωδία	i komodhia	comedy
η κωπηλασία	i kopilasia	rowing
κωφάλαλος	kofalalos	mute (n)

Λ

το λάδι	to ladhi	oil (cooking)
το λάθος	to lathos	mistake/fault
κάνω λάθος	kano lathos	to make a mistake

Λάθος μου. lathos mu	I'm wrong (it's my fault).

Greek	Transliteration	English
ο λαιμός	o lemos	throat/neck
η λάσπη	i laspi	mud
τα λάστιχα	ta lasticha	tyres
το λαχανικό	to lachaniko	vegetable
λείπω (έλειψα)	lipo (elipsa)	to miss; be absent; short of

289

D
I
C
T
I
O
N
A
R
Y

Μου λείπεις. mu lipis		I miss you.
η λειτουργία	i lituryia	service (religious)
η λέξη	i leksi	word
το λεξικό	to leksiko	dictionary
ένα λεπτό	ena lepto	a minute
η λεπτομέρεια	i leptomeria	detail
λεπτός/-η/-ο	leptos/-i/-o	thin/fine
η λεσβία	i lesvia	lesbian
τα λεφτά (pl)	ta lefta	money
λέω (είπα)	leo (ipa)	to say/to tell
λέω ψέμματα	leo psemata	to lie
το λεωφορείο	to leoforio	bus
η λεωφόρος	i leoforos	avenue
η λιακάδα	i liakadha	sunshine
λίγοι/λίγες/λίγα	liyi/liyes/ligha	few/some
λίγο	ligho	a little (amount)
λιγότερος/-η/-ο	lighoteros/-i/-o	less
το λιμάνι	to limani	harbour/port
η λίμνη	i limni	lake
ο λογαριασμός	o loghariazmos	bill (in a restaurant)
ο λόγος	o loghos	reason/cause
το λουκέτο	to luketo	padlock
το λουλούδι	to luludhi	flower
ο λόφος	o lofos	hill
λυπημένος/-η/-ο	lipimenos/-i/-o	sad

M

το μαγαζί	to maghazi	shop
μαγειρεύω (μαγείρεψα)	mayirevo (mayirepsa)	to cook
το μαγιό	to mayio	bathing suit
μαζί	mazi	together
μαθαίνω	matheno	to learn
μακριά	makria	far
μακρύς/-ια/-υ	makris/-ia/-i	long
το μαλλί	to mali	wool
τα μαλλιά	ta malia	hair
η μαμά	i mama	Mum
ο μανάβης	o manavis	greengrocer
μαντεύω	mandevo	to guess
το μαξιλάρι	to maksilari	pillow
το μασάζ	to masaz	massage

Greek	Transliteration	English
μαστουρωμένος/-η	masturomenos/-i	stoned (drugged)
το μάτι	to mati	eye
το μαχαίρι	to macheri	knife
με	me	with
μεγάλος/-η/-ο	meghalos/-i/-o	big/large/great
το μέγεθος	to meyethos	size
μεθυσμένος/-η/-ο	methizmenos/-i/-o	drunk (sloshed)
το μειονέκτημα	to mionektima	disadvantage
η μελανιά	i melania	bruise
το μέλι	to meli	honey
το μέλλον	to melon	future
το μενού	to menu	menu
μένω	meno	to live (somewhere)/ stay
η μέρα	i mera	day
μερικοί/-ες/-α	meriki/-es/-s	some
η μεροληψία	i merolipsia	discrimination
το μέρος	to meros	part/section/place
μέσα	mesa	in/inside
το μεσημεριανό	to mesimeriano	lunch
μετά	meta	after
το μετάλιο	to metalio	medal
η μετανάστευση	i metanastefsi	migration
μετανιώνω	metaniono	to regret
το μετάξι	to metaksi	silk
μεταξύ	metaksi	between
μεταφράζω	metafrazo	to translate
ο μετεωρίτης	o meteoritis	meteor
μετρώ	metro	to count
μέχρι	mechri	until
μη(ν)	mi(n)	not/don't
μη ασφαλές	mi asfales	unsafe
ο μήνας	o minas	month
ο μήνας του μέλιτος	o minas tu melitos	honeymoon
το μήνυμα	to minima	message
η μητέρα	i mitera	mother
μικρός/-η/-ο	mikros/-i/-o	little/small
μιλάω (μίλησα)	milao (milisa)	to speak/talk
ο μισθός	o misthos	salary
μισός/-η/-ο	misos/-i/-o	half
το μνημείο	to mnimio	monument
μοιράζομαι	mirazome	to share (with)
η μόλυνση	i molinsi	pollution

το μολύβι	to molivi	pencil
μόνιμος/-η/-ο	monimos/-i/-o	permanent
μόνος/-η/-ο	monos/-i/-o	alone
μονός/-η/-ο	monos/-i/-o	single
μόνο	mono	only
το μονοπάτι	to monopati	footpath
η μουσική	i musiki	music
το μουσείο	to musio	museum
μπαίνω (μπήκα)	beno (bika)	to enter
το μπαλκόνι	to balkoni	balcony
ο μπαμπάς	o babas	dad
το μπάνιο	to banio	bathroom
η μπαταρία	i bataria	battery
το μποξ	to boks	boxing
μπορώ	boro	to be able (can)
οι μπότες	i botes	boots
το μπουκάλι	to bukali	bottle
μπροστά	brosta	ahead/in front of
το μυθιστόρημα	to mithistorima	novel (book)
μυρίζω	mirizo	to smell
η μυρωδιά	i mirodhia	smell (n)
ο μυς	o mis	muscle
η μύτη	i miti	nose
Μωαμεθανός/-ή	moamethanos/-i	Muslim
το μωρό	to moro	baby

N

ο ναός	o naos	temple
η ναρκομανία	i narkomania	drug addiction
η ναυτία	i naftia	nausea/travel sickness
τα νέα	ta nea	news
νεκρός/-η/-ο	nekros/-i/-o	dead
η νεολαία	i neolea	youth (collective)
νέος/-α/-ο	neos/-a/-o	young
το νερό	to nero	water
το νηπιαγωγείο	to nipiaghoyio	kindergarten
το νησί	to nisi	island
ο νικητής	o nikitis	winner
νοικιάζω	nikiazo	to hire/to rent
ο νόμος	o nomos	law
το νοσοκομείο	to nosokomio	hospital

νότια	notia	south (adv)
ο Νότος	o notos	the south
ο νους	o nus	mind (n)
ντροπαλός/-η/-ο	dropalos/-i/-o	shy
η ντροπή	i dropi	embarassment
το ντουζ	to duz	shower
μια ντουζίνα	mia duzina	a dozen
η ντουλάπα	i dulapa	cupboard/wardrobe
νυσταγμένος/-η/-ο	nistaghmenos/-i/-o	sleepy
η νύχτα	i nichta	night
νωρίς	noris	early

Ξ

ξανά	ksana	again
ξαπλώνω	ksaplono	to lie down
ξεκουράζομαι	ksekurazome	to rest
η ξεκούραση	i ksekurasi	rest/relaxation
το ξενοδοχείο	to ksenodhochio	hotel
ξένος/-η/-ο	ksenos/-i/-o	foreigner/stranger
ο ξενώνας νεότητας	o ksenonas neotitas	youth hostel
ξέρω	ksero	to know
ξεχνώ (ξέχασα)	ksechno (ksechasa)	to forget
ξεχωρίζω (ξεχώρισα)	ksechorizo (ksechorisa)	to separate
τα ξημερώματα	ta ksimeromata	dawn
το ξίφος	to ksifos	sword
το ξύλο	to ksilo	wood
το ξύλο για καύσιμα	to ksilo ya kafsima	firewood
το ξυπνητήρι	to ksipnitiri	alarm clock
το ξυράφι	to ksirafi	razor
ξυρίζομαι	ksirizome	to shave

Ο

ο όγκος	o ongos	volume (cubic space)
ο οδηγός	o odhighos	guide/driver
οδηγώ	odhigho	to drive
ο οδικός χάρτης	o odhikos chartis	road map
η οδοιπορία	i odhiporia	trek
ο/η οδοντίατρος	o/i odhondiatros	dentist
το οδοντικό νήμα	to odhondiko nima	dental floss
η οδοντόβουρτσα	i odhondovurtsa	toothbrush
η οδός	i odhos	street
οδυνηρός/-η/-ο	odhiniros/-i/-o	painful

η οθόνη	i othoni	screen
η οικογένεια	i ikoyenia	family
η οικονομία	i ikonomia	the economy
η οινοποιία	i inopi-ia	winery
όλοι/-ες/-α	oli/-es/-a	all
ολόκληρος/-η/-ο	olokliros/-i/-o	whole/entire
η ομάδα	i omadha	team
η ομοιοπαθητική	i omiopathitiki	homeopathy
όμορφος/-η/-ο	omorfos/-i/-o	beautiful/pretty/handsome
ομοφυλόφιλος	omofilofilos	homosexual
ονειρεύομαι	onirevome	to dream
το όνομα	to onoma	name
το οξυγόνο	to oksighono	oxygen
ο οπαδός	o opadhos	fan (of a team)

Ορίστε; oriste?		Excuse me/Beg your pardon?
η ορχήστρα	i orchistra	band (music)
οργανώνω	orghanono	to organise
ο οργασμός	o orghazmos	orgasm
το όριο ταχύτητας	to orio tachititas	speed limit
η ορειβασία	i orivasia	mountaineering
το οροπέδιο	to oropedhio	plateau
το όρος	to oros	mountain
η οροσειρά	i orosira	mountain range
ο όροφος	o orofos	floor (storey)
το όστρακο	to ostrako	shell
η ουρά	i ura	queue/tail
ο ουρανός	o uranos	sky
ούτε ... ούτε	ute ... ute	neither ... nor
όχι	ochi	no
όχι ακόμα	ochi akoma	not yet

Π

παγκόσμιος/-α/-ο	pangosmios/-a/-o	international
ο πάγος	o paghos	ice
το παγωτό	to paghoto	icecream
το παιδί	to pedhi	child
παίζω (έπαιξα)	pezo (epeksa)	to play
παίρνω (πήρα)	perno (pira)	to take
το παιχνίδι	to pechnidhi	a game

παλιός/-α/-ο	palios/-a/-o	old (objects)
η παλιά πόλη	i palia poli	old city
η παλίρροια	i paliria	tide
το παλτό	to palto	coat
η πάνα	i pana	nappy
το πανεπιστήμιο	to panepistimio	university
το πανηγύρι	to paniyiri	feast
πάντα	panda	always
παντρεύομαι	pandrevome	to marry
πάνω	pano	up
ο παπάς	o papas	priest
τα παπούτσια	ta paputsia	shoes
ο παππούς	o papus	grandfather
παραγγέλνω	paragelno	to order (food etc)
παράγω	paragho	to produce
ο/η παραγωγός	o/i paraghoghos	producer
το παράδειγμα	to paradhighma	example

Για παράδειγμα/παραδείγματος χάρη ...
ya paradhigma/paradhighmatos chari ...
For example ...

το παράθυρο	to parathiro	window
η παραλαβή αποσκευών	i paralavi aposkevon	baggage claim
η παραλία	i paralia	beach/coast/seaside
η παραμονή της Πρωτοχρονιάς	i paramoni tis protochronias	New Year's Eve
η παραμονή των Χριστουγέννων	i paramoni ton christuyenon	Christmas Eve
η παράσταση	i parastasi	performance
παρατώ (παράτησα)	parato (paratisa)	to quit
η παρέα	i parea	company (friends)/ group of friends
το παρελθόν	to parelthon	past (n)
παρκάρω	parkaro	to park
το πάρκο	to parko	a park
παρόμοιος/-α/-ο	paromios/-a/-o	similar
το παρόν	to paron	present (time)
η παρουσίαση	i parusiasi	presentation
το Πάσχα	to pascha	Easter
ο πατέρας	o pateras	father
το πάτωμα	to patoma	floor
παχύς/-ια/-υ	pachis/-ia/-i	thick/fat
πάω (πήγα)	pao (piya)	to go

η πεδιάδα	i pedhiadha	plain (flat area)
η πεζοπορία	i pezoporia	hiking/walking
πεθαίνω (πέθανα)	petheno (pethana)	to die
πεινάω	pinao	to be hungry
πειράζει	pirazi	to mind/bother
πεισματάρης/-α	pismataris/-a	stubborn
ο πελάτης	o pelatis	client
το πέος	to peos	penis
το περιβάλλον	to perivalon	environment
περίεργος/-η/-ο	perierghos/-i/-o	strange
η περιήγηση	i peri-iyisi	tour
περιμένω	perimeno	to wait
το περιοδικό	to periodhiko	magazine
η περίοδος	i periodhos	menstruation/period
ο περίπατος	o peripatos	a walk/stroll
το περίπτερο	to periptero	kiosk
περισσότερος/-η/-ο	perisoteros/-i/-o	more
περνάω καλά	pernao kala	to have a good time
περπατώ	perpato	to walk
η πεταλούδα	i petaludha	butterfly
η πέτρα	i petra	stone
η πετσέτα	i petseta	towel
το πεύκο	to pefko	pine
πηγαίνω (πήγα)	pigheno (pigha)	to go

πηδάω	pidhao	to jump/fuck (slang)
το πιάτο	to piato	plate
η πίεση	i piesi	pressure
πικάντικος/-η/-ο	pikandikos/-i/-o	spicy (hot)
ο πίνακας	o pinakas	painting/blackboard
η πινακίδα	i pinakidha	signpost
πίνω	pino	to drink
η πίπα	i pipa	pipe
η πιπίλα	i pipila	dummy/pacifier
πιστός/-η/-ο	pistos/-i/-o	loyal
η πιστωτική κάρτα	i pistotiki karta	credit card
πίσω	piso	at the back (behind)
η πίτα	i pita	pie
το πλάι	to plai	side
η πλάκα	i plaka	fun/slab (stone)
ο πλανήτης	o planitis	planet

Greek	Transliteration	English
η πλατεία	i platia	town square
η πλάτη	i plati	back (body)
πλατύς/-ια/-υ	platis/-ia/-i	flat (adj)
η πλειοψηφία	i pliopsifia	majority
πλένομαι	plenome	to wash
πλένω	pleno	to wash (something)
το πλεονέκτημα	to pleonektima	advantage
η πληγή	i pliyi	wound
η πληρωμή	i pliromi	payment
πληρώνω	plirono	to pay
πλούσιος/-α/-ο	plusios/-a/-o	rich
το πόδι	to podhi	foot/leg
το ποδόσφαιρο	to podhosfero	football (soccer)
η ποίηση	i pi-isi	poetry
η ποιότητα	i pioita	quality
ο πόλεμος	o polemos	war
η πόλη	i poli	city
πολλοί/-ες/-α	poli/-es/-a	many/a lot
η πολυτέλεια	i politelia	luxury
πολύτιμος/-η/-ο	politimos	valuable
ο πόνος	o ponos	a pain
το ποντίκι	to pondiki	mouse (animal/ computer)
η πορεία	i poria	itinerary/hike
η πόρτα	i porta	door
ο ποταμός	o potamos	river
ποτέ	pote	never
πότε	pote	when

Πότε φεύγει; pote fevyi	When does it leave?

Greek	Transliteration	English
πότε πότε	pote pote	sometimes
το ποτήρι	to potiri	glass (drinking vessel)
το ποτό	to poto	a drink
ο/η πρέσβης	o/i presvis	ambassador
η πρεσβεία	i prezvia	embassy
η πρίζα	i priza	plug (electric)
πριν	prin	before
πριν από	prin apo	ago
το προάστιο	to proastio	suburb
το πρόβατο	to provato	sheep
ο/η πρόεδρος	o/i proedhros	president

προειδοποιώ	proidhopio	to warn
προηγούμενος/-η/-ο	pro-ighumenos/-i/-o	last (previous)
ο προορισμός	o pro-orizmos	destination
η πρόνοια	i pronia	welfare
το προξενείο	to proksenio	consulate
προς	pros	towards
ο προσαρμοστής	o prosarmostis	adaptor
η προσευχή	i prosefchi	prayer
τα προσόντα	ta prosonda	qualifications

| προσοχή! | | |
| prosochi! | Careful! | |

προσπαθώ	prospatho	to try
προστατεύω	prostatevo	to protect
το προστατευόμενο δάσος	to prostatevomeno dhasos	protected forest
το προστατευόμενο είδος	to prostatevomeno idhos	protected species
το πρόστιμο	to prostimo	a fine
πρόσφατος/-η/-ο	prosfatos/-i/-o	recent
πρόσφυγας	prosfighas	refugee
το πρόσωπο	to prosopo	face/person
ο/η πρωθυπουργός	o/i prothipurghos	prime minister
το πρωί	to proi	morning
το πρωινό	to proino	breakfast
η Πρωτοχρονιά	i protochronia	New Year's Day
πρώτος/-η/-ο	protos/-i/-o	first
το πρωτότυπο	to prototipo	original (n)
η πτήση	i ptisi	flight
το πτυχίο	to ptichio	degree
πού	pu	where
που	pu	which/that
το πουκάμισο	to pukamiso	shirt
το πουλί	to puli	bird
το πουλόβερ	to pulover	jumper/sweater
πουλώ	pulo	to sell
η πυξίδα	i piksidha	compass
ο πύργος	o pirghos	tower
ο πυρετός	o piretos	fever
πώς	pos	how

| Πώς λένε ...; | | |
| pos lene ...? | How do you say ...? | |

P

ράβω	ravo	to sew
ο ρατσισμός	o ratsizmos	racism
τα ράφια	ta rafia	shelves
τα ρέστα	ta resta	change (after buying)
η ρόδα	i rodha	wheel
το ρολόι	to roloi	clock/watch
τα ρούχα	ta rucha	clothing
το ρυάκι	to riaki	stream
ο ρυθμός	o rithmos	rhythm/tune/style
ρωτάω	rotao	to ask (a question)

Σ

το Σαββατοκύριακο	to savatokiriako	weekend
το σακκίδιο	to sakidhio	knapsack/rucksack
το σαμπουάν	to sampuan	shampoo
το σαπούνι	to sapuni	soap
η Σαρακοστή	i sarakosti	Lent

| Σαχλαμάρες! sachlamares! | Rubbish! (nonsense) |

ο σεβασμός	o sevazmos	respect (n)
ο σεισμός	o sizmos	earthquake
η σελήνη	i selini	moon
η σελίδα	i selidha	page/sheet of paper
το σεντόνι	to sendoni	sheet (bed)
οι σερβιέτες	i serviettes	sanitary napkins
η σημαία	i simea	flag
σημαντικός/-η/-ο	simandikos/-i/-o	important/significant
σήμερα	simera	today
το σημειωματάριο	to simiomatario	notebook

| Σίγουρα. sighura | Sure. |

ο σιδηροδρομικός σταθμός	o sidhirodhromikos stathmos	railway station
ο σιδηρόδρομος	o sidhirodhromos	railroad
η σκάλα	i skala	stairway
το σκαλί	to skali	step (of a ladder)
η σκέψη	i skepsi	thought
η σκηνή	i skini	stage (theatre)/tent

Greek	Transliteration	English
η σκιά	i skia	shade/shadow
σκίζω	skizo	to tear
σκληρός/-η/-ο	skliros/-i/-o	hard/mean (person)
σκοράρω	skoraro	to score
τα σκουλίκια	ta skulikia	worms
τα σκουπίδια	ta skupidhia	garbage/rubbish
σκοτεινός/-η/-ο	skotinos/-i/-o	dark
σκοτώνω	skotono	to kill
ο σκύλος	o skilos	dog
σοβαρός/-η/-ο	sovaros/-i/-o	serious
το σόου	to so-u	a show
το σουβενίρ	to suvenir	souvenir
ο σουγιάς	o suyias	penknife
σοφός/-η/-ο	sofos/-i/-o	wise
σπάνιος/-α/-ο	spanios/-a/-o	rare
σπάω (έσπασα)	spao (espasa)	break
σπασμένος/-η/-ο	spazmenos/-i/-o	broken
τα σπίρτα	ta spirta	matches
το σπίτι	to spiti	house
σπρώχνω	sprochno	to push
σταματώ	stamato	to stop
ο σταθμός	o stathmos	station
η στάση	i stasi	stop (n)
ο σταυρός	o stavros	cross (religious)
τα σταφύλια	ta stafilia	grapes
στεγνώνω (στέγνωσα)	steghnono (steghnosa)	to dry
στέλνω (έστειλα)	stelno (estila)	to send
στερεός/-α/-ο	stereos/-a/-o	solid
το στήθος	to stithos	chest (part of body)
το στοίχημα	to stichima	bet
το στόμα	to stoma	mouth
ο στομαχόπονος	o stomachoponos	stomach-ache
ο στόχος	o stochos	goal (aim)
το στραμπούληγμα	to strabulighma	sprain (n)
το στρατιωτικό	to stratiotiko	military service
στρίβω	strivo	to turn
στρογγυλός/-η/-ο	strongilos/-i/-o	round
το στρώμα	to stroma	mattress
το στυλό	stilo	pen
ο/η συγγραφέας	o/i singhrafeas	writer
η συγκομιδή φρούτων	i singomidhi fruton	fruit harvest

Συγχαρητήρια!
sincharitiria!   Congratulations!

Greek	Transliteration	English
συγχωρώ	sinchoro	to forgive
ο/η σύζυγος	o/i sizighos	husband/wife
το συμβόλαιο	to simvoleo	contract
η συμβουλή	i simvuli	advice
συμπαθητικός/-η/-ο	simbathitikos/-i/-o	pleasant/likeable
το σύμπαν	to simban	universe
συμπονετικός/-η/-ο	simbonetikos/-i/-o	sympathetic
συμφωνώ	simfono	to agree
ο/η συνάδελφος	o/i sinadhelfos	colleague
τα συναισθήματα	ta sinesthimata	feelings
συναντώ	sinando	to meet
η συναυλία	i sinavlia	a concert
το συνδικάτο	to sindhikato	trade union
η συνέντευξη	i sinendefksi	interview
συννεφιασμένος/-η/-ο	sinefiazmenos/-i/-o	cloudy
το σύννεφο	to sinefo	cloud
τα σύνορα	ta sinora	border/frontier
ο/η συνταξιούχος	o/i sindaksiuchos	pensioner
συντηρητικός/-η/-ο	sindiritikos/-i/-o	conservative
σύντομα	sindoma	soon
ο/η σύντροφος	o/i sindrofos	companion
η σύριγγα	i siringa	syringe
το σύρμα	to sirma	wire
η συστατική επιστολή	i sistatiki epistoli	reference letter
η συστημένη επιστολή	i sistimeni epistoli	registered mail
συστήνω (σύστησα)	sistino (sistisa)	to recommend
συχνά	sichna	often
σφιχτός/-η/-ο	sfichtos/-i/-o	tight
το σφυρί	to sfiri	hammer
σχεδιάζω	schedhiazo	design
σχεδόν	schedhon	almost
η σχέση	i schesi	relationship
το σχήμα	to schima	shape
το σχοινί	to schini	rope
το σχολείο	to scholio	school
το σώμα	to soma	body
σωστός/-η/-ο	sostos/-i/-o	right (correct)

T

η ταινία	i tenia	film/movie
ο ταμιευτής	o tamieftis	cashier
η τάξη	i taksi	class/order

ταξιδεύω	taksidhevo	to travel
το ταξίδι	to taksidhi	journey/trip
οι ταξιδιωτικές επιταγές	i taksidhiotikes epitayes	travellers cheques
το ταξιδιωτικό γραφείο	to taksidhiotiko ghrafio	travel agency
ο ταξιδιωτικός οδηγός	o taksidhiotikos odhighos	travel guide
το τασάκι	to tasaki	ashtray
η ταυτότητα	i taftotita	identification card
ο τάφος	o tafos	grave
το ταχυδρομικό κουτί	to tachidhromiko kuti	mailbox/postbox
το ταχυδρομείο	to tachidhromio	post office
η ταχύτητα	i tachitita	speed
τα τείχη	ta tichi	city walls
τελειώνω	teliono	to end/to finish
τελευταίος/-α/-ο	telefteos/-a/-o	last (final)
το τέλος	to telos	end
το τελωνείο	to telonio	customs
τεμπέλης/-α	tembelis/-a	lazy
το τετράγωνο	to tetraghono	square (shape)
η τέχνη	i techni	art
το τζαμί	to tzami	mosque
το τηλεγράφημα	to tileghrafima	telegram
η τηλεκάρτα	i tilekarta	phonecard
η τηλεόραση	i tileorasi	television
το τηλέφωνο	to tilefono	telephone
τι	ti	what
η τιμή	i timi	price
η τιμή συναλλάγματος	i timi sinalaghmatos	exchange rate
τίποτα	tipota	nothing/anything
ο τοίχος	o tichos	wall
τοπικός/-η/-ο	topikos/-i/-o	local/regional
η τοποθεσία	i topothesia	location
ο τόπος	o topos	place
ο τόπος γεννήσεως	o topos yeniseos	place of birth
οι τουαλέττες	i tualetes	toilets
ο τουριστικός οδηγός	o turistikos odhighos	guidebook
τραβάω	travao	to pull
το τραγούδι	to traghudhi	song
τραγουδώ	traghudho	to sing
η τράπεζα	i trapeza	bank
το τραπέζι	to trapezi	table
η τράπουλα	i trapula	playing cards
ο τραυματισμός	o travmatizmos	injury
τρελλός/-η/-ο	trelos/-i/-o	crazy/mad

τρέχω	trecho	to run
ο τρόπος	o tropos	way (manner)
τρώω	tro-o	to eat
η τσάντα	i tsanda	bag/handbag
η τσέπη	i tsepi	pocket
τα τσιγάρα	ta tsighara	cigarettes
το τσίμπημα	to tsibima	bite (insect)
η τσίχλα	i tsichla	chewing gum
τα τύμπανα	ta timbana	drums
τυπικός/-η/-ο	tipikos/-i/-o	typical
το τυρί	to tiri	cheese
τυφλός/-η/-ο	tiflos/-i/-o	blind
τυχερός/-η/-ο	ticheros/-i/-o	lucky
η τύχη	i tichi	luck
τώρα	tora	now

Υ

η υγεία	i iyia	health

Στην υγειά σου! stin ighia su!	Bless you! (when sneezing)

Στην υγειά σου/σας! stin iyia su/sas!	Good health!; Cheers!

ο/η υπάλληλος	o/i ipalilos	employee
η υπερηφάνεια	i iperifania	pride
η υπηκοότητα	i ipiko-otita	citizenship/nationality
ο υπνόσακκος	o ipnosakos	sleeping bag
η υπογραφή	i ipoghrafi	signature
υπογράφω	ipoghrafo	to sign
το υπόλοιπο	to ipolipo	rest (what's left)
υπομονετικός/-η/-ο	ipomonetikos/-i/-o	patient (adj)
υπόσχομαι	iposchome	to promise
οι υπότιτλοι	i ipotitli	subtitles
υποφέρω	ipofero	to suffer
το υψόμετρο	to ipsometro	altitude

Φ

το φαγητό	to fayito	food
η φαγούρα	i faghura	itch
ο φάκελλος	o fakelos	envelope
οι φακοί επαφής	i faki epafis	contact lenses

Greek	Transliteration	English
ο φακός	o fakos	lens/torch
φανερός/-η/-ο	faneros/-i/-o	obvious
φαρδύς/-ια/-υ	fardhis/-ia/-i	wide
το φαρμακείο	to farmakio	chemist's/pharmacy
το φάρμακο	to farmako	drug (medicine)
το φεγγάρι	to fengari	moon
φέρνω	ferno	to bring
φέτος	fetos	this year
το φθινόπωρο	to fthinoporo	autumn
η φιγούρα	i fighura	figure (body)
η φίλη	i fili	friend (f)/girlfriend
το φιλί	to fili	kiss (n)
το φιλοδώρημα	to filodhorima	tip (gratuity)
ο φίλος	o filos	friend (m)/boyfriend
φιλτραρισμένος/-η/-ο	filtrarizmenos/-i/-o	filtered
φιλώ	filo	to kiss
η φλέβα	i fleva	vein
το φλερτ	to flert	romance
το φλυτζάνι	to flitzani	cup
φοβάμαι	fovame	afraid of (to be)
φοβερός/-η/-ο	foveros/-i/-o	terrible/great (slang)
ο φόβος	fovos	fear
φοιτητής/φοιτήτρια	fititis/fititria	student
φοράω	forao	to wear
το φόρεμα	to forema	dress
ο φόρος	o foros	tax
το φορτηγάκι	to fortighaki	van
το φορτηγό	to fortigho	truck
ο φούρνος	o furnos	bakery/oven
ο φράχτης	o frachtis	fence (gate)
φροντίζω	frondizo	to care (for someone)
φτάνω	ftano	to arrive/reach
τα φτερά	ta ftera	wings
φτηνός/-η/-ο	ftinos/-i/-o	cheap
φτιάχνω	ftiachno	to make
η φτώχεια	i ftochia	poverty
φτωχός/-η/-ο	ftochos/-i/-o	poor
η φυλακή	i filaki	jail/prison
η φυλή	i fili	race (breed)
το φύλο	to filo	sex (gender)
η φύση	i fisi	nature
το φυτό	to fito	plant

φωνάζω	fonazo	to shout
η φωνή	i foni	voice
το φως	to fos	light (sun/lamp)
τα φώτα	ta fota	traffic lights
η φωτιά	i fotia	fire

X

χαζός/-η/-ο	chazos/-i/-o	stupid
χαλαρώνω	chalarono	to relax
το χαλί	to chali	rug/carpet
χαμηλός/-η/-ο	chamilos/-i/-o	low
χαμογελάω	chamoyelao	to smile
χάνω	chano	to lose
το χάπι	to chapi	pill
χαρούμενος/-η/-ο	charumenos/-i/-o	happy
το χαρτί	to charti	paper
το χαρτί υγείας	to charti iyias	toilet paper
ο χάρτης	o chartis	map
τα χαρτομάντηλα	ta chartomandila	tissues
τα χαρτονομίσματα	ta chartonomizmata	banknotes
το χασίσι	to chasisi	hash
τα χείλια	ta chilia	lips
ο χειμώνας	o chimonas	winter
χειροποίητος/-η/-ο	chiropi-itos/-i/-o	handmade
η χειροτεχνία	i chirotechnia	crafts
το χέρι	to cheri	arm/hand
το χιλιόμετρο	to chiliometro	kilometre
το χιλιοστό	to chiliosto	millimetre
χοντρός/-η/-ο	chondros/-i/-o	fat
χορεύω	chorevo	to dance
ο χορός	o choros	dance
το χόρτο	to chorto	grass
χορτοφάγος	chortofaghos	vegetarian
χρειάζομαι	chriazome	to need
τα χρήματα	ta chrimata	money
χρήσιμος/-η/-ο	chrisimos/-i/-o	useful
Χριστιανός/-η	christianos/-i	Christian
τα Χριστούγεννα	ta christuyena	Christmas

| Χρόνια Πολλά! | | |
| chronia pola! | Happy birthday; Many happy returns! | |

| ο χρόνος | o chronos | year/time |

Greek	Transliteration	English
του χρόνου	tu chronu	next year
το χρώμα	to chroma	colour
χρωστάω (χρώστησα)	chrostao (chrostisa)	to owe
η χτένα	i chtena	comb
χτες	chtes	yesterday
χτίζω (έχτισα)	chtizo (echtisa)	to build
ο χυμός	o chimos	juice
το χώμα	to choma	earth (soil)
η χώρα	i chora	country
το χωράφι	to chorafi	field
χωρίζω	chorizo	to part/to separate
το χωριό	to chorio	village
χωρίς	choris	without
ο χώρος	o choros	room/space
ο χώρος κατασκήνωσης	o choros kataskinosis	campsite

Ψ

το ψαλίδι	to psalidhi	scissors
το ψάρι	to psari	fish
ψάχνω (έψαξα)	psachno (epsaksa)	to look for
ψεύτης/ψεύτρα	pseftis/pseftra	liar
ψηλός/-η/-ο	psilos/-i/-o	high/tall
ψηφίζω	psifizo	to vote
τα ψιλά	ta psila	change (spare coins)
το ψυγείο	to psighio	refrigerator
το ψωμί	to psomi	bread

Ω

ο ωκεανός	o okeanos	ocean
οι ώμοι	i omi	shoulders
ωμός/-η/-ο	omos/-i/-o	raw
η ώρα	i ora	time/hour
Τι ώρα είναι; ti ora ine?	What time is it?	
ως	os	until

I
N
D
E
X

FINDER

F
I
N
D
E
R

313

F
I
N
D
E
R

F
I
N
D
E
R

Phrasebooks

Lonely Planet phrasebooks are packed with essential words and phrases to help travellers communicate with the locals. With colour tabs for quick reference, an extensive vocabulary and use of script, these handy pocket-sized language guides cover day-to-day travel situations.

- handy pocket-sized books
- easy to understand pronunciation chapter
- clear & comprehensive grammar chapter
- romanisation alongside script for ease of pronunciation
- script throughout so users can point to phrases for every situation
- full of cultural information and tips for the traveller

'...vital for a real DIY spirit and attitude in language learning'
– *Backpacker*

'the phrasebooks have good cultural backgrounders and offer solid advice for challenging situations in remote locations'
– *San Francisco Examiner*

Arabic (*Egyptian*) • Arabic (*Moroccan*) • Australian (*Australian English, Aboriginal and Torres Strait languages*) • Baltic States (*Estonian, Latvian, Lithuanian*) • Bengali • Brazilian • British • Burmese • Cantonese • Central Asia • Central Europe (*Czech, French, German, Hungarian, Italian, Slovak*) • Costa Rica Spanish • Eastern Europe (*Bulgarian, Czech, Hungarian, Polish, Romanian, Slovak*) • Ethiopian (*Amharic*) • Fijian • French • German • Greek • Hebrew • Hill Tribes • Hindi & Urdu • Indonesian • Italian • Japanese • Korean • Lao • Latin American Spanish • Malay • Mandarin • Mediterranean Europe (*Albanian, Croatian, Greek, Italian, Macedonian, Maltese, Serbian, Slovene*) • Mongolian • Nepali • Pidgin • Pilipino (*Tagalog*) • Portuguese • Quechua • Russian • Scandinavian Europe (*Danish, Finnish, Icelandic, Norwegian, Swedish*) • South-East Asia (*Burmese, Indonesian, Khmer, Lao, Malay, Tagalog Pilipino, Thai, Vietnamese*) • South Pacific (*Fijian, Fijian Hindi, Hawaiian, Kanak, Maori, Niuean, Pacific French, Pacific Englishes, Rapanui, Rarotongan Maori, Samoan, Spanish, Tahitian, Tongan*) • Spanish (*Castilian; also includes Catalan, Galician and Basque*) • Sri Lanka • Swahili • Thai • Tibetan • Turkish • Ukrainian • USA (*US English, Vernacular, Native American languages, Hawaiian*) • Vietnamese • Western Europe (*Basque, Catalan, Dutch, French, German, Greek, Irish*)

LONELY PLANET

Guides by Region

Lonely Planet is known worldwide for publishing practical, reliable and no-nonsense travel information in our guides and on our web site. The Lonely Planet list covers just about every accessible part of the world. Currently there are fifteen series: travel guides, Shoestrings, Condensed, Phrasebooks, Read This First, Healthy Travel, Walking guides, Cycling guides, Pisces Diving & Snorkeling guides, City Maps, Travel Atlases, Out to Eat, World Food, Journeys travel literature and Pictorials.

AFRICA Africa on a shoestring • Africa – the South • Arabic (Egyptian) phrasebook • Arabic (Moroccan) phrasebook • Cairo • Cape Town • Cape Town city map • Central Africa • East Africa • Egypt • Egypt travel atlas • Ethiopian (Amharic) phrasebook • The Gambia & Senegal • Healthy Travel Africa • Kenya • Kenya travel atlas • Malawi, Mozambique & Zambia • Morocco • North Africa • Read This First Africa • South Africa, Lesotho & Swaziland • South Africa, Lesotho & Swaziland travel atlas • Swahili phrasebook • Tanzania, Zanzibar & Pemba • Trekking in East Africa • Tunisia • West Africa • Zimbabwe, Botswana & Namibia • Zimbabwe, Botswana & Namibia Travel Atlas • World Food Morocco
Travel Literature: The Rainbird: A Central African Journey • Songs to an African Sunset: A Zimbabwean Story • Mali Blues: Traveling to an African Beat

AUSTRALIA & THE PACIFIC Auckland • Australia • Australian phrasebook • Bushwalking in Australia • Bushwalking in Papua New Guinea • Fiji • Fijian phrasebook • Healthy Travel Australia, NZ and the Pacific • Islands of Australia's Great Barrier Reef • Melbourne • Melbourne city map • Micronesia • New Caledonia • New South Wales & the ACT • New Zealand • Northern Territory • Outback Australia • Out To Eat – Melbourne • Out to Eat – Sydney • Papua New Guinea • Pidgin phrasebook • Queensland • Rarotonga & the Cook Islands • Samoa • Solomon Islands • South Australia • South Pacific • South Pacific Languages phrasebook • Sydney • Sydney city map • Sydney Condensed • Tahiti & French Polynesia • Tasmania • Tonga • Tramping in New Zealand • Vanuatu • Victoria • Western Australia
Travel Literature: Islands in the Clouds • Kiwi Tracks: A New Zealand Journey • Sean & David's Long Drive

CENTRAL AMERICA & THE CARIBBEAN Bahamas, Turks & Caicos • Bermuda • Central America on a shoestring • Costa Rica • Cuba • Dominican Republic & Haiti • Eastern Caribbean • Guatemala, Belize & Yucatán: La Ruta Maya • Jamaica • Mexico • Mexico City • Panama • Puerto Rico • Read This First Central & South America • World Food Mexico
Travel Literature: Green Dreams: Travels in Central America

EUROPE Amsterdam • Amsterdam city map • Andalucía • Austria • Baltic States phrasebook • Barcelona • Berlin • Berlin city map • Britain • British phrasebook • Brussels, Bruges & Antwerp • Budapest city map • Canary Islands • Central Europe • Central Europe phrasebook • Corfu & Ionians • Corsica • Crete • Crete Condensed • Croatia • Cyprus • Czech & Slovak Republics • Denmark • Dublin • Eastern Europe • Eastern Europe phrasebook • Edinburgh • Estonia, Latvia & Lithuania • Europe on a shoestring • Finland • Florence • France • French phrasebook • Germany • German phrasebook • Greece • Greek Islands • Greek phrasebook • Hungary • Iceland, Greenland & the Faroe Islands • Ireland • Italian phrasebook • Italy • Krakow • Lisbon • The Loire • London • London city map • London Condensed • Mediterranean Europe • Mediterranean Europe phrasebook • Munich • Norway • Paris • Paris city map • Paris Condensed • Poland • Portugal • Portuguese phrasebook • Portugal travel atlas • Prague • Prague city map • Provence & the Côte d'Azur • Read This First Europe • Romania & Moldova • Rome • Russia, Ukraine & Belarus • Russian phrasebook • Scandinavian & Baltic Europe • Scandinavian Europe phrasebook • Scotland • Slovenia • Spain • Spanish phrasebook • St Petersburg • Sweden • Switzerland • Trekking in Spain • Tuscany • Ukrainian phrasebook • Venice • Vienna • Walking in Britain • Walking in Ireland • Walking in Italy • Walking in Spain • Walking in Switzerland • Western Europe • Western Europe phrasebook • World Food Ireland • World Food Italy • World Food Spain
Travel Literature: The Olive Grove: Travels in Greece

INDIAN SUBCONTINENT Bangladesh • Bengali phrasebook • Bhutan • Delhi • Goa • Hindi & Urdu phrasebook • India • India & Bangladesh travel atlas • Indian Himalaya • Karakoram Highway • Kerala • Mumbai (Bombay) • Nepal • Nepali phrasebook • Pakistan • Rajasthan • Read This First: Asia & India • South India • Sri Lanka • Sri Lanka phrasebook • Trekking in the Indian Himalaya • Trekking in the Karakoram & Hindukush • Trekking in the Nepal Himalaya
Travel Literature: In Rajasthan • Shopping for Buddhas • The Age Of Kali

LONELY PLANET

Mail Order

Lonely Planet products are distributed worldwide. They are also available by mail order from Lonely Planet, so if you have difficulty finding a title please write to us. North and South American residents should write to 150 Linden St, Oakland CA 94607, USA; European and African residents should write to 10a Spring Place, London, NW5 3BH; and residents of other countries to PO Box 617, Hawthorn, Victoria 3122, Australia.

ISLANDS OF THE INDIAN OCEAN Madagascar & Comoros • Maldives • Mauritius, Réunion & Seychelles

MIDDLE EAST & CENTRAL ASIA Bahrain, Kuwait & Qatar • Central Asia • Central Asia phrasebook • Dubai • Hebrew phrasebook • Iran • Israel & the Palestinian Territories • Israel & the Palestinian Territories travel atlas • Istanbul • Istanbul City Map • Istanbul to Cairo on a shoestring • Jerusalem • Jerusalem City Map • Jordan • Jordan, Syria & Lebanon travel atlas • Lebanon • Middle East • Oman & the United Arab Emirates • Syria • Turkey • Turkey travel atlas • Turkish phrasebook • World Food Turkey • Yemen
Travel Literature: The Gates of Damascus • Kingdom of the Film Stars: Journey into Jordan • Black on Black: Iran Revisited

NORTH AMERICA Alaska • Backpacking in Alaska • Baja California • California & Nevada • California Condensed • Canada • Chicago • Chicago city map • Deep South • Florida • Hawaii • Honolulu • Las Vegas • Los Angeles • Miami • New England • New Orleans • New York City • New York city map • New York Condensed • New York, New Jersey & Pennsylvania • Oahu • Pacific Northwest USA • Puerto Rico • Rocky Mountain • San Francisco • San Francisco city map • Seattle • Southwest USA • Texas • USA • USA phrasebook • Vancouver • Washington, DC & the Capital Region • Washington DC city map
Travel Literature: Drive Thru America

NORTH-EAST ASIA Beijing • Cantonese phrasebook • China • Hong Kong • Hong Kong city map • Hong Kong, Macau & Guangzhou • Japan • Japanese phrasebook • Japanese audio pack • Korea • Korean phrasebook • Kyoto • Mandarin phrasebook • Mongolia • Mongolian phrasebook • North-East Asia on a shoestring • Seoul • South-West China • Taiwan • Tibet • Tibetan phrasebook • Tokyo
Travel Literature: Lost Japan • In Xanadu

SOUTH AMERICA Argentina, Uruguay & Paraguay • Bolivia • Brazil • Brazilian phrasebook • Buenos Aires • Chile & Easter Island • Chile & Easter Island travel atlas • Colombia • Ecuador & the Galapagos Islands • Healthy Travel Central & South America • Latin American Spanish phrasebook • Peru • Quechua phrasebook • Rio de Janeiro • Rio de Janeiro city map • South America on a shoestring • Trekking in the Patagonian Andes • Venezuela
Travel Literature: Full Circle: A South American Journey

SOUTH-EAST ASIA Bali & Lombok • Bangkok • Bangkok city map • Burmese phrasebook • Cambodia • Hanoi • Healthy Travel Asia & India • Hill Tribes phrasebook • Ho Chi Minh City • Indonesia • Indonesia's Eastern Islands • Indonesian phrasebook • Indonesian audio pack • Jakarta • Java • Laos • Lao phrasebook • Laos travel atlas • Malay phrasebook • Malaysia, Singapore & Brunei • Myanmar (Burma) • Philippines • Pilipino (Tagalog) phrasebook • Read This First Asia & India • Singapore • South-East Asia on a shoestring • South-East Asia phrasebook • Thailand • Thailand's Islands & Beaches • Thailand travel atlas • Thai phrasebook • Thai audio pack • Vietnam • Vietnamese phrasebook • Vietnam travel atlas • World Food Thailand • World Food Vietnam

ALSO AVAILABLE: Antarctica • The Arctic • Brief Encounters: Stories of Love, Sex & Travel • Chasing Rickshaws • Lonely Planet Unpacked • Not the Only Planet: Travel Stories from Science Fiction • Sacred India • Travel with Children • Traveller's Tales

Series Description

travel guidebooks	in depth coverage with background and recommendations download selected guidebook Upgrades at www.lonelyplanet.com
shoestring guides	for travellers with more time than money
condensed guides	highlights the best a destination has to offer
citySync	digital city guides for Palm TM OS
outdoor guides	walking, cycling, diving and watching wildlife
phrasebooks	just don't stand there, say something!
city maps and road atlases	essential navigation tools
world food	for people who live to eat, drink & travel
out to eat	a city's best places to eat and drink
read this first	invaluable pre-departure guides
healthy travel	practical advice for staying well on the road
journeys	travel stories for armchair explorers
pictorial	lavishly illustrated pictorial books
ekno	low-cost international phonecard with e-services
TV series and videos	on the road docos
web site	for chat, Upgrades, destination facts
lonely planet images	on line photo library

LONELY PLANET OFFICES

Australia
PO Box 617, Hawthorn,
Victoria 3122
☎ (03) 9819 1877
fax (03) 9819 6459
email: talk2us@lonelyplanet.com.au

UK
10a Spring Place,
London NW5 3BH
☎ (020) 7428 4800
fax (020) 7428 4828
email: go@lonelyplanet.co.uk

USA
150 Linden St, Oakland,
CA 94607
☎ (510) 893 8555
TOLL FREE: 800 275 8555
fax (510) 893 8572
email: info@lonelyplanet.com

France
1 rue du Dahomey,
75011 Paris
☎ 01 55 25 33 00
fax 01 55 25 33 01
email: bip@lonelyplanet.fr
website: www.lonelyplanet.fr

World Wide Web: www.lonelyplanet.com or AOL keyword: lp
Lonely Planet Images: lpi@lonelyplanet.com.au